Level 2

Beauty Therapy

Francesca Gould

Nelson Thornes

Contents

Introduction   1

G 2 0 Ensure responsibility for actions to reduce risks to health and safety   2

G 4 Fulfil salon reception duties   34

G 8 Develop and maintain effectiveness at work   50

G 1 8 Promote additional services or products to customers   60

A & P Anatomy and physiology   71

B 4 Provide facial skin care treatment   122

B 5 Enhance the appearance of eyebrows and eyelashes   166

B 8 & **B 9** Provide make-up and instruct clients in the use of skin care products and make-up   195

N 2 & **N 3** Provide manicure services and provide pedicure services   242

B 6 Carry out waxing services   281

B 7 Carry out ear piercing   310

S 1 Assist with spa operations   322

B 1 0 Enhance appearance using skin camouflage
Written by Sally-Jane Dawson (this unit is available on the Nelson Thornes hair and beauty website at www.nelsonthornes.com/salon)

Glossary   347

Index   352

Introduction

The world of Beauty Therapy is an exciting one. There have never been so many wonderful opportunities available to the therapist, including working on cruise ships, aeroplanes and in exotic far-away places.

This book has been specially designed to guide you through your Level 2 course with ease and will help you on your journey towards an interesting, challenging and rewarding career in the Beauty Therapy industry. It will assist you in gaining necessary skills and knowledge to achieve your Level 2 qualification.

It is packed full of diagrams and colour photos so you can see exactly what you need to do to carry out the different beauty treatments. There are also activities and tasks to help check your knowledge.

Here are a list of the text features you will use as you work through the book:

UNIT OUTCOMES

Unit outcomes
All units are divided into unit outcomes which match those in your record of assessment book. The first page of each unit lists the relevant learning outcomes.

DON'T FORGET

Don't forget
This feature provides you interesting and useful facts and reminders that will be invaluable to your learning and will enhance your knowledge.

Key terms
During your course you'll come across new words and new terms that you may not have heard before. When these words and terms are first used in the book the key terms feature appears. This gives you a clear definition of the word or term.

HAVE A GO

Have a go
This feature asks you to perform tasks which will help you to understand and remember the information you have learnt. These will help you to apply your learning to your practical work.

Good practice

Good practice
It's important that you always work to high standards and this feature highlights the good practice points that you should follow.

Ask Fran
Your expert author, Francesca Gould, answers all the burning questions you may have as you work through the units and supports you on your way to success!

How are you doing?

How are you doing?
At the end of each unit you will find a list of multiple-choice questions. Answering these will confirm that you have understood what you have read and will check your progress.

Are you ready for assessment?
are
you ready
for assessment?

This feature offers advice on preparing for the different types of assessment you will be required to complete for each unit.

G20 Ensure responsibility for actions to reduce risks to health and safety

UNIT OUTCOMES

On completion of this unit you will:

1. Be able to identify the hazards and evaluate the risks in the workplace

2. Be able to reduce the risks to health and safety in the workplace

3. Know how to reduce risks to health and safety in the workplace

Introduction

key terms

Hazard: a situation that may be dangerous.

Everyone working in a beauty salon must follow health and safety laws and regulations. This will help to ensure a safe and hygienic environment, and so will reduce the likelihood of risks and **hazards** occurring.

UNIT OUTCOME 1

Be able to identify the hazards and evaluate the risks in the workplace

UNIT OUTCOME 2

Be able to reduce the risks to health and safety in the workplace

UNIT OUTCOME 3

Know how to reduce risks to health and safety in the workplace

Health and safety

Anyone running a beauty business must take health and safety seriously, as poor practices may result in the business being closed down. All staff should be continually assessing potential hazards in the workplace in order to reduce health and safety risks. This is known as **risk assessment**. The table overleaf shows some possible hazards that might occur in the salon and the action you should take to reduce the risk.

A risk assessment form is used to record any possible causes of harm and the likelihood of harm occurring.

key terms

Risk assessment: to observe any potential hazard that could result in injury, illness or a dangerous situation.

Risk Assessment
Company/Organisation: Assessor:
Activity/Task *Complete the relevant details of the activity being assessed.*
Hazards *All hazards associated with the activity should be entered here.*
Those at risk *Staff, public and others.*
Current control measures *List current control measures.*

With these controls the risk is (circle)	Unacceptable	Further controls required	Adequately controlled

Further control measures required
List further action needed to adequately control risks.

Date					
Initial					

Use a new box each time this assessment is reviewed

Sample risk assessment form

3

Hazards in the salon	Action you should take	Risk factor to person
Children in the salon	If children are allowed in the salon, make sure all lids are secure on products and stored out of reach.	High risk – child could possibly swallow some dangerous chemicals or suffer a skin reaction if a product is applied to their skin.
Client suffers an allergic reaction	Ensure you give an allergy test, particularly if carrying out treatments such as eyelash tinting or applying artificial lashes. If an allergic reaction does occur, ensure the product is removed immediately. A cool compress can then be applied to soothe the area.	High risk – client may need to be taken to hospital if the reaction is severe.
Faulty couch or chairs	Inform the manager immediately.	High risk – person could fall off and suffer a bad injury.
Faulty electrical equipment	Inform the manager immediately.	High risk – person could suffer an electric shock.
Fire	Do not use a fire extinguisher unless you are trained to do so. Get outside quickly and call the fire and rescue service.	High risk – can cause respiratory problems, burns and even death.
Floors – spillage	Clear it up immediately.	High risk – person could slip and suffer an injury.
Items obstructing doorway	Remove items at once.	High risk – person may trip over them.
Trailing lead	Tidy and secure the lead immediately.	High risk – person may trip over it and suffer an injury.
Clients walking bare-footed on the floor	Give the client disposable slippers or ensure they place their feet onto a couch roll or a towel.	Medium/low risk – may cross-infect and pass on conditions such as athlete's foot and verrucas.
Tissue or cotton wool contaminated with blood	Put on disposable gloves and put it into a sealed bag. Dispose of it hygienically.	Medium/low risk – may cause **cross-infection** if touched.
Poor ventilation when strong-smelling chemicals are being used during treatment	If windows or doors cannot be opened, discuss with your manager what further action can be taken.	Low risk – therapist and client may suffer with headaches and nausea.

key terms

Cross-infection: passing on infection, either by direct person-to-person contact, or by indirect contact such as by using contaminated make-up tools.

High risk situation

Laws and regulations

There are many laws and regulations (rules and restrictions) in place to help minimise the risk of health and safety hazards. Beauty therapists need to be aware of the following legislation (laws) and guidelines.

Good practice

It is now illegal to smoke in virtually all 'enclosed' and 'substantially enclosed' public places and workplaces. Employers and managers need to follow the smoke-free law and ensure that signs are displayed stating 'no smoking' on the business premises.

Health and Safety at Work Act (HASAWA) (1974)

This Act is the main piece of UK legislation covering health and safety in the workplace. It makes sure that employers and employees maintain high standards of health and safety in the workplace.

Employers are responsible for the health and safety of anyone who enters their premises. If an employer has more than five employees, the workplace must have a health and safety policy, which all staff must be aware of.

Both employers and employees have responsibilities under this Act.

Employers must ensure the following.

- The workplace does not pose a risk to the health and safety of employees and clients.
- Protective equipment is provided.
- Dangerous substances are used, handled and stored safely.
- All equipment must be safe and have regular checks.
- There must be a safe system of cash handling, such as when taking money to the bank.
- Staff should be aware of safety procedures in the workplace, and have the necessary information, instruction and training.

Employees' responsibilities include the following.

- To follow the health and safety policy.
- To read the hazard warning labels on containers and follow their advice.
- To report any potential hazard, such as glass breakage or spillage of chemicals, to the relevant person in the workplace.

DON'T FORGET

The Health and Safety Executive (HSE) is the UK body responsible for enforcing health and safety at work legislation.

Broken glass is a potential hazard!

Health and Safety Information for Employees Regulations (1989)

These regulations require employers to display a poster telling employees what they need to know about health and safety in the workplace.

Health and Safety poster

DON'T FORGET

Health and safety rules and regulations must be displayed in the salon.

Workplace (Health, Safety and Welfare) Regulations (1992)

These regulations require employers to make sure that the workplace is safe and suitable for the jobs being carried out there, and does not present risks to employees and others. These regulations cover:

- maintenance of the workplace, equipment, etc.

- adequate ventilation

- lighting

- indoor temperature

- cleanliness and waste materials

- workstations and seating

- facilities to rest and to eat meals.

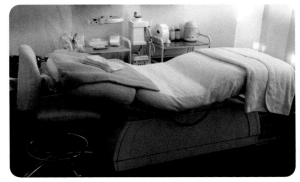

Beauty treatment room

Management of Health and Safety at Work Regulations (1999)

These regulations place a duty on employers to assess and manage risks to their employees, and to others, arising from work activities. Employers are required to carry out risk assessments and put procedures in place to deal with dangerous situations, such as fire, gas explosion, **electrocution**, or escape of toxic gases or fumes. They are also required to make sure that their employees have adequate information and training to be able to carry out their jobs safely. Employees are required to work safely and inform their employer of any potential risks to health and safety in the workplace.

Good practice

Employees must notify the employer, or the person in charge of health and safety, of any serious or immediate danger to health and safety.

Health and Safety (Display Screen Equipment) Regulations (1992 and 2002)

These regulations cover requirements for working with computers, laptops, touch-screens and other similar devices that contain a display screen. The main health risks associated with display screen equipment (DSE) are muscle and skeletal disorders (aches and pains), stress, eyestrain and headaches. Employers must ensure that:

- employees are given adequate breaks

- the workstation can be adjusted to suit the height of the employee, and is also safe

- appropriate information, instruction and training are provided.

Receptionist booking appointment onto computer

Health and Safety (First Aid) Regulations (1981)

These regulations require employers to provide adequate and appropriate equipment, facilities and trained people, so that first aid can be given to employees, or others, if they are injured or become ill in the workplace.

A place of work must have an appointed person to take charge of first-aid arrangements.

There are no set rules regarding the contents of a first-aid box. However, the following is suggested for up to 50 persons.

- 40 plasters

- 6 individually wrapped triangular bandages

- 8 individually wrapped medium sterile wound dressings
- 4 individually wrapped large sterile wound dressings
- 6 safety pins
- 4 sterile eye pads
- 10 individually wrapped cleaning wipes
- 2 pairs of latex gloves
- 1 pair paramedic shears (used to cut fabric)

First-aid box

Good practice

It is recommended that you do not keep tablets and medicines in the first-aid box.

The table below gives some basic first-aid advice, which will be useful for you to know when working in a salon. But remember first aid should be carried out by someone who is qualified. Make sure you know who is qualified in your place of work.

Type of accident	Action you should take
Allergies	If the skin is red, itchy and inflamed after using oil or cream the person may have an allergy. First, remove the product using water. If possible, apply a cold compress or cold pack to reduce any swelling.
Burns	The affected area should be held under a cold, running tap for at least 10 minutes. If the burn is serious, medical attention should be sought. However, it can be loosely covered with a sterile dressing in the meantime.
Cuts	Rinse the cut under a running tap. If there is bleeding, a sterile gauze or a pad of cotton wool can be placed over the wound. Keep the affected part lifted, if possible, and apply pressure for a few minutes. Seek medical attention if the bleeding does not stop. Remember to put on disposable gloves before touching the wound.
Dizziness	The person should be positioned with their head down between their knees. This will help blood to flow to the head.
Electric shock	The person must not be touched until disconnected from the electricity supply. A qualified person can give artificial respiration. Call for an ambulance.
Epilepsy	If a person is having an epileptic seizure, remove any items around him or her that could cause injury. Check airway is clear.
Fainting	Lie the person flat and elevate the legs by, for example, placing pillows under the lower legs. This will increase the flow of blood to the head.
Fall	Do not move the person if he or she complains of back or neck pain. Cover him or her with a blanket and call an ambulance.
Nosebleeds	Sit the person in the chair with their head bent forward. Ask them to firmly pinch the soft part of the nose until bleeding stops.
Objects in the eye	Twist a dampened piece of cotton wool or tissue and try to move the object to the inside corner of the eye. Otherwise wash out the eye with eye solution or clean water.

Reporting of Injuries, Diseases and Dangerous Occurrences Regulations (RIDDOR) (1995)

Minor accidents should be entered into a record book, stating what occurred and what action was taken. Ideally all concerned should sign the report. If, as a result of an accident at work, anyone is off work for more than three days, is seriously injured, has a type of work-related disease certified by a doctor, or even dies, then the employer should send a report to the local authority Environmental Health Department as soon as possible.

ACCIDENT REPORT		
Details of the accident	Date:	Time:
Name of injured person:		
Injury:		
How the accident happened:		
Signed:		
Details of the accident	Date:	Time:
Name of injured person:		
Injury:		
How the accident happened:		
Signed:		

Sample of accident report form

Fire Precautions Act (1971)

This Act requires that all staff are trained in the fire and emergency evacuation procedure and that the premises must have fire escapes. It states that:

- there must be adequate fire-fighting equipment in good working order

- clearly marked fire exit doors should remain unlocked and must not be obstructed

- smoke alarms must be used and regularly checked

- all staff must be trained in fire drill procedures and this information should be displayed at the workplace

- a fire risk assessment must be carried out.

DON'T FORGET

The fire evacuation procedure should be displayed in the salon.

Fire exit signs

Fire extinguishers

There are four main types of fire extinguisher: foam, powder, carbon dioxide and water. Foam, powder and carbon dioxide extinguishers smother the fire and deprive it of oxygen, while a water extinguisher removes the heat.

Fire extinguishers are colour coded for different types of fire.

- Red (contains water): this extinguisher is used for solids such as wood, paper, clothing and plastics. Do not use for electrical fires.

- Cream (contains foam): this can be used to put out fires caused by solids such as paper, wood and plastic, and flammable liquids. Do not use for electrical fires.

- Blue (contains dry powder): this is often described as 'multi-purpose' because it can be used to put out fires caused by solids such as paper, wood and plastic, as well as flammable liquids and flammable gases. It can also be used for electrical fires.

- Black (contains carbon dioxide): this fire extinguisher is ideal for fires involving electrical equipment and will also extinguish flammable liquids.

Good practice

The fire extinguisher should be used by a person trained in its use.

Fire blankets are used to put out small fires. These consist of a sheet of fire retardant material. The blanket covers the fire and helps prevent oxygen from fuelling the flames, and so the fire is put out.

At the end of a working day, the following checks will help to prevent the risk of fire either starting or spreading quickly.

- Make sure all windows and doors are closed.

- Check all highly flammable products and items are safely stored.

- Switch off all electrical equipment and preferably unplug it.

- Make sure all flammable and combustible waste is removed to a safe place.

DON'T FORGET

Water – Red
Foam – Cream
Dry powder – Blue
Carbon dioxide (CO_2) – Black

Fire extinguishers

DON'T FORGET

All fire extinguishers are now coloured red, except for a patch or band of colour indicating their contents.

Fire blanket

Control of Substances Hazardous to Health (COSHH) (2004)

COSHH covers hazardous substances, which can cause ill health. Hazardous substances, such as nail polish remover, essential oils and hydrogen peroxide, must be used and stored safely. Hazardous substances can harm the body in different ways: for example, by causing skin irritation, by being swallowed (ingested), or by inhalation which can damage the lungs. All containers that contain potentially harmful substances must be clearly labelled. Below are some hazard symbols which you may see on containers in the salon. Manufacturers often give safety information regarding their products.

HAVE A GO

Make a list of all the substances and products used in the salon. Collect as much information as you can on each substance, from manufacturers' instructions, suppliers' catalogues and material safety data sheets, and research the risks associated with them.

Hazard symbols

Therapist wearing PPE

Chemicals (Hazard Information and Packaging for Supply) Regulations (2002)

These regulations require suppliers to classify, label and package dangerous chemicals and provide safety data sheets for them.

Personal Protective Equipment (PPE) at Work Regulations (2002)

These regulations require employers to provide appropriate clothing and equipment for their employees. Personal protective equipment (PPE) protects employees against risks to their health and safety. It includes safety glasses, aprons, disposable gloves and face masks.

Provision and Use of Work Equipment Regulations (PUWER) (1998)

These regulations require that equipment provided for use at work, including machinery, is safe and in good order. In a salon, equipment would include couches, chairs and electrical items. Employees should have adequate information and training on the use of work equipment to prevent accidents occurring. Also, equipment should be regularly inspected and records kept of inspections.

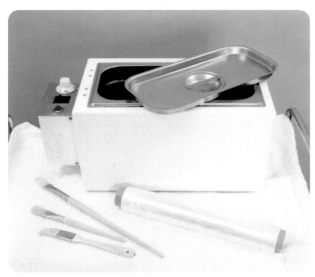

Paraffin wax heater

Electricity at Work Act (1989)

This Act is concerned with safety while using electricity. Any electrical equipment must be checked regularly to make sure it is safe. All checks should be listed in a record book and would be important evidence in the event of any legal action. There should be a system where visual inspections are carried out on electrical equipment, known as Portable Appliance Testing (PAT). Employers need to decide the frequency of PAT testing based on their risk assessment.

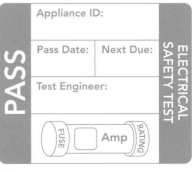

PAT label

Manual Handling Operations Regulations (1992)

Incorrect lifting and carrying of goods can result in injuries such as back injury. Employers must assess the risks to their employees and make sure they provide training if necessary.

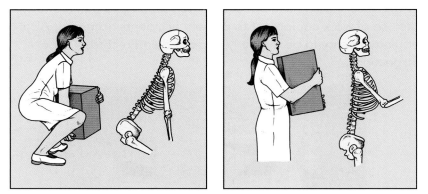

When lifting, keep your knees bent and your back straight at all times to avoid injury

key terms

Clinical waste: refers to waste products that cannot be considered general waste. It may contain needles, blood or other bodily fluids, and so may be hazardous.

Sharps box: a special container, usually coloured yellow, which is used to dispose of sharp items such as needles.

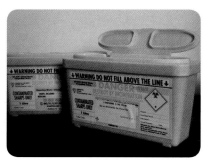

Sharps box

Control of Noise at Work Regulations (2005)

These regulations require employers to take action to protect employees from hearing damage, that could be caused by loud machinery, for example. Loud noises can damage hearing. If people are having difficulty hearing each other, or have to shout to be heard at a distance of one metre, it is likely that the noise levels are damaging. Personal protective equipment, such as ear plugs, can be provided to employees if it is impossible to reduce the noise levels.

Environmental Protection Act (1990)

This Act ensures safe disposal of contaminated **clinical waste**, such as items containing blood. Consult your local authority to find out their procedure for dealing with it. Contaminated waste is usually placed into a yellow bin with a yellow plastic liner. Any sharp objects, such as broken glass or used needles, must be put into a **sharps box**.

Protection of Children Act (1999)

Employers involved in the care of children (anyone under 18 years old) should check the names of people they intend to employ to make sure they are not included in a list called the Protection of Children Act List or List 99. This list contains names of individuals considered unsuitable to work with children.

Consumer Protection Act (1987)

This Act provides the customer with protection when buying goods or services (such as beauty treatments) to make sure that products are safe for use on the customer during the treatment, or are safe to be sold as a retail product.

Cosmetic Products (Safety) Regulations (2004)

These regulations relate to the Consumer Protection Act (1987) and require that cosmetics and toiletries are tested and safe for use.

Local Government Act (1982)

By-laws are laws made by your local authority (council) and are mostly concerned with hygiene practice. Different councils around the UK will have different by-laws. Advice can be sought by contacting your local Environmental Health Officer.

Local Government (Miscellaneous Provisions) Act (1982)

A therapist must apply for a licence from the local Environmental Health and Trading Standards Department if needles are used for any treatments such as ear piercing. For more information see **Unit B7: Carry out ear piercing**.

Cosmetics must be tested to ensure they are safe to use

Insurance

Employers Liability (Compulsory Insurance) Act 1969

Employers must take out insurance policies in case of claims by employees for injury, disease or illness related to the workplace. It protects an employer against any claims made by an employee. A certificate must be displayed at work to show that the employer has this insurance.

Other types of insurance include:

- public liability insurance: this insurance protects you if a client or member of the public becomes injured on your premises, for example, if they fall off the couch

- product liability insurance: this type of insurance protects you against claims arising from products used by clients if they cause any damage or injury. A product must be 'fit for purpose'. If you supply a faulty product, a client may try to claim from you first, even if you did not manufacture it

- treatment liability insurance: this insurance protects you in the event of a claim arising from malpractice. It covers the therapist for damage to clients caused by a treatment.

Codes of practice and codes of ethics

Industry codes of practice for hygiene in salons and clinics

VTCT in association with the Federation of Holistic Therapists publishes the code of practice. The code of practice is concerned with hygiene in the salon and gives guidelines for the therapist. Local by-laws also contain these guidelines to ensure good hygienic practice and avoid cross-infection.

Industry code of ethics

A code of ethics is a set of guidelines that a professional beauty therapist must follow.

A beauty therapist must follow the industry code of ethics

- All health, safety and hygiene legislation must be adhered to and the therapist should be adequately insured.
- The best possible treatment should be given to the client.
- The client should be respected and their dignity maintained at all times.
- A therapist should never claim to cure a condition.
- A therapist should not treat a client who is contra-indicated to treatment. (See below.)
- All clients should be treated in a professional manner, regardless of their race, gender or creed.
- All information given, written or verbal, is confidential and should not be disclosed to anyone without written permission, except when required to do so by law.
- Records of treatments carried out should be kept up to date and complete.
- Further training should be undertaken to enhance skills.
- Therapists should be members of a professional beauty association.

Contra-indications

A **contra-indication** is a reason (usually medical) why a therapist may not be able to provide treatment to a client. General contra-indications can affect the whole body, for example, high blood pressure. However, most contra-indications only restrict treatment, which means that treatment can go ahead but the affected area is avoided, for example a small area of

key terms

Contra-indication: any medical reason, or other factor, that would either prevent or restrict treatment.

bruising. Contra-indications will mostly be discovered during a consultation.

> **Good practice**
>
> Never inform the client that they may have a nasty medical condition! It would be unprofessional, may be incorrect, and could cause unnecessary worry. The client should be referred to their doctor.

Consultation

The consultation involves discussing the treatment with the client so that they are fully aware of the procedure, how much it will cost and how long it will take (**service time**). It also enables the therapist to find out about the client's expectations of the treatment (what they hope to gain from the treatment).

The consultation may be held in the reception area or in a treatment room. It should be carried out in a quiet, private place, as personal information is discussed. As always, it is vital that the therapist looks professional and behaves in a professional manner in order to reassure the client that they will be receiving a good service.

As well as finding out if the client has any contra-indications to treatment, the therapist may ask questions about the client's lifestyle, general health, and current beauty routines.

Record card/consultation form

During the consultation, a **record card/consultation form** will be completed for each client or, if the client is a regular visitor to the salon, their previous card/form will be used.

The record card/consultation form will show the client's personal details (name, address, date of birth, etc.) and any information that is gathered from the consultation. It also shows any treatments that the client has, any products that are recommended to them, and any purchases made.

If the client has any unwanted **contra-actions** (reactions) to a treatment, this should also be recorded on the record card/consultation form. It is important to do this for insurance purposes, and in case of any future action that may be taken against you by the client.

key terms

Service time: commercially acceptable time to carry out a treatment.

Record card: also known as a **consultation form**. It includes the client's name, address, date of birth, contact details and health questionnaire. The client should sign and date the record card before any treatment takes place.

Contra-action: a reaction that happens during or after treatment. This may be an unwanted reaction, such as irritation caused by a product, or a desirable reaction, such as erythema (reddening of the skin) following a facial.

Good practice

Always note any unwanted contra-actions to products on the client's record card/consultation form. This will ensure you do not use the same product again if they return for treatment.

If the client returns to the salon for further treatments, the therapist will be able to look at their client's record card/consultation form to see if they have any contra-indications or allergies, or anything else the therapist would need to know before giving a treatment.

The information gathered from the consultation is used to make a **treatment/service plan** for the client, which may also be written on the record card/consultation form.

Always ensure the client signs the record card/consultation form, as this may be a requirement of your salon's insurance company.

Good practice

If the client is under the age of 16, you will need to get permission from their parent/guardian in order to carry out a treatment. The parent/guardian will also need to be present while the treatment is being carried out, and they will need to sign a **consent form**. The consent form should be kept for three years so it can be inspected if necessary.

Go to www.nelsonthornes.com/salon/free-resources for an example of a consultation form.

During a consultation with a client, it may become apparent that the client has a contra-indication to treatment, such as **diabetes**, which requires a doctor's advice before the treatment can be carried out. A standard letter can be given to their doctor, or posted, enclosing a stamped addressed envelope. The doctor need only sign their name to advise their patient if they think there is a medical reason why treatment should not go ahead.

Good practice

Make sure you also send a leaflet, which briefly explains the treatment, as the doctor may not know what the treatment involves.

key terms

Treatment/service plan: the therapist puts together a plan of action that includes choice of products, client preferences and so on, to ensure the best possible treatment is given and that it meets with the client's expectations.

Consent form: a form, usually pre-prepared, that shows the date, name, date of birth, address and contact numbers for the client, the details of the treatment being carried out, and the signature of the parent/guardian. Sometimes, instead of there being a separate consent form, the consultation form will include a paragraph asking the parent/guardian to sign the form if the client is under 16 years of age.

Diabetes: condition caused by insufficient production of the hormone insulin, or tissues that do not respond to insulin. In people with diabetes, the skin may be paper thin and, because of poor circulation, healing may also be poor. There may also be loss of skin sensation.

[Address of salon]

[Date]

Dear Dr [name]

Your patient [name] of [his/her address] has informed me that he/she is suffering from [for example, diabetes].

Please advise me if, in your view, there is any reason why your patient should not have [for example, massage] treatment.

Thank you

Yours sincerely

[your signature]

[your name printed]

- -

Doctor's advice

I believe [name of client] would/would not be suitable for having [for example, massage] treatment.

Doctor's signature .... Date ....

Sample letter to doctor

Note that doctors often do not know what a beauty treatment involves, and therefore cannot give permission for treatment to go ahead; they can only advise their patient. A doctor's insurance does not cover them for giving permission or consent regarding beauty therapy treatments.

The treatment room

The treatment room must be clean, tidy, and all the equipment must be in good working order. The couch may have a plastic cover to help protect it from products such as wax. Clean towels are often placed over the top of couches for client comfort and hygiene. Therapists commonly use couch roll, also known as paper roll, to put on top of the towels. Couch roll is easily replaced after each client. There must be sufficient lighting. A magnifying lamp is useful to do close-up work, such as eyebrow shaping. It is important that the room is warm, as clients will not relax and enjoy the treatment if they feel cold. The trolley or workstation must be well presented, with all products, tools and equipment cleaned and ready to use.

Treatment room

Good practice

If a client is pregnant or has high or low blood pressure, raise the back of the couch slightly so they do not lie flat.

Personal presentation

Wearing the correct protective clothing and behaving in a professional manner will help to reduce health and safety risks.

Personal presentation should be taken very seriously and the therapist should ensure the following.

- Nails are clean and short – to prevent accidental scratching to the client, and also because the free edge contains germs that could cause cross-infection.

- Hair is tied back – this gives a professional look as well as being more hygienic.

- If necessary, wear protective items such as disposable gloves when carrying out certain treatments, such as bikini line waxing.

- Wear sensible shoes – this will help prevent conditions such as bunions developing. As well as being uncomfortable, high-heeled shoes are a health and safety hazard, as you are more likely to trip over when wearing them. Closed-toe shoes are preferred in order to protect your feet, e.g. if you were to spill hydrogen peroxide when preparing for an eyelash tint.

- Wear minimum jewellery – jewellery, such as rings, will hold bacteria and may scratch the client during treatment.

Professional-looking therapist

Professional behaviour

- Wash hands before and after each treatment.

- Be tidy.

- Store hazardous products according to the manufacturer's instructions.

- Make sure you maintain a good posture to help avoid aches and pains.

- Follow correct lifting procedures.

- Make sure you understand how to use electrical equipment safely. If you are unsure, you should discuss the matter with your manager.

- Make sure everything is kept scrupulously clean.

- Dispose of all waste hygienically. Dispose of contaminated waste as recommended by your local authority.

Posture

A good posture means that the body is aligned and balanced so that muscles only need to carry out minimum work to maintain it. It will ensure muscles and joints are working efficiently so that the body remains free from muscular tension, strains, stiffness and pain. Good posture will help encourage efficient breathing and aid digestion, as the organs will not be compressed or restricted owing to bad posture and tightened muscles.

Correction of posture

To help correct posture take into account the following points.

- The head should be up with chin in.

- Shoulders should be back, but down and relaxed.

- Abdominal muscles should be pulled in.

- Buttock muscles should be tightened and tucked in.

- Knees should be slightly bent.

- The weight of the body should be evenly distributed on both feet.

Good practice

Be aware of your posture when sitting. Make sure your chair has a good back support and try not to slouch. Keep the chest up and shoulders back.

Avoiding cross-infection

There is a lot that can be done to prevent cross-infection occurring in the salon. This includes:

- regular washing of hands
- placing paper roll on the couch and trolley
- making sure clients stand on paper roll or towels when barefoot
- using disposable items
- using spatulas to remove products from containers
- wearing disposable gloves
- special disposal of contaminated items
- cleaning, disinfecting and sterilising tools, items and work surfaces.

Therapist placing paper roll on couch

Cleaning, disinfection and sterilisation

Cleaning

Cleaning is a process that removes substances such as dirt, including some **microorganisms**. Microorganisms include fungi, bacteria and viruses. Cleaning is an essential step before **disinfection** or **sterilisation** is carried out. It does not necessarily destroy all microorganisms, despite a clean-looking area. When cleaning, make sure the water is warm and also use a detergent.

> **Good practice**
>
> Store cleaned equipment in a clean drawer and avoid putting contaminated items into the drawer.

Disinfection

Disinfectants reduce the number of harmful microorganisms to a level where they can no longer cause disease. However, they do not kill spores, which are produced by certain bacteria and can grow to become bacteria that may then cause disease. The extent to which disinfection is successful depends on how dirty the item is and how many microorganisms are present. It is important to clean the article first, before disinfecting it.

Some examples of disinfectants are alcohols, chlorine and ultraviolet (UV) radiation.

key terms

Microorganisms: tiny living organisms including bacteria, viruses and fungi.

Disinfection: a process that reduces the number of harmful microorganisms to a level where they can no longer cause disease.

Sterilisation: a process that kills microorganisms to prevent cross-infection.

DON'T FORGET

Equipment is only as hygienic as the environment in which it is stored.

Ultraviolet radiation

The **ultraviolet (UV) cabinet** is used to sanitise items such as brushes, tweezers and manicure tools. It uses short-wave UV radiation. Items such as metal tools should be firstly wiped with an **antiseptic**. Only the side the UV rays touch will be sanitised, so the item will need to be turned over. It takes around 20 minutes to sanitise tools. The UV cabinet is also ideal for storing tools that have been cleaned and disinfected.

Antiseptics

Antiseptics are substances that have disinfection effects but can be used safely on the skin. They kill, or affect the growth and action of, most disease-causing bacteria, viruses and fungi.

Good practice

UV radiation is damaging to the eyes, so do not look directly at the light.

Good practice

Store disinfected items inside a disinfected, sealed container for up to a day. If the items are left for longer than this, bacteria will start to build up on them again. They will be clean but not disinfected.

Good practice

Disinfecting wipes are a hygienic and quick way of cleaning surfaces.

Sterilisation

Sterilisation destroys microorganisms and their spores. Heat treatment is the most commonly used method of sterilisation. Some different types of steriliser are described below.

Autoclave

The autoclave is an effective method of sterilisation. Water is boiled under pressure inside a container. Items to be sterilised are placed into the upper chamber of the autoclave in removable trays and the water is contained in the lower part. It is useful for sterilising small metal tools. The water boils at around 121°C, and the resulting steam is hot enough to sterilise the contents. The sterilisation process takes about 15 minutes.

> ### key terms
>
> **Ultraviolet (UV) cabinet:** a cabinet with an ultraviolent lamp producing rays that prevent the growth of bacteria. It provides a hygienic environment for storage of equipment. Equipment such as manicure tools, tweezers and brushes can be stored in the cabinet.
>
> **Antiseptic:** a substance which can be applied to the skin, to destroy and prevent the growth of harmful microorganisms. Alcohol is a common antiseptic.

UV cabinet

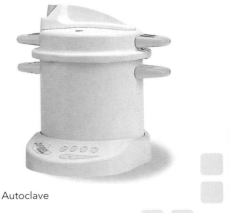

Autoclave

Dry-heat steriliser

Dry heat sterilisers are similar in shape to a microwave but contain stainless steel metal trays to place items upon, a thermostat and a timer. The unit sterilises at temperatures of 160°C to 180°C, which are reached within 15 minutes. It is suitable for metal, glass and delicate items.

Dry-heat steriliser

Glass-bead steriliser

This type of steriliser contains beads that are heated and help to destroy microorganisms and spores. Glass beads are heated to 250°C to effectively destroy all germs. This method is effective for sterilising small, solid metal and glass implements in seconds. It is suitable for sterilising scissors, tweezers and cuticle tools.

Glass-bead steriliser

> **Good practice**
>
> If an item cannot be properly cleaned, it should be treated as 'single use'.

Infectious and non-infectious skin conditions

Beauty therapists mostly carry out treatments that involve the skin, therefore it is important to know which skin conditions are infectious in order to avoid cross-infection.

Infectious skin conditions can be classified as: bacterial infections, viral infections, fungal infections and infestations. Infectious conditions can be caught by direct contact with an infected person. Some can also be caught by indirect contact with contaminated items, such as towels, coins and door handles, which can store microorganisms such as bacteria.

Non-infectious skin conditions include pigmentation disorders, allergies and cancers.

Bacterial infections

Bacteria are tiny single-celled organisms that can multiply very quickly. They are capable of breeding outside the body, so can be caught easily by direct contact (e.g. touching someone) or by touching a contaminated article (e.g. a towel).

There are two types of bacteria: **pathogenic** and **non-pathogenic**. Infections occur when harmful bacteria (pathogens) enter the skin through broken skin or hair follicles. The most common are listed below.

> **key terms**
>
> **Pathogenic:** a pathogen is able to cause a disease, such as a pathogenic bacteria.
>
> **Non-pathogenic:** not capable of causing disease.

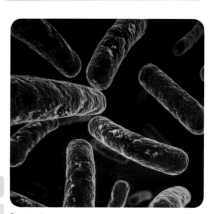

Bacteria

Boils and carbuncles

A boil is an infection of the hair follicle, which begins as a tender, red lump and develops into a painful pustule containing pus. It extends deep into the skin's tissue. Once a head is formed, the pus is discharged, leaving a space, so scarring of the skin often remains after the boil has healed. Carbuncles are a group of boils involving several hair follicles. Poor general health and inadequate diet are factors that increase the chances of developing boils. Sufferers are treated with antibiotics. Boils are infectious, so the area affected should be avoided during treatment. Boils can be dangerous if they occur on the upper lip, in the nose or near to the eyes or brain. In such cases clients should be referred to their doctor.

Boil

Styes

A sty is a small boil on the edge of the eyelid and is caused by an infection of the follicle of an eyelash. The area becomes inflamed and swollen and there may be pus present. Styes are infectious and are mostly caused by bacteria entering the skin, so it is important that the eyelid area is kept clean to prevent them occurring. A doctor may prescribe antibiotics if the infection spreads.

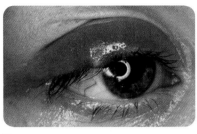
Styes

Conjunctivitis

This is inflammation of the conjunctiva, the membrane covering the eye. The inner eyelid and eyeball appear red and sore. It is caused by an infection following irritation to the eye, such as grit or dust that enter the eye, and is further aggravated by rubbing. Pus is often present and may ooze from the area. Conjunctivitis is infectious and cross-infection can occur through using contaminated towels or tissues.

Conjunctivitis

Impetigo

This infection begins when bacteria invade a cut, cold sore or other broken skin. It can be seen as weeping blisters that form golden/yellow-coloured crusts. The area around the crusts is inflamed and red. Impetigo is highly infectious and spreads quickly on the surface of the skin. Usually the outbreaks are among children and often go hand in hand with lice infestations. If this condition is suspected, the sufferer must be referred to the doctor and treated with antibiotics.

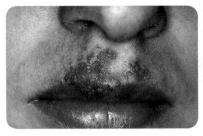
Impetigo

Folliculitis

Folliculitis is a common skin condition and can be caused by a bacterial or fungal infection of the hair follicles. Symptoms include skin inflammation, red swellings (papules) and pus-filled swellings (pustules). It can be a side effect of certain medicines such as steroids. The area should be avoided during treatment.

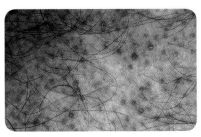
Folliculitis

Viral infections

Although very small, viruses are responsible for a great deal of human disease. Cells in the body are taken over by invading viruses and so break down. Viruses need living cells in which to live and multiply – they cannot live outside their host. Many viruses take up residence along nerve pathways, which accounts for the pain associated with viral infections such as shingles. They can be transmitted by direct and indirect contact.

Cold sores

Cold sores are a common skin infection caused by the herpes simplex virus. It is usually passed on in early childhood, probably after being kissed by someone with a cold sore. The virus passes through the skin, travels up a nerve and lies dormant at a nerve junction. When the virus is stimulated, it travels back down the nerve and forms a cold sore. It begins as an area of **erythema** (redness) on the skin, which blisters and forms a crust, usually around the mouth. Cold sores often appear after a period of stress. They can also be triggered by exposure to bright sunlight, menstruation or may accompany colds and flu. Cold sores are highly infectious so the area must be avoided during treatment.

Warts

Warts include the common wart (verruca vulgaris). They are firm, raised, pink or skin-coloured lumps with a bumpy surface that may look like a cauliflower. They are often seen alone or in groups on the hands, elbows or knees, and will generally disappear on their own within two to three years. Warts are caused by infection with the human papilloma virus (HPV), which can take anything from one month up to two years after contact to cause a wart to form. The virus is spread by direct contact with an infected person, or by touching damp surfaces carrying the virus, such as swimming pool floors and changing rooms, which have been in contact with a person who has warts.

Plantar warts, also known as verrucas (or verrucae), appear on the soles of the feet and grow inwards. Plantar warts are painful and can be differentiated from corns and calluses as they contain areas of black speckling and fine bleeding points. They should be removed medically, although they sometimes disappear by themselves.

Warts and verrucas are infectious and so should not be touched.

Fungal infections

Disease causing (pathogenic) fungi produce infectious conditions. Microscopic fungi spores reproduce by the process of cell

key terms

Erythema: erythema is redness of the skin due to increased blood circulation.

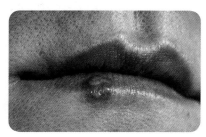

Cold sore

Warts

key terms

Vitiligo: vitiligo causes the skin, and sometimes the hair, to turn white in patches. This is due to melanoctyes (pigment cells) being either damaged or destroyed. It is thought that the body's own immune system attacks the pigment cells.

division. Fungi need other cells to survive and often affect dead tissue, such as hair and nails.

Ringworm (Tinea corporis)

Ringworm is a fungal infection (not caused by a worm) and is sometimes caught through touching animals. It affects the horny layer of the skin and shows itself as red, scaly, circular patches that spread outwards. The centre of the patch heals, forming a ring shape. It usually appears on the trunk of the body, the limbs and the face. Ringworm is highly infectious so the area must be avoided during treatment and the client should be referred to their doctor.

Infestations

Animal parasites also cause disorders of the human skin.

Scabies

The scabies mite burrows into and lays its eggs in the horny layer of the skin. It can affect most areas of the body, although it is commonly found in the webs between the fingers and in the crease of the elbow. There is a four-to six-week incubation period before the outbreak. The female mite leaves a trail of eggs and excrement in the skin, which appears as wavy greyish lines. The condition is very itchy and highly infectious. No treatment should be given and the client should consult their doctor.

Pigmentation disorders

Chloasma

This condition shows itself as patches of increased pigmentation on areas of the skin, often the face. This can be caused by sunburn, pregnancy or the contraceptive pill. This condition is not infectious and treatment can be carried out.

Vitiligo

This condition shows itself as a complete loss of colour in areas of the skin. The affected areas have either lost their pigment or were never pigmented. The lightened patches of skin are very sensitive to sunlight and burn easily. The cause of **vitiligo** is unknown. This condition is not infectious and treatment can be carried out.

Freckles

Freckles (ephelides) show themselves as small, pigmented areas of skin. The UV rays from sunlight stimulate the production of melanin and therefore either darken freckles or create new ones. Freckles are not infectious and can be worked over during treatment.

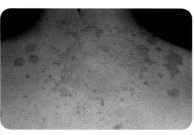

Ringworm

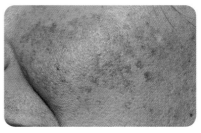

Scabies

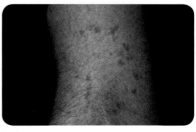

Chloasma

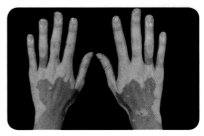

Vitiligo

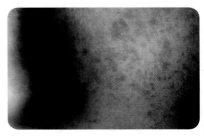

Freckles

Skin allergies

An allergy is an abnormal response by the body's immune system to a foreign substance (allergen). Some individuals can react to ordinary substances that are harmless to most people. Irritation to the skin causes some of its cells to release a substance called histamine, which causes the skin to become warm, red and swollen. An irritated skin caused by an allergy is not infectious, but it is advisable not to work over the affected area.

Urticaria

Urticaria is often called nettle rash or hives. A red rash develops that is very itchy and disappears completely within minutes, or gradually over a number of hours. There are numerous causes of urticaria. It can occur as an allergic response to substances such as certain foods and drugs, or it can be caused by heat, cold, sunlight, scabies, insect bites and contact with plants. This condition is not infectious, but it is advisable not to work over the affected area during treatment.

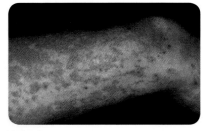

Urticaria

Dermatitis

Dermatitis is an inflammation of the skin caused by contact with external substances. Common irritants are detergents and dyes, but materials such as nylon and wool, and chemicals found in perfumes can produce allergic reactions that can lead to dermatitis. Symptoms include erythema (redness), itching and flaking of the skin and, in severe cases, blisters can develop. Although the condition is not infectious, it is advisable not to work over the affected area until it has cleared up.

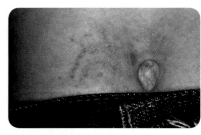

Dermatitis

Eczema

Eczema is an inflammation of the skin that features itchy, dry, scaly red patches. Small blisters may burst, causing the skin to weep. Hereditary factors or external irritants such as detergents, cosmetics and soaps can cause eczema. Internal irritants such as dairy products can also be a trigger. This condition is not infectious, although it is advisable to avoid working over the affected areas during treatment, especially if there is weeping or bleeding.

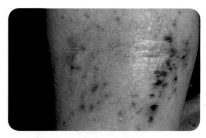

Eczema

Sebaceous gland disorders

Milia

If skin keratinises over the hair follicle, it causes sebum and other substances to accumulate and become trapped in the hair follicle. It is the keratinised skin cells that cause the hard lump. A milium (plural: milia) can be seen as a small white spot, so is often termed a white head, and mostly accompanies dry skin. This condition is not infectious and treatment can be given.

Milia

Comedones

Comedones (singular: comedo), also known as blackheads, occur when sebum becomes trapped in a hair follicle. Keratinised cells mix with the sebum and form a plug. The head of the comedo becomes black in colour because it combines with the oxygen in the air (oxidises). Comedones generally occur on greasy skin types and are not infectious. Treatment can be given.

Acne vulgaris

Acne is a common complaint that usually affects teenagers. It is caused by an overproduction of sebum, usually caused by stimulation of the sebaceous glands by hormones called testosterone and progesterone. During adolescence, the levels of these sex hormones rise. The sebum, along with dead skin cells, becomes trapped in the openings of the sebaceous glands and, if they become infected, red and swollen spots will appear. Comedones (blackheads) also form and, if they become infected, the typical red and swollen spot appears. The spots are mainly found on the face, neck and back. Acne is not infectious, but a treatment may need to be modified to suit the client's needs.

Rosacea

This condition is often referred to as **acne rosacea**. It mainly affects people over the age of 30, and is more common in women than men. Rosacea affects the nose, cheeks and forehead, giving a flushed, reddened appearance. The blood vessels, which are dilated in these areas, produce a butterfly shape. Pus-filled spots may appear, and the affected area may also become lumpy because of swollen sebaceous glands. Triggers include eating spicy or hot food, drinking alcohol and stress. It is not an infectious condition, but care needs to be taken when working over the affected areas. It is advisable to avoid the area if a client has a severe case of rosacea.

Skin disorders involving abnormal growth

Psoriasis

In people with psoriasis, the skin cells reproduce too quickly in certain areas of the skin. This results in thickened patches of skin, which are red, dry, itchy, and covered in silvery scales. Psoriasis may be mild and only affect the elbows and knees, or may cover the whole body, including the scalp. The cause is unknown, although the condition tends to be hereditary and stress can be a factor. Psoriasis is not infectious, so treatment can be given providing there is no bleeding or weeping; the client will not feel any discomfort.

Comedones

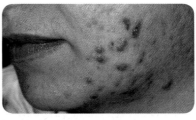

Acne vulgaris

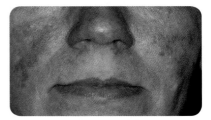

Rosacea

key terms

Acne rosacea: a common disorder that causes redness on the nose, cheeks and forehead and, if not treated, red solid bumps and pus-filled pimples can develop. The nose may become bulbous and swollen looking. Broken capillaries are also associated with this condition.

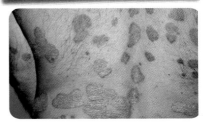

Psoriasis

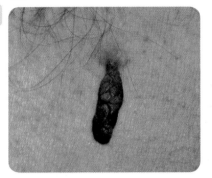

Skin tags

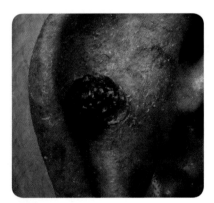

Skin cancer – carcinoma

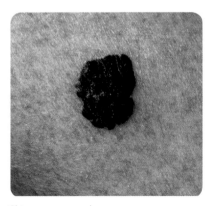

Skin cancer – melanoma

Skin tags

Skin tags can affect most parts of the body, and are often found on the neck. They are made of loose fibrous tissue, which protrudes out from the skin, and are mainly brown in colour. They are harmless and are not infectious. Removal of skin tags can be carried out by a doctor or certain beauty clinics. It is advisable not to work over the skin tags as it may be uncomfortable for the client.

Skin cancer

Skin cancer is an abnormal and uncontrolled growth of cells in the skin. There are three main types of skin cancer, named after the types of skin cell from which they develop.

Basal cell carcinoma and squamous cell carcinoma

Basal cell and squamous cell carcinomas account for 95 per cent of all skin cancers. They are usually found on areas of the body often exposed to the sun, such as the face, neck, arms and hands. These cancers are often painless and begin as small, shiny, rounded lumps, that form into ulcers as they enlarge. They appear to be brought on by UV light and are usually seen in fair-skinned people. They are not infectious but should be avoided during treatment.

Melanoma

A melanoma is a skin growth caused by overactivity of the melanocytes, usually the result of excessive exposure to the sun. Melanocyte overactivity may be benign (not harmful), as in a mole, or malignant (cancerous) as in a malignant melanoma. Although rare and not infectious, malignant melanomas are extremely dangerous. They can occur anywhere on the body but often at the site of a mole. They are usually irregular in outline, patchy in colour, itchy or sore and may bleed. They spread very quickly and need prompt medical attention.

The danger signs to look out for are:

- any new moles that appear
- a mole that gets bigger
- a mole that bleeds, itches or ulcerates
- a mole that gets darker or lighter in colour.

Good practice

Of course, you must never tell a client that you think they may have skin cancer. However, you should advise them to see their doctor.

For more information about the skin see the **Anatomy and physiology** unit.

How are you doing?

1 Which Act ensures that employers and employees maintain high standards of health and safety in the workplace?

a Environmental Protection Act

b Consumer Protection Act

c Health and Safety at Work Act

d Health and Safety (First Aid) Regulations

2 If a client fainted, what immediate action would you take?

a Give them a glass of water

b Try to stand them up

c Lie them flat and place a pillow under the lower legs

d Sit them in a chair

3 What do the initials COSHH stand for?

a Control of Substances Hurtful to Health

b Control of Substances Helpful to Health

c Control of Situations Hazardous to Health

d Control of Substances Hazardous to Health

4 Which of the following would you **not** find contained within a fire extinguisher?

a Water

b Petrol

c Carbon dioxide

d Foam

5 Which Act states that fire exit doors must be clearly marked?

a Fire Precautions Act

b Fire Protection Act

c Fire Purpose Act

d Fire Prevention Act

6 Which of the following is **not** a hazard symbol?

a Toxic

b Corrosive

c Highly flammable

d Very fragile

7 A reason why a therapist may not be able to provide treatment to a client is called a:

a contra-action

b contra-indication

c contra-association

d contra-treatment

8 Which of the following will help to prevent cross-infection occurring?

a Wearing disposable gloves

b Using clean towels

c Using disposable items

d All of the above

9 What is the correct definition of sterilisation?

a A process that reduces numbers of harmful microorganisms

b A type of antiseptic that is used to clean the skin

c A process that destroys microorganisms and their spores

d A process that kills all bacteria

10 Which of the following skin conditions is caused by a virus?

a Cold sore

b Athlete's foot

c Impetigo

d Dermatitis

are you ready *for* assessment?

The evidence for this unit must be gathered in the workplace (salon) or realistic working environment (training centre).

Simulation (role play) is not allowed for any performance evidence (such as carrying out a treatment) within this unit.

You must ensure health and safety is followed in your practical work at all times, and that you have met the required standard for this unit.

You must achieve all outcomes, assessment criteria and range statement to pass this unit.

Assessing your practical work

All evidence can be gathered while carrying out beauty therapy treatment in your place of work or training centre. You can demonstrate outcomes by any of the following.

- Observation by your assessor in your place of work or training centre. Your assessor will watch you carry out treatments and other relevant tasks, and will sign off an outcome when it is achieved.

- Signed statement by a colleague or line manager who has witnessed your successful performance of activities in your place of work.

- Documentary or other product-based evidence.

- A report written by yourself and supported by your colleagues.

- You can be asked questions.

- Evidence can be gathered during a discussion.

In this unit you must show you are capable of all practical outcomes on at least **three** separate occasions.

Assessing your knowledge and understanding

You will be guided by your tutor and assessor on the evidence that needs to be produced.

Your knowledge and understanding will be assessed using the assessment tools listed below.

■ Portfolio of evidence

■ Oral questioning

G4 Fulfil salon reception duties

DON'T FORGET

People make their judgements within the first four seconds of entering a salon, so first impressions really do count.

Introduction

An efficiently run reception area helps to ensure the success of the salon. A receptionist is expected to greet clients and handle enquiries, make appointments, answer the telephone, deal with payment, and deal with retail sales and stock control.

UNIT OUTCOME 1

Be able to maintain the reception area

First impressions

The receptionist has a very important role to play in the running of the beauty salon, and may be the first person the client sees and speaks to. If the receptionist is unprofessional, the client may be put off visiting for treatment.

Everyone working in a beauty salon must be mindful of their appearance, and the receptionist is no exception. If the

The receptionist must be professional

receptionist is dirty and scruffily dressed, it will reflect badly on the salon. The client's first impression of the salon may be the reception area, so it is important that it is kept clean and tidy. The retail shelves should be fully stocked and the products attractively presented so they are eye-catching.

The receptionist not only greets clients, but also has many other duties, including:

- making appointments
- dealing with enquiries, which may be face-to-face, by telephone or email
- taking messages
- making phone calls, and sending text message and emails
- escorting the client to their therapist
- taking and dealing with payment
- ensuring the reception area is fully equipped with the necessary stationery and materials
- ensuring shelves are fully stocked with retail products
- keeping the reception area and product displays clean, neat and tidy at all times
- providing the therapists with client record cards/consultation forms (which need to be kept organised in a card index box or filing cabinet)
- providing clients with information regarding products for sale and assisting with selling the products
- dealing with complaints and compliments.

Reception area

All staff, including the receptionist, should help to ensure the salon is kept tidy and safe at all times. A client may leave crumbs on the floor, magazines in a mess, or there may be coffee spills or record cards/consultation forms left lying around. This type of mess is unacceptable and must be dealt with quickly.

Put yourself in your client's position – how would you like to be treated, and how would you expect a professional reception area to look?

Stationery and materials

The receptionist needs to ensure the reception area contains everything necessary to allow smooth running of the salon. A disorganised receptionist will affect the whole salon and result in dissatisfied staff and clients. Stationery and materials required in the reception area include:

- pens, pencils and eraser
- treatment price lists
- product price lists
- appointment book
- appointment cards
- pre-treatment and aftercare advice leaflets
- client record cards/consultation forms
- gift vouchers
- samples and testers
- stock sheets
- till cashing-up sheets
- message pad to record messages
- calculator
- first-aid kit
- accident report book.

Treatment price lists briefly discuss each treatment and include information such as: the price of each treatment, how long it will take to carry out, the salon's opening hours, current special offers, the salon address, telephone number and email address.

Reception items

Messages

The receptionist will be expected to take down messages for staff and clients. It is important that information such as who the message is for and from, the date and time, details of the message and contact details are written down on a message pad. The message should be quickly passed to the appropriate person.

Sienna's Beauty Salon

For: Sienna

Date: 14 February

Time: 2 pm

Message: Please can you call Mrs Canes regarding a facial product she bought from the salon?

Tel no: 0117 9758444.

Taken by: Charlotte

Sample message pad

UNIT OUTCOME 2

Be able to attend to clients and enquiries

UNIT OUTCOME 6

Understand communication methods

---

key terms

Body language: how people interpret the movements and gestures of a person's body. For example, a slouched receptionist with folded arms may be interpreted as being unfriendly, bored and disinterested in dealing with the client. Positive body language with good eye contact sends the correct signals.

Communicating with the client

Greeting and talking to clients not only involves using verbal skills, but also non-verbal skills such as listening and using **body language**. When talking to your client ensure you give good eye contact and smile regularly. Ensure you hold a good posture, which involves sitting with your back straight. If you slouch with your arms folded, your client may think you are not interested in dealing with their enquiry. Careful listening is a skill, and it is surprising how many people are not very good at doing it. When talking to your client, allow them to finish their sentences without interruption. If you do not listen properly, this is annoying for the client, and you may make a mistake because you have not fully understood their request. Remember, it can be very irritating for the therapist if appointments are incorrectly booked, or if an unsuitable product has been sold to a client.

Ensure you give good eye contact and smile when talking to clients

Good practice

Clients like to feel special. If they tell you, for instance, they are taking a holiday on a cruise liner, make sure you note this on their record card/consultation form. You can ask them how they got on the next time they visit.

Client relaxing in reception area

When a client arrives for an appointment, make sure you give them your full attention and make good eye contact. Help them take off their coat and hang it up. While escorting a client to a reception chair, the receptionist, in a very friendly manner, will often say something like:

> 'Please take a seat, the therapist will be with you shortly. Would you like a magazine to read and something to drink?'

If the client is too early, or has to wait a while for their treatment, always ask them if they would like a beverage, such as tea or coffee or a soft drink. The client may also be offered a drink while having a treatment such as a pedicure.

Good practice

A client's coat should be hung up upon arrival. The receptionist can also help a client put on their coat as they leave.

It is common for a salon, especially if it is positioned on a busy main street, to have 'passing trade', which refers to people who are passing the salon and walk in to request a treatment or buy a product. They may want an appointment at that moment, so the receptionist should do their best to find an available therapist and a time on the appointment sheet to carry out the treatment.

Answering the telephone

Do not answer the telephone while someone is standing at the reception desk. If a client comes to the reception desk and you are already talking on the telephone, ensure you acknowledge them with a smile. Do not make a gesture with your hand, encouraging them to sit down on a chair – it is extremely annoying for a client.

When answering the telephone, smile!

When answering the telephone, do so with a smile on your face. When you do this the sound of your voice changes, making you sound more positive, happy and pleasant. If a caller asks you to repeat the business name or your name, you have probably spoken too quickly or mumbled. Always give your full attention to the caller. Do not find other things to do at the same time, such as sorting out leaflets, otherwise you will be more likely to make mistakes and perhaps enter an incorrect appointment.

When answering the telephone most receptionists in salons will use a greeting similar to this one.

> 'Good morning, Sienna's Beauty Salon. My name is Charlotte. How may I help you?'

Good practice

Answer a ringing telephone or an email message as soon as possible. Nobody likes to be kept waiting.

Dealing with an unhappy client

The receptionist should follow the salon policy regarding complaints.

- Always remain calm, polite and listen carefully to what the client has to say.

- Ensure that you fully understand the complaint and state the main facts back to the client so they know you are clear about the situation.

- Never be rude, awkward or raise your voice.

- You may be able to sort out the situation so the client is satisfied with the outcome. If you are unsure of how to handle the matter, or if the client is still dissatisfied, contact your supervisor for help.

- Write details of the complaint onto the client record card/consultation form, stating the time and date, details of the complaint and the outcome.

Ensure you fully understand what the complaint is

Good practice

Even though you may feel your client is being very unreasonable, never raise your voice or get angry with them. It is unprofessional and gives a bad impression of the business.

Making appointments

An appointment page helps members of staff to quickly and easily see which clients are booked in for treatments on that day. Many salons will use a computer booking system instead of using sheets of paper. A computer system is also useful for communicating special offers and newsletters to clients, and for monitoring **stock levels**, product orders and **sales figures**.

Note that any client information stored either on the salon's computer system or on record cards/consultation forms is covered by the Data Protection Act. This Act controls how personal information is used and protects against misuse of personal details. It also gives people the right to insist that any information that others keep about them is accurate.

The appointment system will be prepared many weeks in advance. When a client has a treatment, for instance waxing, they may want to rebook another appointment for six weeks later. There will be a procedure regarding making appointments in every salon. The information written into an appointment book includes the therapist's name, the client's name, their contact details, and the treatment they are receiving.

Good practice

Occasionally a receptionist or therapist may forget to write down the contact details of a client on the appointment page. So, a well organised record card/consultation form system can help the receptionist locate a client's contact details, if they are an existing client.

Note that the appointment page is divided into 15-minute intervals, so if a client requires an eyebrow tidy, only one of the 15-minute slots will be needed and therefore filled in. A waxing treatment may take about half an hour, so two 15-minute slots would be booked out.

G

4

When making an appointment with a client, always repeat the treatment details, appointment date and times, and the contact number at the end of the conversation. This will help to avoid any confusion and an incorrect booking being made. Always give a client an appointment card, as this will help act as a memory jogger. Also, many salons will email, text or phone their client shortly before the treatment to remind them.

DON'T FORGET

The appointment page is a record of staff and clients present in the salon, so it is useful in case of emergency.

BK – Back massage
B/L – Bikini line
FBM – Full body massage
C – Cancel
Day: Saturday

DNA – Did not arrive
EBS – Eyebrow shape
EBT – Eyebrow tint
ELT – Eyelash tint
Date: 14th February

EP – Ear piercing
EXT – Extensions
FLW – Full leg wax
F/MAN – French manicure
U/A – under arm

	Charlotte	Sienna	Jayne	Madeline
9.00	Mrs Kaur			
9.15	1/2 leg wax DNA		Mr Canes	MR SHORT
9.30	B/L 60435	MRS LUCAS	Pedicure	BK MASSAGE
9.45		F/MAN	BK	+ MANICURE
10.00		0797 63704	0777 49639	0777 34944
10.15			////////	////////
10.30	MS BESSEX		////////	////////
10.45	FACIAL			
11.00	0117 930349	Ms Mansell	MRS HOUSE	
11.15	////////	Make-up	ELT 0117 932349 C	
11.30		lesson		////////
11.45	Ms Jay EP 32398	0117 956728		LUNCH
12.00		Mrs Thompson	Mrs Gould	
12.15		FLW	Aroma	////////
12.30	////////	0117 60395	FBM 63974	
12.45	LUNCH	////////	////////	MRS STOCKS
1.00		////////	LUNCH	NAIL/EXT
1.15	////////	LUNCH	////////	07890 33204
1.30	Mrs Edwards	////////	////////	
1.45	Manicure	////////	////////	
2.00	EBS	MS BISHTON	Mrs Hodges	
2.15	0117 967529	BRIDAL	EBT/ELT	
2.30	0776 39546	TOP TO TOE	EBS 61398	
2.45		07890 32395		
3.00	Mrs Bedale		MS FUDGE	Ms Smith
3.15	FLW B/L		FACIAL	Make-up
3.30	U/A		ELT	U/A wax
3.45	0117 969348		EBS	0779 63248
4.00	Ms Armstrong		0117 63298	////////
4.15	F/MAN		0779 23698	
4.30	0117 949326			Mrs Bridgeman
4.45	////////			Manicure C
5.00				0779 88467
5.15				////////
5.30				
5.45				

Sample appointment page

HAVE A GO

Make a list of all the treatments provided by your salon, including their service times, and practise making appointments onto an appointment page.

Sample appointment card

When a client arrives for an appointment, the receptionist will often strike out their name in the appointment book, using a tick, so all staff know they have turned up.

Remember the following when booking appointments.

- Use a pencil so that it can easily be rubbed out if necessary. If a client cancels, another client can be booked into their place.

- Make sure the correct amount of time is given to each treatment. Too little time and the therapist will fall behind. Too much time and the salon loses money.

- Book out lunch and break times for staff.

- Ensure your writing is clear and easily understood.

- Give an appointment card to every client.

- Use abbreviations of treatments on the appointment page, for instance, EBS stands for eyebrow shape and HLW stands for half leg wax. Different salons may use different abbreviations.

Appointment problems

Unfortunately, problems do sometimes occur regarding appointments, and the receptionist is responsible for helping to sort them out. Problems that can arise include:

- double booking – two clients have arrived for the same time slot with the same therapist

- client arrives late – a client's treatment time will probably have to be shortened as a result

- staff sickness – if a therapist has a column full of clients booked in and there is no cover, the receptionist will need to contact all of the clients to cancel their treatments.

Salons will use different letters on an appointment page to represent different situations, for instance:

- C – cancelled

- L – late

- FTA – failed to arrive.

The letters will be written in pencil, in case they need to be rubbed out and another client booked in the place.

Cancellation charge

Many salons will state on their treatment price lists that there will be a cancellation charge if a client misses an appointment and fails to give 24 hours notice. A text message, phone call or email reminding the client of their treatment 24 hours beforehand will help prevent this situation arising.

Skin sensitivity test

A receptionist can be trained to carry out a skin sensitivity test if a client is making an appointment for certain treatments, such as an eyelash tint or artificial lashes. The test involves placing a small amount of a product behind the client's ear or on their inner arm. The client is then asked to leave the product on their skin for 24–48 hours to see if a reaction occurs. If it does, then the treatment may not be able to go ahead, but the therapist may be able to advise an alternative treatment.

It is very important to write down details of the test, such as the time, date and the result, on the client's record card/consultation form and store it away safely.

UNIT OUTCOME 4

Be able to handle payments from clients

UNIT OUTCOME 8

Understand how to calculate and take payments

Handling payment from customers

A client can pay for their treatment by different methods, including:

- cash
- cheque
- debit card
- credit card
- gift voucher.

Cash

Most clients will not pay by cash, but if someone chooses to do so, be aware that some banknotes may be fake. There are some checks that you can carry out to ensure that notes are genuine.

- Check the watermark by holding the paper up to the light. Real notes will have the watermark, a picture of the Queen's head, in the paper.

Ask Fran

Q: What should I do if a client insists they gave me £20 when they only gave me £10?

A: Inform the client tactfully that you believe it was £10, and that you will notify them if there is a discrepancy when the till is checked at the end of the day. Make sure you have the client's contact details.

When a client gives you a banknote, do not put it into the till until you have given change. This saves confusion, as the client may believe they have paid you £20, but you can show them the note they actually gave you.

- There should be a hologram effect in the mid-left section of the note.

- A metallic strip must run through the paper and should be intact.

- Fake notes often feel different to real notes: genuine notes are printed on very fine paper, fake notes will feel thicker.

- Real notes are made in such a way that the ink rises off the paper, which gives a slightly bumpy feel. A fake note may feel smooth and flat.

Some salons may use counterfeit money detectors, such as special pens that work by a chemical reaction between the pen ink and the paper – if the money is fake, a brown mark will appear on the note. Ultraviolet (UV) detectors are also used to identify fake banknotes by checking fluorescent features on notes.

The police can provide a list showing details of forged bank notes, so businesses can look out for these forgeries when taking payment.

Cheques

When a client pays by cheque, make sure there is also a cheque guarantee card. This card helps to guarantee that their bank will pay up to the amount shown on the card.

The cheque must be filled out with:

- the name of the salon

- the correct date

- the correct amount in both words and numbers

- the client's signature.

The receptionist must check:

- that the client's signature on the cheque matches the one on the guarantee card

- that the account number on the cheque is the same as the one on the card

- the date on the card – to ensure that it has not expired.

The receptionist must also write the number of the cheque guarantee card on the back of the cheque. If the client does not have a cheque guarantee card, or enough money in the bank to pay what they owe to the salon, the cheque will 'bounce' and so the salon will not receive any money.

Filled in cheque

Debit cards

Debit cards act like automatic cheques and include Switch/ Maestro and Solo. A cheque can take around five days to clear, but with a debit card the money is debited (taken out) of the client's account immediately, through a telephone connection (**chip and PIN**), using an **EPoS system** (electronic point of sale). The salon can only take this payment if they have an electronic terminal. The company that processes the card will charge a small fee to the salon for each card transaction.

Credit cards

A client may choose to pay for their treatment by using a credit card. The card company pay the bill and the client pays the credit card company back, either at the end of the month or in monthly instalments. A percentage of the total bill is charged to the salon.

Debit and credit cards

key terms

Chip and PIN: a security system for ensuring that the holder of a debit or credit card is the owner. Cards have a silicon chip where the four-digit personal identification number (PIN) of that card is stored. When the card is used, the owner enters the PIN into a keypad and this number is compared with the one stored on the chip.

EPoS system: this system handles the calculations involved in sales of services and products, including change given and total amounts. It issues receipts, and keeps track of stock levels and customer information.

DON'T FORGET

Debit and credit cards can be used to make payments for treatments over the telephone.

Gift vouchers

Gift vouchers are often bought by customers to give as presents, especially at certain times of the year, such as Mother's Day and Christmas. The gift vouchers will contain information such as the salon name, the date, the amount of treatment purchased, and the expiry date (vouchers are often valid for about six months). They may contain serial numbers so that they cannot be reused.

BL♪NK

This voucher entitles: ....

treatments to the sum of £ ....

Signed: .... Date: ....

valid for 6 months from the date of purchase

Sample gift voucher

DON'T FORGET

A float is a certain amount of cash that is kept in the till to be able to provide change to clients.

DON'T FORGET

Every sale that is put through the till will provide a receipt to give to the client, and the total amount taken for the day will be entered onto the till's audit roll.

Cashing-up

At the end of the day, cashing-up takes place. This involves ensuring the money in the till matches the recorded amount taken, although cash for the float will be disregarded. The money is often taken to a bank or collected by a special security company.

UNIT OUTCOME 7

Understand salon services, products and pricing

Services

Services are beauty treatments provided by the salon. The receptionist is expected to know all the services provided and be able to fully explain the treatment to clients. The treatments will be listed on a treatment leaflet.

Products

A beauty salon business can make a lot of money by selling beauty products, which will probably be located on a retail stand in the reception area. If the products are placed neatly and in an attractive way, they are more likely to catch the attention of the client and be purchased. The receptionist will not be popular if the retail stand contains few products, or products that are messily displayed and have a layer of dust on them. The receptionist needs to regularly check stock and take a note of products that are the top sellers. If certain products do not sell very well, putting on a special offer may help to boost sales of that particular line.

Good practice

Always remove a faulty product from the display, otherwise a client may be annoyed that they have to return it to the salon, or they could even be injured as a result of using it.

Salon products displayed in the reception area

Rotating stock – which means putting older stock at the front of the retail stand and putting new stock towards the back – will help to ensure that older stock is purchased first. This is particularly important if the products contain expiry dates.

Clients will regularly ask the receptionist questions about products and treatments, so the receptionist must have good knowledge of them all. It is also important to tell clients about promotions and offers to help boost sales.

UNIT OUTCOME 5

Understand salon and legal requirements

Pricing

Services and products should be clearly priced. It is illegal to mislead people regarding pricing.

Services carried out in salons and products displayed for retail come under legal requirements from different Acts. For more information about these Acts see **Unit G20: Ensure responsibility for actions to reduce risks to health and safety**. Also see **Unit G18: Promote additional services or products to customers**.

How are you doing?

1 Which of the following is **least** likely to be found at a reception area?
   a An eraser
   b Eyelash tint
   c Appointment cards
   d A wax heater

2 Which of the following is **not** a main duty of the receptionist?
   a Making appointments
   b Taking telephone messages
   c Providing aftercare advice
   d Providing gift vouchers

3 Which legislation deals with the storage of client's personal details?
   a Manual Handling Operations Regulations
   b Data Protection Act
   c Sale of Goods Act
   d RIDDOR

4 If the appointment page is set out in 15-minute slots, how many slots would you book out for an hour treatment?
   a One
   b Two
   c Three
   d Four

5 What is a cash float?
   a Cash used for items such as milk and magazines
   b Money that is put into a till at the beginning of the day or week, to allow change to be given to customers
   c A fake banknote
   d The total amount of cash taken at the end of a working day and paid into a bank

6 What is petty cash?
   a A small amount of money that is used to buy small items required by the salon, such as milk and stamps
   b A large amount of money that is kept in the safe and taken to the bank at the end of the day
   c Money used to pay wages
   d The change given to the client after paying for a treatment

7 A debit card can be described as which of the following?
   a A plastic card that credits the holder's account within a few days through an EPoS system
   b A credit card that debits the holder's account immediately through an EPoS system
   c A plastic card that debits the holder's account immediately through an EPoS system
   d A credit card that credits the holder's account immediately through an EPoS system

8 What is a PIN?
   a Personal Identification Number
   b Personal Indication Number
   c Probable Indemnity Number
   d Practical Introduction Number

9 Which of the following would be found on a debit card?
   a Client's address
   b Client's telephone number
   c Client's date of birth
   d Client's signature

10 Which of the following legislation is relevant to working in a salon?
   a Health and Safety at Work Act
   b Supply of Goods and Services Act
   c Fire Precautions Act
   d All of the above

are you ready *for* **assessment**?

The evidence for this unit must be gathered in the workplace (salon) or realistic working environment (training centre).

Simulation (role play) is not allowed for any performance evidence within this unit.

You must practically demonstrate in your everyday work that you have met the required standard for this unit.

All outcomes, assessment criteria and range statements must be achieved.

No mandatory (compulsory) written questions are required with this unit.

Assessing your practical work

Your assessor will observe your performance of a practical task, such as carrying out reception duties.

Your assessor will sign off an outcome when all criteria have been competently achieved.

On occasions, some assessment criteria may not naturally occur during a practical observation. In such instances you will be asked questions to demonstrate your knowledge in this area. Your assessor will document the criteria that have been achieved through oral questioning.

In this unit you must demonstrate competent performance of all practical outcomes on at least **three** occasions. These observations must cover all four main outcomes of this unit (i.e. the first four outcomes stated at the beginning of this unit).

Assessing your knowledge and understanding

You will be guided by your tutor and assessor on the evidence that needs to be produced.

Your knowledge and understanding will be assessed using the assessment tools listed below.

- Oral questioning
- Portfolio of evidence

G8 Develop and maintain effectiveness at work

On completion of this unit you will:

1. Be able to improve personal performance at work

2. Be able to work effectively as part of a team

3. Understand salon roles, procedures and targets

4. Understand how to improve performance

5. Understand how to work with others

Introduction

DON'T FORGET

A trade test is given by a potential employer to assess your beauty therapy skills.

This unit will help you to understand how you can improve your standard of work, and the importance of working as a team.

There is a lot of competition for jobs, so gain as much knowledge and experience as you can. This will raise your confidence and increase your chances of getting a job.

A potential employer will probably ask you to demonstrate your beauty skills. This is known as a 'trade test', which means the employer will observe you as you carry out a treatment such as waxing. If they are not impressed with your skills as a therapist, then your knowledge and attitude alone is unlikely to get you the job.

Working in a salon with other therapists is a great way to learn new techniques, pick up bits of advice and to learn by other therapists' experience.

UNIT OUTCOME 1

Be able to improve personal performance at work

UNIT OUTCOME 4

Understand how to improve performance

Working as a team

Improving your skills

Training providers, such as beauty colleges, offer invaluable beauty training, but you will also learn a great deal from beauty exhibitions, beauty magazines, and also by doing work experience. If you work for a salon, they may send you on training courses, or teach you how to carry out new treatments within the salon, and how to use the salon's products. Your confidence will grow, and your skills will improve, as you gain experience. While training, offer treatments to family and friends, and evaluate the treatments you give. Consider how you could have provided a better service.

Taking the initiative at work will impress those around you. This means that if a job needs to be done, perhaps cleaning a workstation, you do it on your own initiative, without being asked.

Don't forget to take responsibility for everything you do in the salon, and do not blame others for mistakes. Learn by your mistakes and remember that everyone makes them, so be sympathetic to others when they make mistakes too.

Use your own initiative!

Your strengths and weaknesses

Identifying your own strengths and weaknesses can help you to assess areas where improvement is required, and where further training would help. We all have strengths and weaknesses – nobody is good at everything. Your strengths will probably be tasks you enjoy, perhaps meeting people or carrying out certain treatments. Your weaknesses may be things like poor timekeeping when doing certain treatments, or having an untidy treatment area – both of which can be rectified easily. It's great that you have strengths, but you need to work on your weaknesses. A manager can help you recognise your strengths and weaknesses, and can make useful suggestions to help you improve certain areas.

Your employer will regularly carry out a work appraisal, which will help you to understand your strengths and weaknesses, and they will give you advice to help you improve your quality of work.

Work appraisals

To assess your progress at work, ask yourself regularly if you have given 100 per cent to your work. If not, think about how you could improve your performance. What action could you take to help you reach your goals? Do you need more training or support?

A work appraisal may occur every year, or more frequently, and will usually be carried out by a manager. A good appraisal will be helpful, motivational, and focus on the future. It may include your

HAVE A GO

Make a list of your strengths and weaknesses, particularly in a work context. This isn't easy to do. Think about how you could improve any weaknesses.

DON'T FORGET

Everyone has strengths and weaknesses. We can all improve on any areas of weakness.

An appraisal

manager's opinion of how they think you are getting on. There may be some constructive criticism, but this shouldn't be upsetting. Consider it as feedback, not failure. Perhaps you need a bit more practice at something, or some additional training. Don't be afraid to give your opinions and ask questions about the appraisal.

Before your appraisal, you will probably be asked to fill out an appraisal form, which will contain questions similar to the following.

- Has the past year been good/bad/satisfactory or otherwise for you – and why?
- What do you consider to be your most important achievements over the past year?
- What aspects of the job do you find most difficult?
- What aspects of the job interest you the most and least?
- What actions could be taken, by you and your employer, to improve your performance?

When you have completed your appraisal, you may want to make some goals to help you improve aspects of your work, and also to consider what you would like to do in the future. These could be short-term, medium-term or long-term goals. Some examples are given below.

Short-term goals (weeks)

- Sell more facial products
- Carry out manicure treatments in a shorter time
- Improve client care skills

Medium-term goals (months)

- Do ear piercing training
- Increase overall product sales
- Increase client base

Long-term goals (years)

- Work on a cruise liner
- Open my own salon

These will help you to think about what you want to achieve, and to prioritise the actions you should take.

If you have long-terms goals, consider the steps you need to take to reach them. Do you want to remain with the same employer and become a manager? Do you want to travel? Do you want to open your own salon? These things require planning.

During the appraisal, you can ask for further training to gain further qualifications or experience, even if you plan to take this knowledge elsewhere in the future.

UNIT OUTCOME 2

Be able to work effectively as part of a team

UNIT OUTCOME 5

Understand how to work with others

Being part of a team

Good teamwork depends on working with others and supporting them with their roles. If you are able to contribute positively in a team environment, you will be valued by your work **colleagues**. Working as part of a team is an important skill and can be learnt over time.

Most of us don't get to choose who we work with, so you may have to be more flexible if you have a colleague who isn't supportive and is difficult to get on with. Occasionally clients may also prove difficult to work with, but being a professional will mean you are calm and respectful at all times. Remember that your goal is to do the best work possible and help to ensure that the client returns for further treatment.

The role of the manager is to give orders to people, and it is not always easy to do what you are told. If you are asked to carry out a duty, you should do it without moaning or arguing. You will learn some valuable skills at your training centre regarding working as a team. Beauty students will often play the role of salon manager, and the other students will be expected to work as a team and support their manager. Rather like playing a team sport, you are expected to help and support each other. You can help other members of your team, for example, by offering to tidy another therapist's workstation if she is running late in preparation for the next client. Or ask your colleague if they would like a drink, especially if working in hot conditions. If therapists do not work together, and perhaps do not get on, this will be noticed by clients, which could affect the business.

key terms

Colleague: a person you work with.

One therapist giving support to another

Good practice

Think about the needs of other therapists. A busy day can mean little time for breaks, so colleagues will be grateful if you regularly offer fresh water to drink, or ask them if they need help with tidying and so on.

To build trust you need to openly discuss any matters and listen carefully to what colleagues say. It is important that you recognise one another's strengths and respect your differences. If you have a problem with a colleague, calmly ask them to discuss the situation with you. It may be the result of a minor matter or miscommunication. If this doesn't work, it is advisable to privately and calmly explain your concerns to your manager. The situation needs to be sorted out so that it does not get any worse and cause a problem in the salon. The manager can monitor the situation and help sort out the matter if necessary.

Health club

UNIT OUTCOME 3

Understand salon roles, procedures and targets

Roles

When you apply for a job, the company will provide a job description (either written or verbal), which informs you of the therapist's roles and responsibilities. The following is an example of a job description provided by a health club that requires a beauty therapist.

Job description

Job title: Beauty Therapist

Reporting to: Health Club Manager

Job scope
- Work under the general guidance and supervision of the health club manager.
- Ensure the highest standard of customer care and services at all time.

Key responsibilities
- Actively promote marketing activities set out by manager.
- Promote the sale of beauty products in conjunction with beauty treatments.
- Handle payments made for beauty therapy treatments/ products.
- Record details of all treatments given to each client.
- Manage stock control accounting systems.
- Cashing up.

Self-management
- Comply with health club rules and regulations and provisions contained in the employment handbook.
- Comply with company grooming and uniform policies.
- Comply with timekeeping and attendance standards.
- Take part in training and development programmes, and maximise opportunities for self-development.

Customer service
- Give clients your full attention.
- Carry out a service within a reasonable time and to a high standard.
- Maintain a high level of knowledge to enhance the client experience.
- Demonstrate a service attitude that goes beyond expectations.

Health, safety and security
- Ensure the highest standards of hygiene, cleanliness and tidiness in the beauty salon at all times.
- Show understanding and awareness of all policies and procedures relating to health and hygiene, and understand fire safety, emergency and evacuation procedures.

General
- Perform all tasks at the level of the role, as directed by your line manager, in pursuit of the achievement of business goals.
- Show the desire and ability to improve your knowledge and abilities through on-going training.
- Be able to work as part of a diverse team with colleagues from different viewpoints, cultures and countries.

An employer will probably require the following skills as well. So, if there are any that you don't already have, you will need to learn or practise them.

- Basic numeracy and literacy
- Experience in the beauty industry
- Ability to carry out instructions
- Desire and ability to learn
- Ability to ask for help
- Ability to communicate clearly
- Ability to clean and restock
- Ability to plan and prioritise
- Ability to organise self
- Ability to multi-task
- Flexibility and adaptability
- Ability to build rapport
- Attention to detail
- Excellent listening skills
- Problem-solving skills
- Ability to work under pressure
- Passion and enthusiasm
- Positive attitude
- Excellent sales techniques
- Ability to work independently, without constant supervision
- Being customer focused
- Ability to anticipate client needs
- Openness to new ideas
- Cultural awareness

You can see that there are many other attributes an employer requires, besides being competent in carrying out beauty treatments.

Ask Fran

Q: What would I do if a salon manager wanted me to carry out a treatment that I wasn't qualified to do?

A: Do not carry out job roles you are not qualified to do. You could harm others and get into trouble. The Beauty Therapy National Occupation Standards are standards that inform the beauty therapist what skills they must be able to carry out, and what things they must know and understand. Be honest with your employer from the start about what skills you have. Employers will want to see your beauty certificates and will probably keep a copy of them for insurance purposes.

Contract of employment

When you accept a job offer, you will probably have to sign a **contract of employment**. This is a **legally binding** document which sets out your job description and conditions of work, such as pay and holiday entitlement. It also discusses disciplinary rules, for instance, what would happen in the case of theft.

Job interview

Procedures

Each salon will have their own procedures, which means a salon's way of doing certain things, such as dealing with staff and client complaints.

If an employee has a problem at work, and is unhappy with the way they are being treated, they may decide to follow the company's appeals and grievance procedure.

Appeals and grievance procedure

The purpose of the grievance procedure is to help ensure that grievances (complaints) are dealt with and sorted out by discussion between the aggrieved employee (e.g. beauty therapist) and their manager. Grievances are concerns, problems or complaints made by an employee and must be made in writing.

Codes of conduct

Remember, beauty therapists are expected to act in a professional way at all times and should follow these general codes of conduct.

- Be courteous and respectful at all times.
- Always remain calm and seek the advice of your supervisor if necessary.

- Never argue in front of clients.

- Do not gossip about anybody.

- Always be punctual – try not to keep a client waiting.

- Retain client modesty at all times.

- Have high standards of dress and personal hygiene.

- Always ensure equipment is safe and in good working order.

- Keep the conversation to a professional level.

- Always make sure you do your very best when carrying out a treatment.

Remember to act professionally at all times

Targets

A salon is a business, and running a successful one is tough, especially as there is so much competition. The salon owner will want to generate as much income as possible, which means many clients may be booked in, and they will want to sell as many products as they can too. The salon owner and managers may set targets to motivate staff to sell as much as possible. The target will be set over a period of time, maybe a month, and will be agreed between you and your manager. The more products that you sell, the more money or other incentives, such as free products, you will get, and the more income the salon will generate. If you prove to be a good salesperson, it may help you climb the career ladder. There are good jobs for exceptional salespeople, which involve selling beauty products and equipment, and that pay a good salary and include benefits such as a company car and pension.

How are you doing?

1 If you have a disagreement with your work colleague, you should:

   a complain about your colleague to your other colleagues

   b discuss it with your manager

   c discuss it with your colleague and try to sort out the matter in a friendly manner

   d ignore you colleague for as long as possible

2 A contract of employment is:

   a a complete list of all the beauty treatments you are required to carry out

   b an agreement between an employer and employee that details the rights, responsibilities and duties agreed between them

   c a legal document that discusses the employees' roles and responsibilities

   d a full job description that discusses hours of work, products used and the pay structure

3 A trade/skills test requested by a beauty employer requires you to:

   a perform a certain beauty treatment, such as waxing, to show you can competently carry it out

   b answer a series of multiple-choice questions about beauty treatments and products used

   c carry out a trial work period in a salon

   d all of the above

4 A code of conduct:

   a is a set of rules to ensure professional and appropriate behaviour of an individual

   b refers to specific jargon and language used in a salon

   c helps to ensure all legal and safety requirements are complied with

   d is a document you sign when you begin employment

5 A method of evaluating a person's work performance in a salon is called a:

   a work apparel

   b skills appraisal

   c conduct assessment

   d work appraisal

are **you ready** *for* **assessment?**

The evidence for this unit must be gathered in the workplace (salon) or realistic working environment (training centre).

Simulation (role play) is not allowed for any performance evidence within this unit.

You must practically demonstrate in your everyday work that you have met the required standard for this unit.

All outcomes, assessment criteria and range statements must be achieved.

No mandatory (compulsory) written questions are required with this unit.

Assessing your practical work

Your assessor will observe your performance of a practical task, such as offering a colleague a drink, or helping them to set up their treatment area.

Your assessor will sign off an outcome when all criteria have been competently achieved.

On occasions, some assessment criteria may not naturally occur during a practical observation. In such instances you will be asked questions to demonstrate your knowledge in this area. Your assessor will document the criteria that have been achieved through oral questioning.

In this unit you must demonstrate competent performance of all practical outcomes on at least **one** occasion.

Assessing your knowledge and understanding

You will be guided by your tutor and assessor on the evidence that needs to be produced.

Your knowledge and understanding will be assessed using the assessment tools listed below.

- Oral questioning
- Portfolio of evidence

G18 Promote additional services or products to customers

Introduction

All salons want to be busy and successful. This requires a lot of hard work by all members of staff who, to help ensure salon success, are encouraged to promote additional services and products to clients. It is important that staff make the clients

Promoting products to a client

aware of the treatments provided by the salon and the products it sells. A client is likely to try out other treatments and buy products if told about them, which means more income for the salon. Beauty is a competitive industry, so promoting services and products to clients will help a business to thrive.

While working as a beauty therapist, your manager may set you targets to increase both sales and your **client base** in order to generate more income for the salon.

key terms

Client base: the individuals who regularly visit a beauty therapist for treatments.

Good practice

While providing a client with a drink, why not also give them a brochure to read: perhaps one that contains the latest treatments or products on offer in the salon.

UNIT OUTCOME 1

Be able to identify additional services or products that are available

UNIT OUTCOME 2

Be able to inform customers about additional services or products

Knowledge of services and products

You must have an excellent knowledge of the products and treatments available in your salon in order to sell them to your client effectively. This will come with experience while working as a beauty therapist. If you feel you lack knowledge, take the necessary steps to get it. You could:

- ask senior therapists
- read product labels
- undertake training
- try samples and use the products
- read training manuals
- attend beauty exhibitions and ask lots of questions
- read industry magazines.

A product range

To be able to sell products effectively you need to know:

- what the product is
- what it is for
- how it should be applied
- the active ingredients it contains
- if it has been tested on animals
- the range of products
- the cost.

Continuing professional development (CPD)

Product companies often provide training when their products are used in the salon. This is a good opportunity for therapists to update their skills and so increase their confidence and knowledge.

Therapist training for a new selling skill

Selling products

It can be daunting selling products to clients, but it can also be rewarding for you both. For instance, the client's skin can be greatly improved by using the correct products for their skin type. The client will not only benefit from using the products but will also acquire their therapist's support and knowledge. The client can be shown how to apply products properly and informed how they benefit the skin.

When selling a product, it is important to talk about its features and benefits. A feature is an aspect or characteristic of a product, such as its size, smell or special ingredients. The features of a product provide benefits to the customer. A benefit describes an advantage of using a product. For instance, the benefit of using a moisturiser with an **SPF (sun protection factor)** is that it will help to protect the skin against the damaging effects of the sun.

Also, ensure you show the client how and when to use the product. Feeling the texture of the product, and also smelling it, can help the client make a decision as to whether they will purchase it or not. Giving samples can also be an effective way of encouraging clients to buy.

Remember, if you believe in your product, it shouldn't be too hard to help your client believe in it too.

Good practice

Ensure there are testers and samples available, so clients can try some on their skin and also smell them.

You may earn a **sales commission** for selling products, which will help to increase your wages. Some salons may offer other incentives, such as free products, to motivate therapists to sell more.

Carrying out a beauty treatment is usually time consuming and hard work compared to making profit by selling products. Although many people find selling techniques difficult, it is an important skill, and one that can be learnt.

Good practice

Remember to record all client sales on their record card/ consultation form.

Knowledge of other product ranges

Skin care products can be bought at supermarkets, pharmacies and even airports. It is important that you know about other products available so you can encourage the client to buy from the salon instead.

Most salons supply 'professional only' product ranges, which means they are only sold through approved salons. Your client may be tempted to buy 'professional products' on internet sites like eBay, so they need to be reminded that the products could be out of date, or even fake.

If the client buys from the salon, they are not only buying the product but also your professional knowledge.

key terms

SPF (sun protection factor): this is a rating given to sun creams, which tells you how much protection they provide from the burning (UVB) rays of the sun. For example, if a person normally burns in the sun after 15 minutes of exposure, a lotion with an SPF of 4 allows them to stay out four times longer (i.e. one hour) in the sun without burning.

Sales commission: percentage of money earned from every product sold.

Therapist selling products

DON'T FORGET

If you believe passionately in your products, make sure you share your enthusiasm with your clients. Enthusiasm is often contagious.

UNIT OUTCOME 3

Be able to gain customer commitment to using additional services or products

Sales techniques

Being able to sell is a great skill, and will make you a valuable employee. This does not mean you should be ruthless and insincere when selling products or services. You should always aim to be professional, tell the truth, and advise about the best possible treatments and products for your client.

A fine balance has to be drawn between encouraging the client to buy a product or treatment, and being too pushy. How would you feel if someone tried to force you into buying something you did not want or could not afford? Would you go back to the salon – probably not! When selling a product or treatment, try not to use too much jargon, such as long chemical names, as you will probably lose the client's attention and so may lose a sale.

Empathy is the ability to understand the thoughts, feelings and motives of another person. Empathy is very important in professional selling. Listening carefully to what your client has to say will help you to empathise and, depending on the information the client has given, know how to proceed with the sale. The client should sense that you care and understand about their needs and are not just looking for a sale.

The best salespeople are good at identifying their customer's needs, building trust, and dealing with questions regarding the product or service. Ensure you keep good eye contact with your client. If you start looking around or fidgeting, you may distract them and give the impression you are uncomfortable.

Good practice

Never assume a person cannot afford to buy products or treatments just because they are scruffily dressed. Making an incorrect assumption may lose income for the salon.

Closing the sale

Closing the sale is the point at which you believe the client is ready to purchase a treatment or product. When customers are ready to buy, they may indicate this by asking questions such as:

'How much do I need to apply?' or 'Which colour suits my skin?'. People only ask questions when something interests them. Other signs include comments such as: 'really?' or 'good idea'. Do not respond to questions with 'yes' or 'no', instead ask carefully chosen questions, such as: 'What do you use to moisturise your face currently?' You can then discuss the features and benefits of a particular moisturiser that the salon sells.

Why not set targets for yourself – how many treatments and products can you sell today? If, for instance, a paraffin wax treatment hasn't been carried out for a while, challenge yourself to get a client to book an appointment to receive one.

DON'T FORGET

Your personality determines about 80 per cent of your sales success, so ensure you are both friendly and knowledgeable.

Good practice

Ask other members of your team about their sales techniques, which treatments and products they have successfully sold, and how.

UNIT OUTCOME 4

Understand how to promote additional services or products to customers

Promoting treatments and products

A good time to suggest other treatments and products to a client is while providing homecare advice. If a client has a manicure treatment, why not ask if they would like to buy nail polish and other nail products too? Listen carefully to what the client says and maintain good eye contact. Your client may give you clues as to other treatments or products that may be of interest. However, ensure you discuss these matters at the right time as it may be annoying for a client if they are having a relaxing back massage and you are trying to sell them nail polish!

Building a good, trusting relationship with your client will help you both to communicate effectively, enabling you to inform the client of the benefits of other treatments and products, and the client to feel at ease asking questions about them.

Remember, if clients are not aware that your salon provides certain treatments, it's unlikely they will book in for them, so it's your job to inform them.

Closing the sale

Building a good, trusting relationship with your client is important

DON'T FORGET

If a client mentions a special event coming up, such as a wedding, this would be a good time to discuss other treatments, such as eyelash tinting and make-up.

If your client is going to a party, or on holiday, why not suggest some additional treatments or products? The client may not consider having artificial lashes, for instance, unless it is suggested by the therapist. The client will be pleased with the result, as artificial lashes will help to draw attention to the eyes, and you will generate extra income for the salon. Of course, if required a sensitivity test must be carried out before a treatment can be given.

The following treatments and products could be recommended to clients for special events.

Holiday

- French manicure
- Waxing
- Eyelash and eyebrow tinting
- Manicure and pedicure
- Skin care products that help to protect the skin from the sun

French manicure

Party

- Evening make-up
- Artificial lashes
- File and polish
- Manicure
- Nail extensions
- Make-up and nail products

Good practice

If clients have little time, perhaps only a lunch hour, you can suggest services that take only a short time to carry out, such as an eyebrow shape.

Promotional campaigns

You can also run promotional campaigns at specific times to introduce new treatments and products. It is common to link this to seasonal opportunities such as Christmas and Mother's Day.

Also, plan to position products according to when clients will be most likely to buy them. For example, moisturisers can be placed in a prominent position in winter, and products that protect the skin from the sun can be displayed in the summer. This is called **merchandising strategy**.

Link selling

If a client decides to buy a cleanser, for example, ensure she is aware of other related products she can also buy, such as a toner and moisturiser, which will all work together to benefit the skin. This is known as link selling. On a retail stand, items such as a cleanser will often be placed next to toners to encourage the client to buy more than one product.

DON'T FORGET

Ensure clients are aware that you sell gift vouchers or cards, particularly at certain times of the year, such as Mother's Day, Father's Day and Christmas, when sales of them will increase as people buy them as presents.

key terms

Merchandising strategy: a method of promoting particular products by, for instance, placing them in a prominent position.

HAVE A GO

Carry out role play with a colleague. Pretend to sell various products and discuss how it will benefit your client. Ask your colleague to ask different questions about the product, so you can practise giving knowledgeable and professional answers.

Be aware that many clients are concerned about what chemicals are contained within products and if they have been tested on animals.

Facial products on a retail stand

'Not tested on animals' logo

Ask Fran

Q: What is meant by consumer rights?

A: These are laws which protect the buyer (consumer) when buying goods. The products should be of satisfactory quality (free of faults) and fit for purpose (it should do what it is supposed to do). If a buyer is given a sample, the goods purchased must match the sample. If you give either verbal or written information about a product, the information must be truthful, accurate and not misleading.

key terms

Consumer rights: what the consumer can expect when they buy the product. Consumer rights include protection from hazardous goods, and false and misleading claims in advertising and labelling practices. Consumer rights are protected by consumer law.

Legislation relating to selling treatments and products

See **Unit G20: Ensure responsibility for actions to reduce risks to health and safety**, for more information regarding legislation that relates to beauty treatments and products.

The following table shows some of the laws that relate specifically to selling.

Trades Description Act (1968)	This Act makes it an offence for a seller to make false or misleading statements, either verbal or written, about goods and services.
Sale of Goods Act (1979)	This Act provides protection against goods that are of poor quality. 'Quality' refers to its fitness for purpose (it does what it is supposed to do) and appearance.
Prices Act (1974 and 1975)	This Act ensures that prices of products are clearly shown and are not misleading to customers.
Consumer Protection Act (1987)	This Act provides the customer with protection when buying goods or services (such as beauty treatments), to make sure that products are safe for use on the customer during the treatment, or are safe to be sold as a retail product.
Cosmetic Products (Safety) Regulations (2008)	Cosmetic products must be safe and correctly labelled. The following should be included on a label: • ingredients • shelf life • storage instructions • warnings and precautions • manufacturer's name and address.
Supply of Goods and Services Act (1982)	This Act aims to protect customers against receiving a poor service, such as a beauty treatment. The service should be carried out with reasonable care and skill. It should be carried out in a reasonable time and at a reasonable cost.

Cosmetic products are formulated to have a long shelf life, so will keep their quality for a long time, but if a product has a limited shelf life (less than 30 months) it has to be labelled with a 'best before' date.

Good practice

Each product should be clearly priced.

How are you doing?

1 What is link selling?

   a When a client asks for a product, the salesperson suggests other related products, for example, cleansers and toners

   b When you try to sell the same product to two or more clients

   c Selling many products from different ranges

   d All of the above

2 Which of the following is a positive sign indicating that a client may be interested in purchasing a product?

   a Good eye contact

   b Folding their arms

   c Looking at their watch

   d Reaching for their coat

3 Why is it important to have an excellent knowledge of the products and treatments you provide in the salon?

   a To appear knowledgeable and professional to your clients

   b To help you to sell products

   c To help give your client correct information

   d All of the above

4 Which Act helps to protect the customer from unsafe services and products?

   a Trades Description Act

   b Consumer Protection Act

   c Data Protection Act

   d Prices Act

5 What is CPD?

   a Consumer product data

   b Consumer price detector

   c Continuing professional development

   d Cosmetic product development

are you ready *for* **assessment**?

The evidence for this unit must be gathered in the workplace (salon) or realistic working environment (training centre).

Simulation (role play) is not allowed for any performance evidence within this unit.

You must practically demonstrate in your everyday work that you have met the required standard for this unit.

All outcomes, assessment criteria and range statements must be achieved.

No mandatory (compulsory) written questions are required with this unit

Assessing your practical work

Your assessor will observe your performance of a practical task, such as selling a product to a customer.

Your assessor will sign off an outcome when all criteria have been competently achieved.

On occasions, some assessment criteria may not naturally occur during a practical observation. In such instances you will be asked questions to demonstrate your knowledge in this area. Your assessor will document the criteria that have been achieved through oral questioning.

In this unit you must demonstrate competent performance of all practical outcomes on at least **three** separate occasions.

Assessing your knowledge and understanding

You will be guided by your tutor and assessor on the evidence that needs to be produced.

Your knowledge and understanding will be assessed using the assessment tools listed below.

■ Oral questioning

■ Portfolio of evidence

Anatomy and physiology

A&P

Introduction

It is important to understand the effects that beauty treatments have on the face and body. Having a good knowledge of anatomy and physiology will allow you to give the best possible treatment.

Cells

Like the bricks of a house, cells are the building blocks of the body. The body is made up of over 100,000 billion cells. Different cells have different functions – such as skin, muscle, blood and fat cells – and can vary in size and shape. Cells contain chromosomes, within the cell **nucleus**, which are strings of DNA (deoxyribonucleic acid), and carry all the information needed to make an entire human being.

> **key terms**
>
> **Nucleus:** the part of the cell that contains DNA and is responsible for growth and reproduction of the cell.

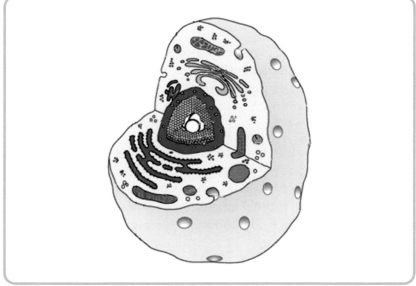

Cross-section of a cell

> **DON'T FORGET**
>
> *A cell is surrounded by a cell membrane, which allows certain substances in and out of it.*

> **DON'T FORGET**
>
> *A nerve cell (neuron) can be as long as a metre!*

For cells to produce energy to carry out their work – such as muscle cells helping to create muscle movement – they require fuel. The food we eat provides the fuel. It is absorbed from the intestines into the bloodstream and then passes to the cells of the body. Glucose is the fuel mostly used by cells. Glucose is a type of sugar that is produced when the body breaks down carbohydrates, from foods such as potatoes and bread. Fats and proteins can also be used for fuel if glucose is not available.

Oxygen is also vital for cells to burn up the glucose. Oxygen enters the body through the lungs, passes into the bloodstream, and is carried in the blood to the cells. Cells use the glucose and oxygen to make energy for the cell's activities.

Beauty treatments, such as facial massage, help to stimulate the blood circulation, thereby increasing oxygen to the area being treated.

Tissue

Cells divide (in a process called **mitosis**) and create new cells. This leads to a big group of cells being formed, which is known as tissue. Connective tissue is the most abundant and widespread type of tissue in our bodies. The function of connective tissue is to protect, support and bind together. Different types of connective tissue are listed below.

Areolar tissue

Areolar tissue is widely distributed throughout the body. It has the function of connecting skin to other tissues and muscles. Areolar tissue also contains stretchy fibres of **elastin** protein.

Fibrous tissue

Fibrous tissue is found in muscles, bones, **tendons** (which join muscle to bone) and ligaments (which join bone to bone). Fibrous tissue is made up of collagen fibres. Collagen is a type of protein that helps to give strength to the tissues.

Adipose tissue

Adipose tissue consists of fat cells. This fatty tissue is found in most parts of the body. It helps to support and protect organs, such as the kidneys, and forms a protective covering for the whole body, to help protect against injury. It also provides insulation to keep the body warm and is stored energy if the body requires it.

Liposuction

Liposuction, also known as lipoplasty, is an operation that can remove small areas of fat by suction through a tube. It is commonly carried out on the abdomen, hips, thighs and buttocks. The body doesn't replace fat cells, so there should be a long-lasting change in the body shape, especially if an individual

key terms

Mitosis: the division of a cell into two identical daughter cells. It is the process by which the body grows and replaces cells.

Elastin: a protein that allows many tissues in the body, such as the skin, to resume their shape after being stretched.

Tendon: a tough band of inelastic tissue that attaches muscle to bone.

DON'T FORGET

We are all born with a certain number of fat cells. When we put on additional weight, we do not make more fat cells, but our existing fat cells become larger.

exercises, eats a healthy diet, and maintains a healthy weight after the operation. However, putting on weight can cause the remaining fat cells to enlarge.

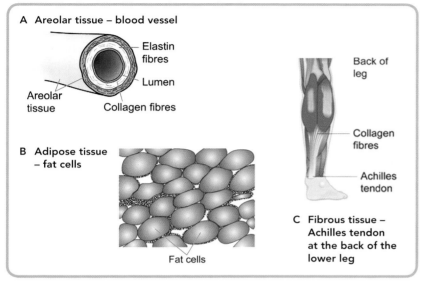

Different types of connective tissue: areolar, adipose and fibrous

The skin

The skin is the largest organ in the body and forms a protective, waterproof covering over the entire surface of the body. It is thinnest on the eyelids and thickest on the soles of the feet. The skin is continually shedding and renewing itself. It is made up of layers called the epidermis and dermis.

Most treatments will affect the skin, so it is essential to have a good understanding of its structure and function, and how certain treatments can benefit it.

Epidermis

The upper portion of the skin is known as the epidermis and it consists of five layers.

Horny layer (stratum corneum)

The top layer of the epidermis is called the horny layer, and consists of flat, overlapping, keratinised cells. Keratin is a protein responsible for the hardening process (keratinisation) that cells undergo when they change from living cells, with a nucleus, to dead cells, without a nucleus. Cells that have undergone keratinisation are therefore dead.

The keratinised cells help to prevent bacteria entering through the skin, and protect the body from minor injury. Cells of the

DON'T FORGET

The skin is the largest organ in the body.

DON'T FORGET

Stratum is the Latin word for layer.

DON'T FORGET

Exfoliation involves the removal of dead cells by methods such as dermabrasion, and applying exfoliating scrubs and alpha hydroxy acids (AHAs).

DON'T FORGET

About 80 per cent of house dust consists of dead skin cells.

horny layer are continually being rubbed off the body by friction, and are replaced by cells from the layers beneath. The shedding of dead skin cells is known as desquamation.

Clear layer (stratum lucidum)

The clear layer is found below the horny layer and consists of dead, keratinised cells without a nucleus. The cells are transparent, which allows the passage of sunlight into the deeper layers. This layer is only found on the fingertips, the palms of the hands and the soles of the feet.

Granular layer (stratum granulosum)

The granular layer contains cells that have a granular appearance. As the cells die, they fill with tiny granules called keratohyalin and so keratinisation begins to take place. This layer consists of living and dead cells.

Prickle cell layer (stratum spinosum)

In the prickle cell layer, the cells are living. The cells interlock by fine, arm-like threads, which give them a prickly appearance.

Basal layer (stratum germinativum)

The basal layer is the deepest layer in the epidermis and is in contact with the dermis directly beneath it. In this layer, the cells are alive, contain a nucleus, and divide (using mitosis) to make new skin cells. As new cells are produced, they push older cells above them towards the surface of the skin, until they finally reach the horny layer. It takes three to six weeks for the skin cells to be pushed up from the basal layer to the horny layer.

> **DON'T FORGET**
>
> The outer surface of the skin helps to kill harmful bacteria.

> **DON'T FORGET**
>
> Black skin has a thicker horny layer than white skin.

> **DON'T FORGET**
>
> The top three layers of the epidermis contain dead skin cells.

> **DON'T FORGET**
>
> Psoriasis is a skin condition where the skin cells divide too quickly, which results in the build-up of dead skin cells.

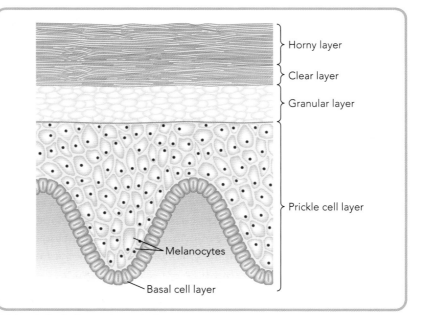

Epidermis (including melanocytes)

Skin pigmentation

Cells called melanocytes are found within the basal layer and produce granules of **melanin**. Melanin is responsible for the pigment (colour) of the skin and is stimulated by ultraviolet (UV) rays from the sun. This is why the skin develops a tan after sunbathing. The function of melanin is to protect the deeper layers of the skin from damage. Approximately one in every ten basal cells is a melanocyte.

Everyone has the same number of melanocytes, but they produce varying quantities of melanin. This determines the depth of skin colour – more melanin is produced in black skins than white skins. This extra protection means that less UV light passes through to the dermis below, which is why black skins tend to age more slowly than white skins.

Dermis

Below the epidermis lies the dermis, which connects with the basal layer. It consists of two layers.

The dermis also contains **hair follicles**, sebaceous glands, sweat glands and arrector pili muscles.

Papillary layer

The papillary layer is the upper layer, and it contains small tubes called capillaries, which carry blood and **lymph**. It also contains nerve endings. This layer provides nutrients for the living layers of the epidermis.

Blood

Blood provides the skin with oxygen and nutrients. The living cells of the skin produce waste products such as **carbon dioxide** and metabolic waste. These waste products pass from the cells and enter into the bloodstream to be taken away and removed by the body.

Lymph

Lymph is carried in tubes called lymphatic vessels, which include lymphatic capillaries. Lymph is a fluid that contains lots of white blood cells, which help us to fight infections. The lymphatic vessels also drain away excess fluid.

Nerves

Sensory nerve endings are found all over the body, but are particularly numerous on our fingertips and lips. These nerves will make us aware of feelings of pain, touch, heat and cold by sending messages through sensory nerves to the brain.

Messages are sent from the brain through **motor nerves**. Motor nerves stimulate the sweat glands, arrector pili muscles and sebaceous glands to carry out their functions.

key terms

Melanin: a pigment responsible for skin and hair colour. Vitiligo is a skin condition in which there is a lack of melanin.

Hair follicle: a tube-like opening from which a hair grows.

Lymph: a watery, colourless fluid that plays an important role in protecting the body from infection.

Carbon dioxide: a gas that is found in the atmosphere, and is breathed out by humans during respiration.

Sensory nerves: nerves that pass messages to the brain and make us aware of feelings of heat, cold, touch and pain.

Motor nerves: nerves that cause movement when stimulated.

DON'T FORGET

Carotene is a pigment which adds yellow colour to the skin.

DON'T FORGET

The epidermis and dermis are joined by a layer called a basement membrane.

key terms

Acid mantle: a slightly acidic oil layer on the skin's surface, made from sebum and sweat, which protects against harmful bacteria, viruses and other contaminants that might penetrate the skin.

pH: the measure of the acidity or alkalinity of a solution. The pH of the skin is 5.5, which is slightly acidic.

DON'T FORGET

Products such as soaps should have a pH that is similar to that of the skin, otherwise they can cause drying of the skin and destroy the acid mantle.

DON'T FORGET

Overproduction of sebum can result in the formation of spots, and lead to a condition called acne vulgaris.

Reticular layer

The reticular layer is the lower layer, and it contains many connective tissue fibres. Collagen gives skin strength, and elastin gives it elasticity. Wavy bands of tough collagen fibres restrict the extent to which the skin can be stretched, and elastin fibres return the skin back to shape after it has been stretched.

Stretch marks

Stretch marks may be caused by the sudden stretching of the skin, such as during pregnancy or fast weight gain. The collagen and elastin fibres in the dermis may become thin and overstretched, and some of them may break if the body grows rapidly. This breakage of fibres allows blood vessels underneath to show through, which is the reason why stretch marks will firstly appear red in colour. After a time, the blood vessels shrink leaving only the fat underneath to show through, therefore the stretch marks will be a silvery white or grey colour. People who produce a large amount of a hormone called cortisol are more likely to develop stretch marks, because cortisol reduces the amount of collagen in the skin.

Sebaceous glands

Sebaceous glands are small, sac-like structures that produce a substance called sebum. Sebum is a fatty substance and is the skin's natural moisturiser. These glands are found all over the body, but are most numerous on the scalp, and areas of the face such as the nose, forehead and chin. Hormones control the activity of these glands: in puberty, we tend to produce more sebum, so skin becomes greasy; as we get older the secretion of sebum decreases, causing the skin to become drier.

Sebum and sweat mix together on the skin to form an **acid mantle**. The acid mantle maintains the **pH** of the skin at 5.5–5.6. This helps to protect the skin from harmful bacteria. Some soaps can affect the acid mantle and cause irritation and drying of the skin.

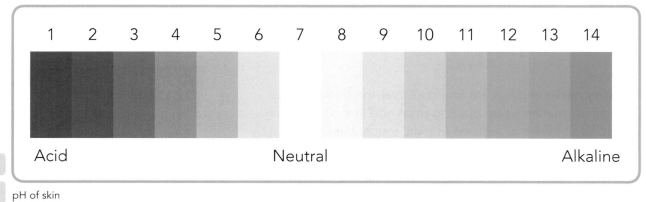

| 1 | 2 | 3 | 4 | 5 | 6 | 7 | 8 | 9 | 10 | 11 | 12 | 13 | 14 |

Acid   Neutral   Alkaline

pH of skin

Sweat glands

There are two types of sweat gland (sudoriferous glands) in the body.

Eccrine glands

Eccrine glands excrete sweat and are found all over the body. The sweat duct opens directly on to the surface of the skin through an opening called a pore. Sweat is a mixture of water, salt and toxins. Black skins contain larger and more numerous sweat glands than white skins.

Apocrine glands

Apocrine glands are found in the armpits, around the nipples, and in the groin area. These glands are larger than eccrine glands and are attached to the hair follicle. They secrete a milky substance. Chemical substances, called pheromones, which are present in this milky substance, are thought to play a part in sexual attraction between individuals, and in the recognition of mothers by their babies. Apocrine glands are controlled by hormones and become active at puberty. Body odour is caused by the breaking down of the apocrine sweat by bacteria.

Arrector pili

Arrector pili are small muscles attached to the hair follicles. When we are cold, the contraction of these muscles causes the hairs to stand on end. This results in the appearance of goose bumps. Air is trapped between the skin and hair and is warmed by the body heat. This can help to keep the body warm.

Subcutaneous layer

The subcutaneous layer is situated below the dermis. It consists of adipose tissue (fat) and areolar tissue. The adipose tissue helps

DON'T FORGET

Excessively oily skin is known as seborrhoea, and is caused by the sebaceous glands producing too much oil (sebum). This skin look shiny and feels greasy, and there may be spots present.

DON'T FORGET

Toxins are expelled from the body through sweat; therefore the skin helps to detoxify the body.

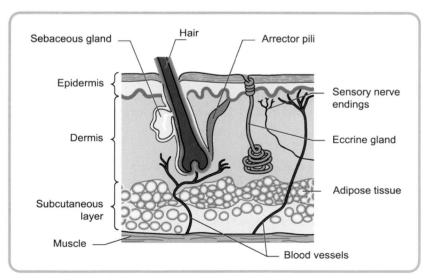

The skin and its structures

to protect the body against injury and acts as an insulating layer against heat loss, helping to keep the body warm. The areolar tissue contains elastic fibres, making this layer elastic and flexible. Muscle is situated below the subcutaneous layer and is attached to bone.

Functions of the skin

Sensation

The skin contains sensory nerve endings that send messages to the brain. These nerves respond to touch, pressure, pain, cold and heat, and allow us to recognise objects from their feel and shape.

Heat regulation

It is important for the body to have a constant internal temperature of around 37 °C. The skin helps to maintain this temperature by:

- vasoconstriction: this occurs when the body becomes cold. The blood vessels constrict (tighten), reducing the flow of blood through the capillaries. Heat loss from the surface of the skin is therefore reduced.

- vasodilation: this occurs when the body becomes too hot. The capillaries widen and the blood flow increases. This allows heat to be lost from the body by radiation. The loss of heat from the body will help to cool it down.

- goose bumps: contraction of the arrector pili muscles when the body is cold causes the hairs to stand on end, keeping a layer of warm air close to the body. This was probably of more use to our distant ancestors, who were generally hairier.

- shivering: shivering when we are cold helps to warm the body, as the contraction of the muscles produces heat within the body.

- sweating: in hot conditions the rate of sweat production increases. The eccrine glands excrete sweat on to the skin surface and heat is lost as the water evaporates from the skin.

Absorption

The skin is largely waterproof and absorbs very little, but certain substances are able to pass through the basal layer. Certain medications, such as hormone replacement therapy (HRT) can be given through patches placed on the skin. UV rays from the sun are also able to penetrate through the basal layer to the dermis beneath.

DON'T FORGET

The skin helps to regulate body temperature.

DON'T FORGET

The skin prevents harmful germs and chemicals from getting into the body.

Protection

The skin protects the body by keeping harmful bacteria out and providing a covering for all the organs inside. It also protects underlying structures from the harmful effects of UV light. The other functions of the skin also help to protect the body.

Excretion

Eccrine glands excrete sweat on to the skin's surface. Sweat consists of 99.4 per cent water, 0.4 per cent toxins and 0.2 per cent salts.

Secretion

Sebum is a fatty substance secreted from the sebaceous glands on to the skin's surface. It keeps the skin flexible, helps to waterproof it, and also reduces the loss of moisture from the skin, helping to ensure it doesn't become dry.

Vitamin D

The skin uses UV rays from the sun to make a form of vitamin D called cholecalciferol. Vitamin D is essential for healthy bones – deficiency can cause rickets, a condition in which the bones are not formed properly.

For information about conditions associated with the skin, see **Unit G20: Ensure responsibility for actions to reduce risks to health and safety**.

Hair

Most of the body is covered by hairs, with the exception of the palms of the hands and the soles of the feet. Hairs mainly consist of the protein **keratin** and grow out from follicles. Follicles are deep pits that extend into the dermis. Hairs help to keep the body warm and are also a form of protection. The eyelashes prevent substances from entering the eyes, and the hairs that line the nose and ears help to trap dust and bacteria.

Structure of the hair

The bulb is found at the base of the hair and has an upper and lower part. The matrix is the lower part of the bulb, and this is where cell division takes place to create the hair. When cells reach the upper part of the bulb they quickly fill with keratin and die. Melanin can be found in the upper part of the bulb and will determine the colour of hair. The hair bulb surrounds the dermal papilla, an area containing many blood vessels, which provides the necessary nutrients needed for hair growth.

DON'T FORGET

Melanin protects the body by absorbing the UV rays from sunlight.

DON'T FORGET

The lips do not contain sebaceous glands, so should be protected to prevent them from becoming dry.

DON'T FORGET

The skin is able to make vitamin D because of the action of sunlight.

DON'T FORGET

SHAPES VitD will help you to remember the functions of the skin.

key terms

Keratin: a hard, waterproof protein that is found in hair and nails.

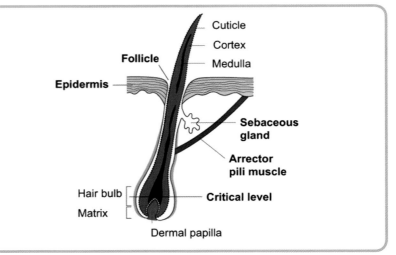

Structure of the hair

key terms

Terminal hair: a type of thick hair that grows on the head, eyebrows, underarm and pubic regions.

The hair is made up of three layers.

Cuticle

The cuticle is the outer part of the hair and consists of a single layer of scale-like cells. These cells overlap rather like tiles on a roof. No pigment is contained within this layer.

Cortex

The cortex lies inside the cuticle and forms the bulk of the hair. It contains melanin, which determines the colour of the hair: the darker the hair the more melanin it contains. When melanin is no longer produced, the hair will become white. The cortex also helps to give strength to the hair.

Medulla

The medulla is the inner part of the hair and is not always present (thick hair usually contains a medulla, but fine hair often lacks a medulla). Air spaces in the medulla determine the shine of the hair which is caused by the reflection of light.

Types of hair growth

There are different types of hair growth.

Lanugo

Lanugo hair is the hair found on the foetus and is usually shed by about the eighth month of pregnancy.

Vellus

Vellus hair is soft and downy and is found all over the body, except on the palms and soles of the feet. This hair is short and mostly does not contain melanin. It is possible, however, for a vellus hair when stimulated to become a **terminal hair**.

Terminal

Terminal hair is longer, coarser, and the follicles are deeper than vellus hair. These hairs are generally found on the head, eyebrows and eyelashes, under the arms, and in the pubic region. However, this depends on the hairiness of the individual: any thick, visible hair is classed as terminal. Terminal hairs found at the bikini line and underarm areas will often have deep follicles. When these hairs are removed during treatments, such as waxing, there may be some spotting of blood caused by slight damage to the follicle.

Stages of hair growth

It takes up to seven years for the fully grown terminal hair to be shed and be replaced by a new hair. The hair grows in three stages: anagen, catagen and telogen. All hairs will be at different stages of growth at any one time.

Anagen

This stage is the active growing stage. It lasts from two to six years and accounts for 85 per cent of hairs at any one time. The hair bulb surrounds the nutrient-giving dermal papilla, and a hair begins to grow from the matrix in the bulb. The anagen stage ends when the hair begins to separate from the dermal papilla and so no longer receives nutrients.

Catagen

This stage is the transitional stage and lasts for about two weeks. Only 1 per cent of hairs will be at this stage. The hair is now fully grown and cell division has stopped. The hair has separated from the papilla and the follicle begins to shrink.

Telogen

This is the stage at which the hair rests, and lasts for about three to four months. About 14 per cent of hairs will be at this stage. The resting hair will either fall out or be pushed out by a new hair growing beneath it.

> **DON'T FORGET**
>
> *When a hair in anagen stage is pulled out, it often contains a bulb and whitish-coloured sheath. A hair in catagen or telogen stage will not have a bulb.*

> **DON'T FORGET**
>
> ***ACT*** *will help you to remember the three stages of growth:*
> ***A****nagen –* ***A****ctive growing stage*
> ***C****atagen –* ***C****hanging stage*
> ***T****elogen –* ***T****ired stage*

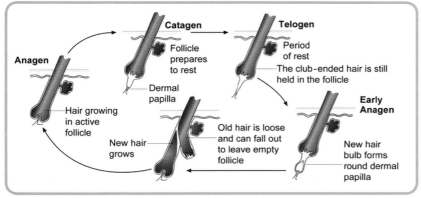

Stages of hair growth

Factors that affect hair growth

- Pregnancy – levels of hormones called oestrogen increase during pregnancy and can cause the stimulation of hair growth, resulting in excess hair growth either on the head or body.

- Having thick black hair – this grows faster than fine blonde hair

- Stress – during times of stress, such as losing a job, divorce or bereavement, the body may produce chemicals that affect the hair follicles and cause temporary loss of hair on the head or body.

- Age of an individual – hair growth slows down as we get older.

- Hereditary factors – growth patterns may be passed down from parents.

- Illnesses and certain medications, for example, alopecia.

Conditions associated with the hair

Alopecia

Alopecia is the term for loss of hair. Alopecia totalis is total hair loss from the scalp. Alopecia areata is a form of patchy baldness. Many women suffer from some degree of alopecia in their lives, especially after the menopause. During pregnancy, scalp hair grows thicker than normal, but afterwards a decrease in hormones may cause a sudden loss of hair. Usually the loss is not noticeable because new hairs will be growing. Common reasons for hair loss include hereditary factors (these usually affect men), severe illness and stress.

Hirsutism

This is an abnormal growth of excess hair, which follows a male pattern of hair growth. It is caused by hormones called androgens. These hormones are made in larger amounts in men, but small amounts are also produced in women. The cause of hirsutism can be an abnormally high level of androgens, or normal levels of androgens but hair follicles that are oversensitive to them. Levels of androgens can increase at puberty, pregnancy, menopause and at times of stress, so all these conditions can lead to hirsutism. **Hirsutism** can also be caused by medical conditions such as ovarian cysts and anorexia nervosa.

Nails

Nails are formed from hard, keratinous cells and also contain some water and fat. Nails help to protect the ends of fingers and toes, and fingernails are useful for picking up small objects.

DON'T FORGET

The number and distribution of hair follicles are the same in both sexes, but because men produce larger amounts of androgens than women, they tend to be hairier.

key terms

Hirsutism: excessive hair growth in women in areas where usually only men grow hair, such as the chin. Some women with hirsutism have a condition in which the ovaries do not work properly, called polycystic ovary syndrome (PCOS).

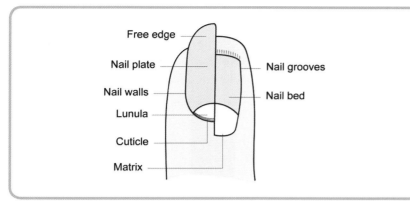

The nail and its structures

Free edge

The free edge is an extension of the nail plate and is the part that we cut and file. If you have long enough nails, look at the palm of your hand and see the nail protruding over the fingertips – you will be looking at the free edge.

Nail plate

This is the tough part of the nail that we can see. It appears pink in colour because of the blood vessels in the nail bed below it. It contains no blood vessels or nerves, so can be cut without pain. Its function is to protect the nail bed beneath it.

Nail walls

These are overlapping folds of skin found at the side of the nails which protect the edges of the nail plate.

Nail grooves

Grooves at the side of the nails, between the nail plate and nail wall, act as guide lines for growing nails so that they grow in a straight line.

Nail bed

The nail bed is found underneath the nail plate and is rich with nerves and blood vessels. The nail bed and nail plate contain grooves and ridges, which enable them to adhere perfectly with each other.

Lunula

The lunula is crescent-shaped and mostly white in colour. It is found at the base of the nail plate. It has no specific function.

> **DON'T FORGET**
>
> *The hyponychium (hi-po-nick-ee-um) is the skin found under the free edge. It helps prevent dirt and bacteria from entering under the nail.*

Cuticle

The cuticle is the overlapping skin at the base of the nail. It prevents bacteria, and any other harmful substance, from entering the matrix and causing infection.

Matrix

Cell division takes place in the matrix to form the nail plate. It is an area richly supplied with nerves and blood vessels. Injury to this area can mean temporary or permanent damage to the growing nail.

It takes about five to six months for the nail to grow from the matrix to the free edge. Diet, injury, health and age are all factors related to poor nail growth and an unhealthy appearance of the nail.

For information about conditions associated with the nails, see **Unit N2 and N3: Provide manicure services and provide pedicure services**.

The skeletal system

The skeletal system consists of the bones and joints of the body. There are 206 bones in the body, which continue to grow up to the ages of 18–25. After 25 years old the bones stop growing, although they can still continue to thicken.

Bone is living tissue and is constantly being built up and broken down. It is made up of 30 per cent living tissue and 70 per cent minerals and water. The minerals include mainly calcium and phosphorus.

Functions of the skeleton

- Shape/support: the skeleton gives the body its shape and supports the weight of all the other tissues.

- Attachment for muscles and tendons: bones provide the attachment point for the tendons of most skeletal muscles.

- Development of blood cells: red blood cells, white blood cells and platelets are produced within the red bone marrow of the bone.

- Protection: bones help to protect vital organs from injury. For example, the ribs protect the heart and lungs and the skull protects the brain.

DON'T FORGET

The cuticle is also known as the eponychium (ep-oh-nick-ee-um).

DON'T FORGET

There are 206 bones in the adult body.

DON'T FORGET

SAD PAM will help to remind you of the functions of the skeleton.

- Allows movements of the body: when skeletal muscles contract, they pull on bones to produce a movement.

- Mineral store: bones store the minerals calcium and phosphorus, which are important for the strength of the bone. If these minerals are required elsewhere in the body, the bones can release them into the bloodstream.

Bones

Bone tissue

There are two types of bone tissue: compact and cancellous (spongy).

Compact bone tissue

Compact bone tissue is hard and dense. It provides strength, support and protection. Under a microscope, compact bone looks like honeycomb, and many circles can be seen, which contain nerves, lymph capillaries and blood vessels.

Cancellous bone tissue

Cancellous bone has a spongy appearance, and so is often called spongy bone. The spongy bone helps to give great strength, but also keeps the skeleton light. The cancellous bone is filled with red bone marrow. Red bone marrow produces billions of red blood cells every day in adults.

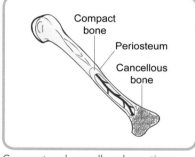

Compact and cancellous bone tissue

Types of bone

Almost all bones are designed to meet a particular need in the body. There are five main types of bone.

- Long bones, such as the humerus in the arm, have a long shaft and two wider ends. They act as levers to enable the body to move. Other examples of long bones include the tibia, fibula (both found in the lower leg), radius, ulna (both found in the lower arm) metacarpals (found in the hand) and phalanges (found in fingers and toes).

- Short bones are roughly cube-shaped. They are found where strength rather than mobility is required. Bones of the wrists (carpals) and ankles (tarsals) are examples of short bones.

- Flat bones help to protect vital organs in the body. Examples include the skull, which protects the brain, and the ribs, which protect the heart and lungs.

- Irregular bones, such as the vertebrae of the spine (backbone) are found in places where extra strength is needed, and also make good attachment points for muscles.

DON'T FORGET

Around 99 per cent of the calcium in our bodies is found in the bones and teeth. However, the remaining 1 per cent is also very important: its uses include muscle contraction and the passing of nerve messages in the body.

■ Sesamoid bones are small rounded bones that develop in the tendons (fibrous bands that attach muscle to bone). They enable the tendon to move smoothly over certain bones, for example, the patella (knee cap). They are also found in the palms of the hands and soles of the feet. For example, these bones can be found in tendons lying over the joint, under the head of the first metatarsal in the foot. Its purpose is to protect the tendon as it moves over the joint. They may vary in number from person to person and mostly measure only a few millimetres.

Conditions associated with bones

Osteoporosis

Bones are living tissue and are constantly being built up and broken down. Osteoporosis causes the bone to break down faster than it is being formed. This causes the bones to become porous, and thin, so there is an increased risk of fracture. It mainly affects middle-aged and older people and is more common in women than men. Hormones, such as oestrogen in women and testosterone in men, help stimulate the bone-forming cells to

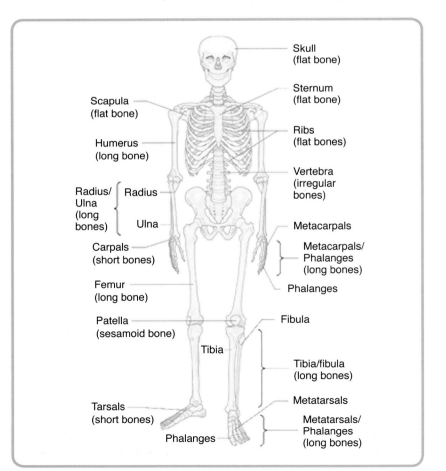

Types of bone

produce new bone tissue. Women produce smaller amounts of oestrogen after the menopause, and men produce smaller amounts of testosterone as they age. As a result, the bone-forming cells become less active, and there is a decrease in **bone mass**.

A well-balanced diet, which includes plenty of vitamin D and calcium, as well as exercise, can help protect against osteoporosis later in life.

Damage to ligaments

Ligaments consist of bands of strong, fibrous connective tissue that are silvery in appearance. They prevent dislocation by holding the bones together across joints, but stretch slightly to allow movement. When excess strain is put on a joint, especially the ankle or knee, the ligaments can become sprained or torn. Injuries to ligaments can be minor or severe, and result in bruising, tenderness and swelling. Minor injury can be treated with ice packs to reduce the swelling, and then bandaged to support the joint. As ligaments have a relatively poor blood supply, they can take a long time to heal when damaged.

Damage to tendons

Tendons consist of white, strong, almost inelastic, fibrous bands. Most muscles are attached to bones by tendons. They vary in length and thickness. When a muscle contracts, the force transmitted through the tendon creates movement at the bone. An example of a tendon is the **Achilles tendon** that attaches from the calf muscle to the back of the foot.

A tendon can become injured if stretched beyond its normal limit. This happens in twisted ankles and sprained wrists, as the body weight is suddenly concentrated in one small area, putting strain on the tendon. The tendon may partially tear when some fibres are torn. There can also be a complete tearing in which the tendon is severed. The tendon can tear away from the bone or muscle, which is extremely painful.

Anatomical terms

To understand these terms, the body has to be in the correct position. Imagine someone standing upright with their arms by their side and palms facing forwards. There is an imaginary vertical line that runs through the middle of the body and is known as the midline.

- Medial: on the inner side of the body. The ulna is on the **medial side** of the forearm. The inside of the leg and foot is the medial side.

key terms

Bone mass: refers to the amount of minerals (mostly calcium and phosphorous) a specific volume of bone contains. A person with low bone mass is at risk from fractures and osteoporosis.

DON'T FORGET

'Osteo' means bone.

key terms

Achilles tendon: a tendon that connects the heel of the foot to the muscles of the lower leg (calf muscles).

Medial side: the medial side of the foot is the inside part of the foot and the lateral side is the outside part of the foot.

DON'T FORGET

Ligaments attach bone to bone. Tendons attach muscle to bone.

key terms

Lateral side: the part of the body that is furthest from the middle of the body and is on the outer side; it is also used to describe the side of a body part, e.g. when describing the foot, 'lateral' refers to the outside of the foot.

- Lateral: towards the outer side of the body. The humerus is lateral to the clavicle. The outside of the leg and foot is the **lateral side**.

- Anterior or ventral: nearer to or at the front of the body. The sternum is anterior to the heart.

- Posterior or dorsal: nearer to or at the back of the body. The heart is posterior to the sternum. The top of the foot is the dorsal surface.

- Plantar: on or towards the sole of the foot.

- Proximal: closest to the midline. In the limbs it is the part nearer to the trunk. The humerus is proximal to the radius.

- Distal: furthest away from the midline. In the limbs it is the part that is further away from the trunk. The phalanges are distal to the carpals.

- Superficial: towards the surface of the body. The skin is superficial to the heart.

- Deep: away from the surface of the body. The heart is deep to the skin.

Bones of the skull and face

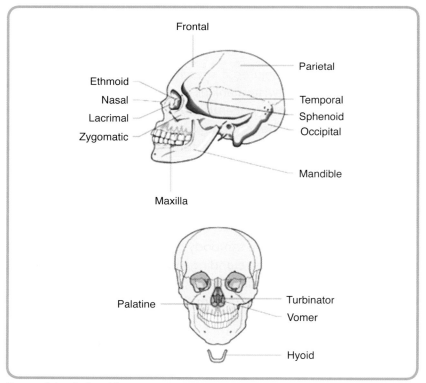

Bones of the skull and face

Bone	Position
Frontal bone	One frontal bone forms the forehead.
Parietal bone (pa-ri-e-tal)	Two parietal bones form the sides and top of the skull.
Temporal bone (tem-por-ral)	Two temporal bones are found at the sides of the skull under the parietal bones.
Occipital bone (ox-ip-i-tal)	One occipital bone forms the back of the skull.
Zygomatic bone (zy-go-mah-tic)	Two zygomatic bones form the cheekbones.
Maxilla (mak-sil-ah)	The maxilla forms the upper part of the jaw.
Mandible (man-dee-bill)	The mandible forms the lower part of the jaw. It is the only movable bone of the skull.
Ethmoid (eth-moid)	One ethmoid bone helps to form the eye socket and nasal cavities.
Sphenoid (sfee-noid)	One sphenoid bone helps to form the base of the skull.
Nasal (nayz-all)	Two nasal bones form the bridge of the nose.
Lacrimal bone (lah-kruh-mul)	Two lacrimal bones make up part of each eye socket.
Turbinates (tur-bin-nuts)	Two turbinated bones make up part of the nasal cavity.
Palatine bones (pal-la-tyne)	Two L-shaped palatine bones form the walls of the nasal cavities and part of the roof of the mouth.
Vomer (voh-mer)	One vomer extends upwards from the hard palate to make the nasal septum.
Hyoid (hi-oyd)	One horseshoe-shaped bone lying in the neck. It is not joined to any other bone. However, it is attached to the temporal bone by ligaments. It is a sesamoid bone.

HAVE A GO

Blow up a balloon and tie its end. Use a marker pen to draw on the following bones: frontal, parietal, occipital, nasal, zygomatic, maxilla and mandible. When the balloon is complete try to remember the name of each bone.

The spine

The spine is also known as the backbone. It is made up of ring-like bones that run from the skull to the pelvis. It holds the head and body upright and allows the body to bend and twist. It also offers protection to the spinal cord, which is a large bundle of nerves that runs through the hollow space in the centre of the spine. The nerves pass messages between the brain and the rest of your body.

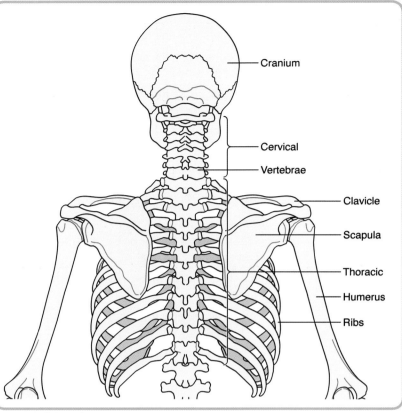

Structure of the spine

Bones of the upper body

Bones of the shoulder girdle

- Clavicle: a long, slender bone, also known as the collar bone.

- Scapula (plural: scapulae): a large, triangular, flat bone, also known as the shoulder blade.

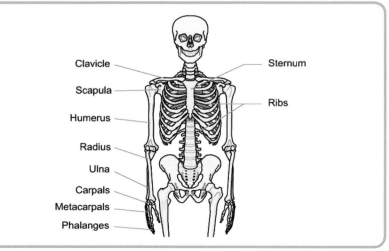

Bones of the upper body

Bones of the thorax

The **thoracic cavity** contains organs such as the heart and lungs, which are protected by the ribcage.

- Ribs: long, curved bones – there are 12 pairs of ribs.
- Sternum: a small, flat bone, also known as the breast bone.

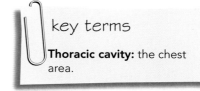

key terms

Thoracic cavity: the chest area.

Bones of the upper limbs

- Humerus: the long bone of the upper arm.
- Radius: the bone situated on the thumb side of the forearm.
- Ulna: the bone situated on the little-finger side of the forearm.

Bones of the wrist and hand

- Carpals: the carpals consist of eight small bones in the wrist, which are closely fitted together and held in position by ligaments. These are:
    - scaphoid (scaf-oid)
    - lunate (lune-ate)
    - triquetrum (tri-kwee-trum)
    - pisiform (pie-see-form)
    - trapezium (trap-ee-zee-um)
    - trapezoid (trap-ee-zoid)
    - capitates (cap-ee-tates)
    - hamate (hay-mate).

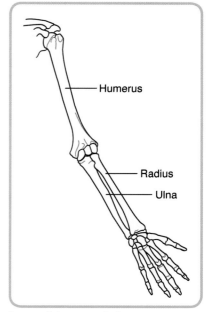

Bones of the upper limbs

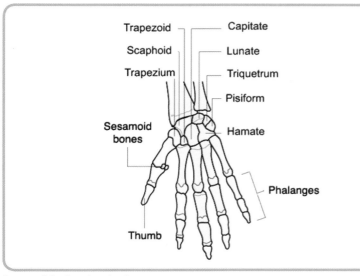

Bones of the hand and wrist

DON'T FORGET

The carpus is the group of bones that makes up the wrist.

■ Metacarpals: the metacarpals consist of five metacarpal bones (long bones), which form the main part of the hand.

■ Phalanges: there are 14 phalanges (fa-lan-geez) in each hand, three in each finger and two in the thumb.

Bones of the lower limbs

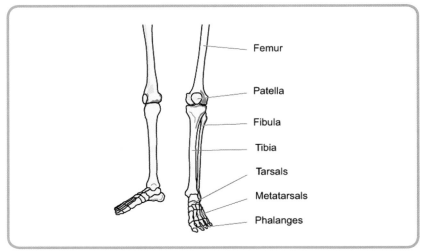

Bones of the lower limbs

■ Femur: the largest bone in the body, which runs from the hip to the knee, also known as the thigh bone.

■ Patella: the knee cap, which articulates with the femur.

■ Tibia: the bone situated on the front of the lower leg, also known as the shin bone.

■ Fibula: the bone situated on the outer side of the tibia and thinner than the tibia.

Bones of the ankle and foot

■ Tarsals: the seven bones of the ankle that form the posterior (back) part of the foot. These are:
  – one calcaneus (kal-kay-nee-us)
  – one talus (ta-lus)
  – one cuboid (cue-boyd)
  – one navicular (na-vik-cue-ler)
  – three cuneiforms (cue-nee-forms).

■ Metatarsals: there are five metatarsal bones, which can be seen on the dorsal aspect of the foot.

■ Phalanges: the 14 phalanges form the toes.

DON'T FORGET

A phalanx (fa-lanks) is any of the bones of the fingers or toes. (plural: phalanges)

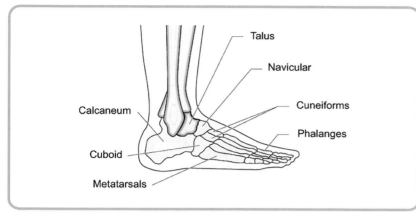

Bones of the foot

Arches of the foot

The bones of the feet fit together to make arches. The arches help to support the weight of the body and provide leverage when walking. Strong ligaments and tendons support the bones that form the arches.

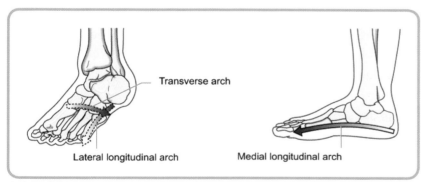

Arches of the foot

The arches of the foot are:

- lateral longitudinal arch: this is on the little-toe side of the foot and begins at the calcaneus. It rises at the cuboid and descends to the two outer metatarsal bones.

- transverse arch: this runs between the medial and lateral aspect of the foot and is formed by the navicular, the cuneiform bones and the bases of the five metatarsals.

- medial longitudinal arch: this is the highest arch on the big-toe side of the foot. It begins at the calcaneus, rises to the talus and descends through the navicular, the three cuneiforms and the three medial metatarsals.

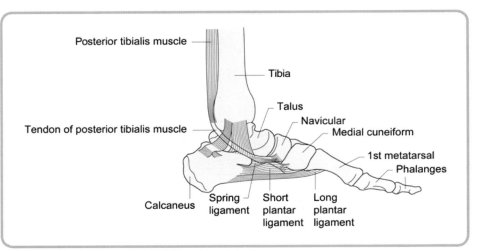

Tendons and ligaments supporting the arches of the foot

Joints of the body

A joint describes the joining (articulation) of two or more bones of the body. There are three main types of joint.

Fibrous or immovable joints
These are fixed joints in which no movement between the joints is possible. Examples are the sutures or joints between the skull bones.

Cartilaginous joints (cart-til-laj-gin-nus)
These are slightly movable joints in which only limited movement is possible. Examples are the joints between the bones of the vertebral column (spine).

Synovial joints (sy-no-vee-all)
These are freely movable joints, of which there are several types, all having similar characteristics. An example is the joint of the knee.

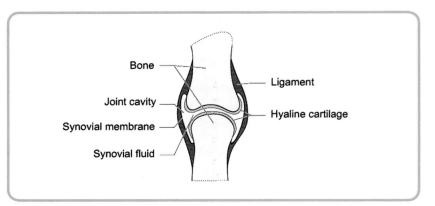

Structure of a synovial joint

In a freely movable joint, ends of the bones are mostly covered by hyaline cartilage. The cartilage helps to reduce friction and acts as a shock absorber during movement. Ligaments are needed to bind the bones together and help prevent dislocation. The space between the bones is called the joint cavity and is enclosed by a capsule of fibrous tissue. The synovial membrane lines the joint cavity and secretes a fluid called synovial fluid, which lubricates the joint and provides the hyaline cartilage with nutrients.

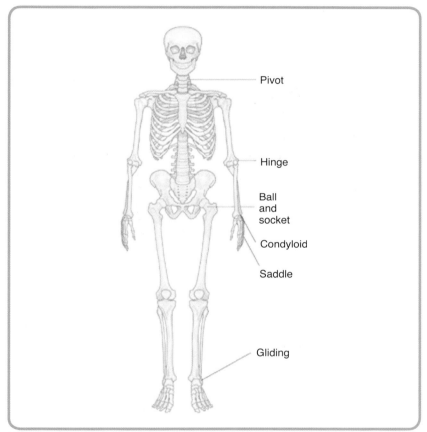

Pivot

Hinge

Ball and socket

Condyloid

Saddle

Gliding

Types of synovial joint

Muscles

There are over 600 muscles in the body, which make up 40–50 per cent of the body weight. The function of the muscles is to produce movement, maintain posture and provide heat for the body.

Therapists are mostly concerned with the skeletal muscles, which are also known as voluntary muscles, as they are under our conscious control. Skeletal muscles are striped in appearance and consist of bundles of muscle fibres enclosed in a sheath (fascia). They allow movement of the body.

Skeletal muscles are richly supplied with blood vessels and nerves. Before movement of a muscle can occur, a message must be sent from the brain through a nerve, which in turn stimulates the muscle to contract. Skeletal muscles bring about movement by exerting a pull on tendons, which cause the bones to move at the joints. The pulling force that causes movement is the result of contraction (shortening) of the muscle.

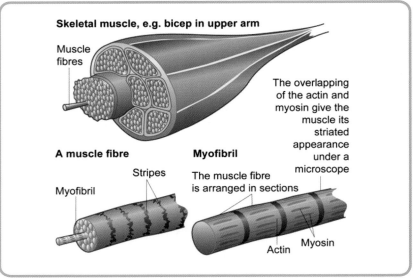

The interior of a muscle

The origin of a muscle is the bone to which it is attached that does not move. The insertion is the bone to which the muscle is attached that does move. For example, the biceps of the upper arm has its point of origin at the shoulder, while the point of insertion is the radius of the lower arm. The insertion is the part farthest away from the spine.

Fascia

Muscles are covered in a layer of fibrous tissue called a fascia (fash-ee-ah). This sheath extends to become tendons and attaches the muscle to bone. The fascia allows the muscles to glide smoothly past each other.

Muscle tone

Muscle is never completely at rest but is in a state of partial contraction. The partial contraction is not enough to move the muscle, but will cause some tension. All skeletal muscles must be slightly contracted if the body is to remain upright. If all of the muscles relaxed, the body would fall to the floor. This continuous slight tension is involuntary and is known as muscle tone. Different groups of muscle fibres contract at different times, which prevents the muscle from becoming fatigued.

Each person's degree of muscle tone varies depending on the amount of activity or exercise they do. People who are sedentary (inactive), and do not exercise, usually have poor muscle tone as the muscle fibres do not contract as far as they should.

Effects of temperature on muscle

Exercise is an effective way of increasing body temperature because when muscles are working they produce heat. When muscle tissue is warm, the muscle fibres contract more easily as the blood circulation is increased. Therefore, the chemical reactions that naturally take place in the muscle cells are speeded up. When muscle tissue is cold, the opposite happens – the chemical reactions slow down and so contraction will be slower. This is why in cold conditions hands may feel stiff when moving them.

Conditions associated with muscles

Muscle strain
Overwork or overstretching of the muscles can cause strain and may result in muscle fibres being torn. It can normally be felt as hardness in the muscle, usually running the same way as the muscle fibres.

Tearing of muscle fibres
Injury to a muscle can cause complete or partial tearing of the muscle fibres. Partial tears result in the tearing of some muscle fibres and will feel very tender and painful, especially when contracting the muscle. Complete tearing involves tearing of all the muscle fibres, which causes the two ends of the muscles to contract away from each other. It is extremely painful and there is complete of loss of function.

Cramp
Cramp is a painful muscle spasm that may arise following exercise. Muscle spasms occur when muscles contract for too long, or when excessive sweating causes water and salt loss. The accumulation (build up) of a substance called lactic acid following vigorous exercise can also cause cramp. Lightly massaging and gradually stretching the affected muscle can relieve the spasm and pain. Sometimes cramp can occur for no reason, for example during sleep, and may be the result of poor muscle tone.

Fibrositis
This is a common muscular condition in which there is a build-up of **urea** and lactic acid inside the muscle, which causes pain and stiffness.

DON'T FORGET

Vigorous exercise can cause minor tearing of muscle fibres. This is thought to be a major reason why muscles become sore and stiff 12–48 hours after exercise.

key terms
Urea: a waste chemical produced from the break down of protein. Urea is taken by the kidneys from the blood and removed from the body by urine.

Muscles of the head, face and neck

Muscle	Position	Action
Frontalis (fron-tal-lis)	Across the forehead	Draws the scalp forward and raises the eyebrows
Corrugator (cor-oo-gater)	Between the eyebrows	Lowers the eyebrows and wrinkles the skin of the forehead, as in frowning
Buccinator (bux-sin-ay-ter)	In each cheek, to the side of the mouth	Compresses the cheeks, as in whistling and blowing, and draws the corners of the mouth in, as in sucking
Risorius (ree-so-re-us)	Extends diagonally from either side of the mouth	Draws the corner of the mouth outwards, as in grinning
Masseter (ma-see-ter)	The cheeks	The muscle of chewing: it closes the mouth and clenches the teeth
Orbicularis oculi (or-bik-cue-la-riss ok-you-lie)	Around the eyes	Closes the eye
Zygomaticus major (zy-go-mat-ti-kus)	Extends diagonally from the corners of the mouth	Lifts the corners of the mouth upwards and outwards, as in smiling or laughing
Mentalis (men-ta-lis)	On the chin	Raises and protrudes the lower lip, wrinkles the skin on the chin
Orbicularis oris (or-bik-cue-la-riss aw-riss)	Surrounds the mouth	For closure and protrusion of the lips, changes the shape of the lips for speech
Temporalis (tem-po-rah-lis)	Extends from the temple region to the upper jaw bone	Raises the lower jaw and draws it backwards, as in chewing
Sternocleidomastoid (sterno-cly-doh-mas-toyd)	Runs from the top of the sternum to the clavicle and temporal bones	Bends the head forward and to the side
Platysma (pla-tis-ma)	Extends from the lower jaw to the chest and covers the front of the neck	Depresses the lower jaw and draws the lower lip outwards, draws up the skin of the chest
Levator anguli oris (le-vay-tor an-goo-lie aw-riss)	On the cheek	Raises the corner of the mouth, as in smiling
Levator labii superioris (le-vay-tor lay-bee su-peer-ree-aw-riss)	On the cheek	Lifts the upper lip, as in smiling
Depressor anguli oris (de-press-or an-goo-lie aw-riss)	On the chin	Draws the corners of the mouth down, as in frowning
Depressor labii inferioris (de-press-or lay-be in-fear-ree-aw-riss)	On the chin	Lowers the bottom lip
Nasalis (nay-sah-lis)	Sides of the nose	Opens the nostrils, as when angry
Procerus (pro-seer-rus)	On the nasal bone	Causes the small horizontal lines between the eyebrows when angry
Occipitalis (ox-ip-i-tah-lis)	At the back of the head	Draws the scalp backwards
Pterygoids (lateral and medial) (terry-goyds)	Outer part of the cheek	Moves the mandible from side to side, as in chewing
Triangularis (tri-ang-goo-lah-riss)	Chin	Lowers the corners of the mouth
Splenius capitis (splen-knee-us cap-pee-tis)	Back of the neck	These muscles work together to move the head to an upright position

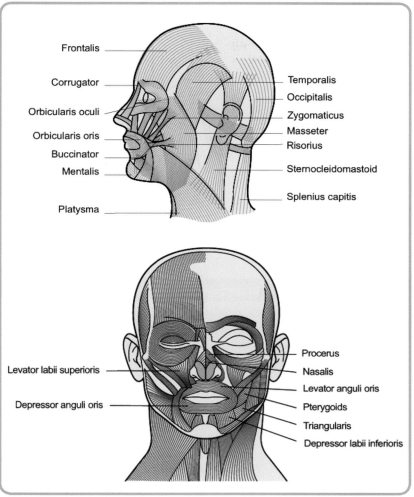

Muscles of the face and neck

Frontalis
Corrugator
Orbicularis oculi
Orbicularis oris
Buccinator
Mentalis
Platysma

Temporalis
Occipitalis
Zygomaticus
Masseter
Risorius
Sternocleidomastoid
Splenius capitis

Levator labii superioris
Depressor anguli oris

Procerus
Nasalis
Levator anguli oris
Pterygoids
Triangularis
Depressor labii inferioris

HAVE A GO

Blow up a balloon and tie its end. Use a black marker pen to draw the following muscles: frontalis, temporalis, orbicularis oculi, buccinator, masseter, mentalis and orbicularis oris. Practise trying to remember the name of each muscle.

Muscles of the anterior aspect of the trunk

Muscle	Position	Origin	Insertion	Action
Pectoralis major (peck-tor-rah-lis may-jor)	Covers the upper part of the thorax	Sternum, ribs and clavicle	Humerus	Adducts (draws towards the body) and medially rotates the arm
Pectoralis minor (peck-tor-rah-lis mine-or)	Small muscle found beneath pectoralis major	Ribs	Scapula	Draws the shoulder downwards and forwards

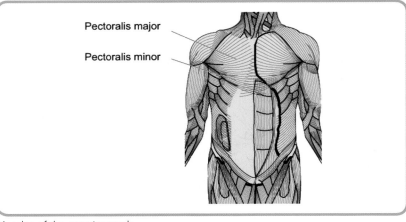

Muscles of the anterior trunk

Muscles of the shoulders

Muscle	Position	Origin	Insertion	Action
Trapezius (tra-pee-zee-us)	Forms a large, kite-shaped muscle across the top of the back and neck	Occipital bone and vertebrae	Scapula and clavicle	Lifts the clavicle as in shrugging, and also draws the head backwards
Deltoid (del-toyd)	A thick, triangular muscle that caps the shoulder	Clavicle and scapula	Humerus	Abducts the arm (draws it away from the body) and draws it backwards and forwards
Coracobrachialis (coh-rah-co-bray-key-ah-liss)	Upper medial part of the arm	Scapula	Humerus	Flexes and adducts the arm
Splenius capitis (splee-knee-us cap-pee-tiss)	Found under the trapezius in the neck	Thoracic/cervical vertebrae	Occipital bone	Helps to hold the neck and head in an upright position and aids rotation of the head
Splenius cervicis (splee-knee-us ser-vis-sees)	Found beneath the splenius capitis	Thoracic vertebrae	Cervical vertebrae	Helps to hold up the head and neck and aids rotation of the head

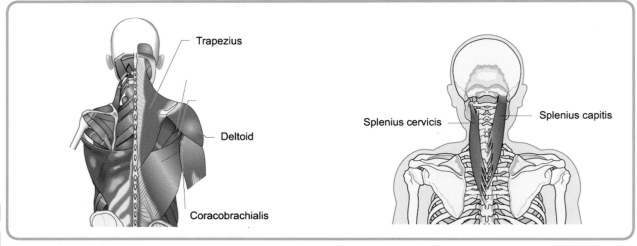

Muscles of the shoulders

Muscles of the upper limbs

Muscle	Position	Origin	Insertion	Action
Biceps brachii (bi-seps bray-kee-eye)	Down anterior surface of the humerus	Scapula	Radius and flexor muscles in forearm	Flexes and supinates the forearm (turns it so palm is facing upward)
Triceps (tri-seps)	Posterior surface of the humerus	Humerus and scapula	Ulna	Extends the forearm
Brachialis (bray-kee-ah-lis)	On the anterior aspect of the humerus beneath the biceps	Humerus	Ulna	Flexes the forearm
Coracobrachialis (coh-rah-co-bray-key-ah-liss)	Upper arm	Scapula	Humerus	Flexes and adducts the arm at the shoulder joint
Flexors (flex-sers) and extensors (ex-sten-sers) of the forearm	Forearm	Flexors – humerus, radius and ulna Extensors – humerus	Carpals, metacarpals and phalanges	Flexors flex the wrist and extensors extend the wrist
Brachioradialis (bray-key-oh-ray-dee-ah-liss)	On the same side as the radius bone of the forearm	Humerus	Radius	Flexes, supinates and pronates forearm (turns it so palm is facing downwards)
Pronator teres (pro-nay-ter terrys)	Anterior side of forearm, across the elbow joint	Humerus and ulna	Radius	Pronates and flexes the forearm

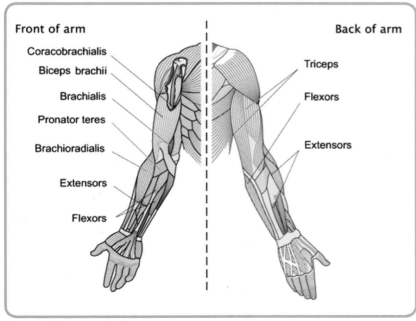

Muscles of the upper limbs

Muscles of the arms and hands

Muscle	Position	Origin	Insertion	Action
Supinator (su-pin-nay-ter)	Forearm	Humerus	Radius	Supinates forearm
Extensor digitorum (ex-sten-sore diji-tor-rum)	Forearm	Humerus	Phalanges	Extends phalanges
Flexor digitorum superficialis (flex-ser diji-tor-rum super-fish-ee-ah-liss)	Forearm	Humerus	Phalanges	Flexes phalanges
Extensor carpi ulnaris (ex-sten-sore car-pee ul-nar-riss)	Forearm	Humerus	5th metacarpal	Extends and adducts hand at wrist joint
Flexor carpi ulnaris (flex-ser car-pee ul-nar-riss)	Forearm	Humerus	Carpals and 5th metacarpal	Flexes and adducts hand at wrist joint
Extensor carpi radialis (ex-sten-sore car-pee ray-dee-al-liss)	Forearm	Humerus	2nd Metacarpal	Extends and abducts hand at wrist joint
Flexor carpi radialis (flex-ser car-pee ray-dee-al-liss)	Forearm	Humerus	Metacarpals	Flexes and abducts hand at wrist joint
Extensor pollicis brevis (ex-sten-sore pol-lee-sis bray-viss)	Forearm	Middle of radius	Phalanx of thumb	Extends phalanx of thumb at metacarpo-phalangeal joint
Muscles of thenar eminence (thee-nar)	On the palm of the hand	Carpals and metacarpals	Phalanx of thumb	The four thenar muscles act on the thumb. Movements include adduction, abduction and flexion of the thumb
Muscles of hypothenar eminence (hi-poe-thee-nar)	On the palm of the hand	Carpals	Phalanx of little finger and the metacarpal near to little finger	The three hypothenar muscles act on the little fingers. Movements include abduction and flexion of the little finger

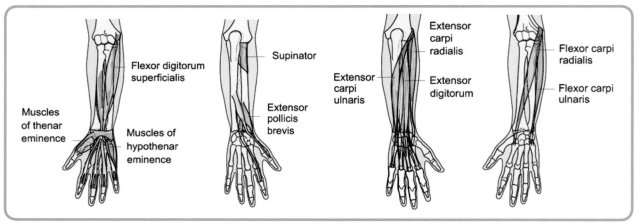

Muscles of the arms and hands

Muscles of the lower limbs

Muscle	Position	Origin	Insertion	Action
Gastrocnemius (gas-troc-nee-me-us)	Back of the lower leg	Femur	Calcaneus in the foot via the Achilles tendon	Plantarflexes the foot (draws the foot downwards)
Soleus (so-lee-us)	At the back of the lower leg, deep to the gastrocnemius	Tibia and fibula	Calcaneus via the Achilles tendon	Plantarflexes the foot
Tibialis anterior (tib-ee-ah-liss an-tear-rhee-er)	Down the shin bone	Tibia	Tarsal and metatarsal bones	Dorsiflexes the foot (draws the foot upwards)
Tibialis posterior (tib-ee-ah-liss pos-tear-rhee-er)	Deepest muscle on the back of the lower leg	Tibia and fibula	Metatarsals, navicular, cuneiforms and cuboid	Plantarflexes and inverts the foot (turns the foot inwards)
Peroneus longus (pear-row-knee-us long-gus)	Down the outside of the lower leg	Fibula	1st metatarsal and cuneiform bone	Plantarflexes and inverts foot (turns foot outwards); supports the transverse and lateral longitudinal arches of the feet
Extensor hallucis longus (ex-sten-sore ha-loo-sis long-gus)	Down the front of the lower leg	Fibula	Phalanx of big toe	Extends the big toe
Flexor hallucis longus (flex-ser ha-loo-sis long-gus)	Outer side and towards the back of the lower leg	Fibula	Phalanx of big toe	Flexes the big toe, inverts and plantarflexes the foot; also supports medial longitudinal arch of the foot
Extensor digitorum longus (ex-sten-sore diji-tor-rum long-gus)	Lateral to the tibialis anterior muscle	Tibia, fibula	Phalanges	Dorsiflexes the foot
Flexor digitorum longus flex-ser diji-tore-rum long-gus)	Medial to the tibialis anterior muscle	Tibia	Phalanges	Plantarflexes the foot

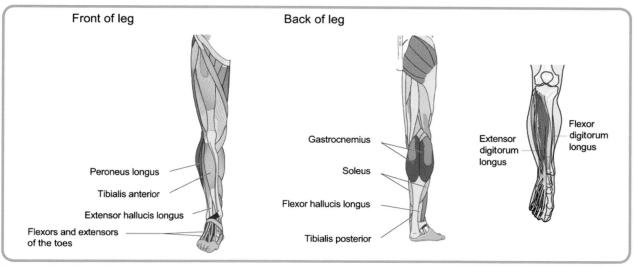

Front of leg

Peroneus longus
Tibialis anterior
Extensor hallucis longus
Flexors and extensors of the toes

Back of leg

Gastrocnemius
Soleus
Flexor hallucis longus
Tibialis posterior

Extensor digitorum longus

Flexor digitorum longus

Muscles of the lower limbs

The cardiovascular system

The cardiovascular system consists of the heart, blood and blood vessels. The function of the heart is to act as a pump to move the blood around the body. The blood carries oxygen and nutrients and is transported in the body by blood vessels.

The heart

The heart is situated between the lungs in the thoracic cavity (chest region), lying slightly to the left of the body. It is roughly the size of its owner's closed fist and is an organ made up mainly of cardiac muscle.

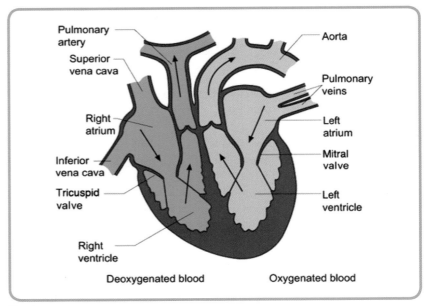

Heart

Blood

Functions of the blood

The blood has several functions.

- It carries oxygen, nutrients, and hormones to the cells of the body. It also transports heat, from the muscles and liver, around the body, which helps regulate the body temperature.

- It removes carbon dioxide and waste from the cells.

- It attacks harmful organisms such as bacteria: the white blood cells protect the body against disease.

- It clots to prevent excess loss of blood if an injury occurs to the body.

Blood plasma

Plasma is the liquid part of the blood and mainly consists of water. Many substances can travel in the blood plasma, including blood cells, hormones, nutrients and the waste products produced by cells.

Blood cells

Red blood cells

Red blood cells (erythrocytes) are button-shaped cells that do not have a nucleus. They are made in the bone marrow and live for about three months. There are approximately five million of these cells in a drop of blood. The function of red blood cells is to carry oxygen around the body and deliver it to the cells. They deliver to nearly all body cells, such as skin and muscle cells. The cells use the oxygen and produce carbon dioxide. Carbon dioxide is carried away by the red blood cells and taken back to the lungs to be breathed out.

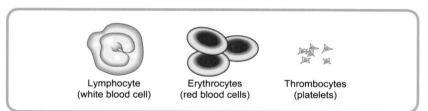

Lymphocyte
(white blood cell)

Erythrocytes
(red blood cells)

Thrombocytes
(platelets)

Blood cells

White blood cells

White blood cells (leucocytes) contain a nucleus and are larger than red blood cells. There are up to 10,000 in a drop of blood. Most types of white blood cell can change their shape, so they are able to squeeze through small spaces. Therefore, white blood cells are able to reach almost anywhere in the body. White blood cells include **lymphocytes** and **monocytes** and their function is to protect us from disease. Lymphocytes do this by producing **antibodies**, while monocytes destroy harmful matter, such as bacteria, by engulfing and digesting them.

Platelets

Platelets (thrombocytes) are tiny fragments of cells, which are smaller than white and red blood cells. They are produced in the bone marrow and live for up to two weeks. There are about 200,000 in a drop of blood. Platelets are involved with the clotting process of the blood following an injury to the body. Their function is to help to prevent loss of blood from damaged blood vessels by forming a plug.

DON'T FORGET

Plasma makes up about 50 per cent of the blood – the rest is blood cells.

DON'T FORGET

There are approximately five million red blood cells in a drop of blood.

key terms

Lymphocytes: white blood cells that produce antibodies.

Monocytes: white blood cells that destroy harmful matter, e.g. bacteria, by engulfing and digesting them. These cells gather around wounds and kill invading bacteria to prevent them from entering the body.

Antibodies: these are chemicals made by the body in response to bacteria and any other harmful matter. They have the function of destroying the harmful matter so that it is no longer a threat to the body.

DON'T FORGET

Haemoglobin is a substance in red blood cells that carries oxygen around the body, and is responsible for the red colour of blood. It contains iron, and if there is an insufficient amount of iron in the diet it may lead to a condition called anaemia. This is where an individual does not have enough red blood cells to carry oxygen around their body efficiently, which can lead to symptoms such as tiredness and shortage of breath.

DON'T FORGET

An increase of monocytes will occur in response to inflammation in the body.

DON'T FORGET

An autoimmune disease is one in which antibodies, produced by the immune system, attack the body's own tissues. Examples include arthritis, psoriasis and multiple sclerosis.

Blood clotting

A blood clot is formed at the site of an injury to the body, and prevents the loss of further blood. If this process did not occur we would bleed to death.

Blood vessels

Blood is transported around the body in a series of pipes called blood vessels. These blood vessels are called arteries, arterioles, capillaries, venules and veins, and form an intricate network within the body.

Arteries

Arteries have thick, elastic, muscular walls, because the blood within them is carried under high pressure owing to the pumping action of the heart. Most arteries carry oxygenated blood away from the heart. Arteries are generally deep-seated, except where they cross a pulse spot, such as the radial artery in the wrist and carotid artery in the neck, where a pulse can be felt. As arteries get further from the heart they branch off and become smaller. The oxygenated blood eventually reaches very small arteries called arterioles.

Capillaries

Arterioles are connected to capillaries. Capillaries are the smallest vessels, about a hundredth of a millimetre thick. Unlike arteries and veins, the walls of the capillaries are thin enough to allow certain substances to pass through them – this is known as capillary exchange. In this way, oxygen and nutrients are delivered to the cells of the body, and carbon dioxide and waste products are removed.

Capillaries also connect with venules. These are blood vessels, larger than capillaries but smaller than veins, which carry deoxygenated blood (containing carbon dioxide and no oxygen) to the veins.

Veins

Blood that is carried in veins is called venous blood and is carried towards the heart. The walls of veins are thinner and less elastic than arteries. Veins mostly carry deoxygenated blood and are nearer the surface of the body than the arteries. Unlike the other blood vessels, veins contain valves, which prevent the blood from flowing backwards.

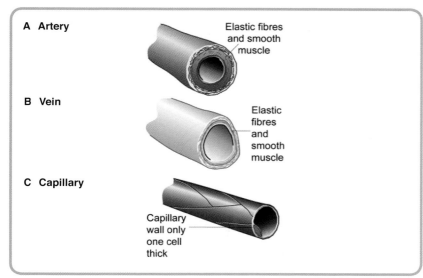

Blood vessels

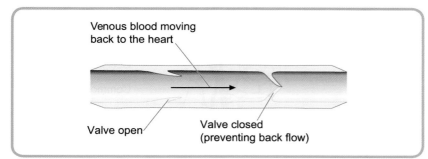

Valves in the veins

Unlike arteries, the veins carry blood at low pressure because they are not helped by the pumping action of the heart. Blood in the veins is moved through the body by the squeezing action of

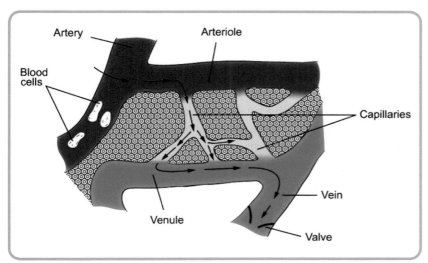

How blood passes from arteries through capillaries to veins

the voluntary muscles, such as during walking, and the involuntary muscles, such as the movement of breathing. Therefore, exercise and massage are particularly useful to help the venous flow.

Blood vessels of the head and neck

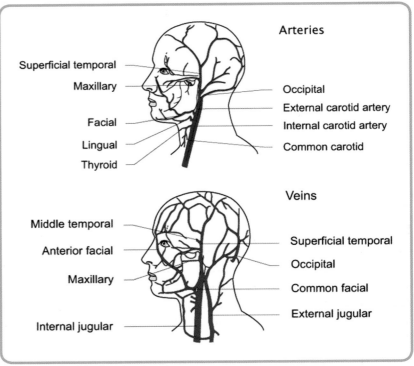

Blood vessels of the head and neck

Arteries – to the head and neck
The blood to the head arrives via the carotid arteries. There are two main carotid (cah-rot-tid) arteries, one either side of the neck.

- The internal carotid artery, which supplies oxygenated blood to the brain.

- The external carotid artery, which carries blood to the more superficial structures of the head – that is, muscle, skin and bone.

Important arteries of the head and neck include the common carotid, the occipital, the superficial temporal, the maxillary, the facial, the lingual and the thyroid arteries. These branch off from the internal and external carotid arteries.

Veins – from the head and neck
Important veins of the head and neck include the middle temporal, the superficial temporal, the maxillary, the anterior facial, the common facial, the internal jugular, the external jugular and the occipital veins.

A
&
P

Blood vessels of the body

■ The aorta is the largest artery of the body. Its diameter is about the size of a ten pence piece. This artery subdivides to become smaller arteries and supplies blood to the whole body.

■ The inferior vena cava is the largest vein in the body, about 3.5 cm in diameter. The superior vena cava has a diameter about the size of a ten pence piece.

■ Other important blood vessels include the pulmonary artery, pulmonary vein, hepatic portal vein, hepatic artery, hepatic vein, renal artery, renal vein.

How the circulatory system works

Blood pressure

A normal blood pressure will measure around 120 mmHg systolic and 80 mmHg diastolic, or 120/80.

Blood pressure is used as an indicator of the health of the blood vessels and heart. Damaged blood vessels that are less elastic, or have a partial blockage, will show a raised blood pressure, and a weak heart will show low blood pressure. People who exercise regularly often have slightly lower than average blood pressure. Exercise helps to strengthen the heart, so it has to do less work to pump the same amount of blood.

High/low blood pressure

High blood pressure (hypertension) is when the blood pressure is consistently above normal. It can lead to strokes and heart attacks, as the heart has to work harder to force blood through the system. High blood pressure can be caused by hereditary factors, smoking, obesity, lack of exercise, eating too much salt, stress, too much alcohol, the contraceptive pill and pregnancy.

Low blood pressure (hypotension) is when the blood pressure is below normal for a substantial time. Blood pressure must be sufficient to pump blood to the brain when the body is in an upright position. If it is not, then the person will feel faint. Some people with low blood pressure may feel faint when sitting up suddenly from the lying position.

Pulse

The pulse can be felt in arteries that lie close to the surface of the body, such as the radial artery in the wrist and the carotid artery in the neck. The number of pulse beats per minute represents the heart rate. The pumping action of the left ventricle in the heart is strong, so it can be felt as a pulse in arteries. The average pulse of an adult at rest is between 60 and 80 beats per minute.

> **DON'T FORGET**
>
> People who exercise regularly often have slightly lower than average blood pressure.

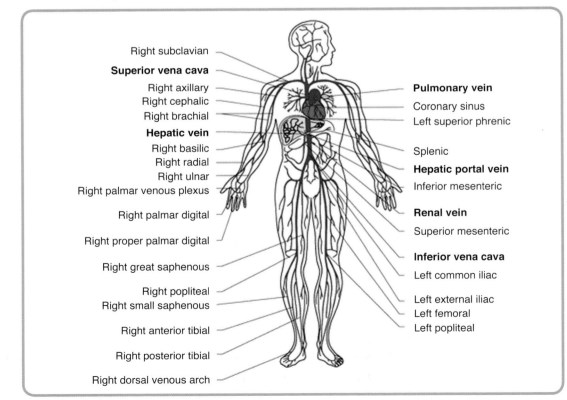

Vertebral
Ascending aorta
Right subclavian
Pulmonary artery
Right brachial
Hepatic artery
Right renal
Abdominal aorta
Right radial
Right ulnar
Right superficial palmar arch
Right deep palmar arch
Right iliac artery
Right deep femoral
Plantar arch

Arch of aorta
Left subclavian
Aorta
Diaphragm
Left axillary
Splenic
Renal artery
Superior mesenteric
Inferior mesenteric
Left common iliac
Left internal iliac
Left external iliac
Left femoral
Left popliteal
Left anterior tibial
Left peroneal
Left posterior tibial
Left dorsal metatarsal

Arteries of the body

Right subclavian
Superior vena cava
Right axillary
Right cephalic
Right brachial
Hepatic vein
Right basilic
Right radial
Right ulnar
Right palmar venous plexus
Right palmar digital
Right proper palmar digital
Right great saphenous
Right popliteal
Right small saphenous
Right anterior tibial
Right posterior tibial
Right dorsal venous arch

Pulmonary vein
Coronary sinus
Left superior phrenic
Splenic
Hepatic portal vein
Inferior mesenteric
Renal vein
Superior mesenteric
Inferior vena cava
Left common iliac
Left external iliac
Left femoral
Left popliteal

Veins of the body

Factors affecting the pulse rate

- Exercise: any form of exercise will cause the pulse rate to increase. During strenuous exercise, the pulse rate can double. However, regular exercise will lower a person's resting pulse rate.

- Emotion: the pulse rate can increase at times of stress, excitement, fear, anger and any other strong emotional states.

- Age: children have a higher pulse rate than adults.

- Drugs: certain drugs can influence the pulse rate.

Conditions associated with blood and blood circulation

Varicose veins

Varicose veins are swollen and enlarged veins, which are usually blue or dark purple. They may also be lumpy, bulging or twisted in appearance. They develop when the valves inside the veins stop working properly. If these valves weaken, or are damaged, they can become permanently dilated (widened), and the blood may flow backwards and can collect in the vein, eventually causing it to be varicose.

Varicose veins commonly occur in the veins near the surface of the leg. They can also occur in the anus and here they are called haemorrhoids or piles. The causes of varicose veins include hereditary factors, ageing, obesity, pregnancy, and jobs that involve long periods of standing. The affected veins must not be touched during beauty treatments.

Thrombosis

A **thrombosis** is a clot of blood that is stationary within an artery or vein. It is dangerous, as it may constrict or cut off the flow of blood. If massage is carried out, there is a risk that the clot may be moved or broken up and taken to the heart, lungs or brain – which could prove fatal.

Embolism

This is the blockage of a blood vessel by a blood clot or foreign material (such as a clump of bacteria or globule of fat) that is contained within the bloodstream. A piece broken away from a thrombosis can be the cause. It circulates in the bloodstream until it becomes wedged somewhere in a blood vessel and blocks the flow of blood. Such a blockage may be extremely harmful.

key terms

Thrombosis: the formation of a blood clot inside a blood vessel, which obstructs the flow of blood through the circulatory system.

Phlebitis (fl-bite-tis)

This is an inflammation of the walls of veins, caused by tiny blood clots. There is redness, tenderness and swelling along the affected veins. No treatment should be given to anyone suffering with this condition.

HIV/AIDS

HIV (Human Immunodeficiency Virus) is the cause of Aids (Acquired Immune Deficiency Syndrome). It is a virus that can be passed on by infected blood, through activities such as sexual intercourse and sharing infected needles. HIV attacks the immune system, therefore the person becomes susceptible to illness.

DON'T FORGET

It is not possible to contract HIV through touching.

Good practice

There is no risk of passing HIV on to clients while working as a beauty therapist, because only sterile needles and piercing equipment is used.

key terms

Hepatitis: occurs when there is inflammation of the liver, often caused by a virus. There are different kinds of hepatitis.

Hepatitis A, B and C

Hepatitis is inflammation of the liver, often caused by a virus. There are different types of virus responsible for hepatitis.

- Hepatitis A virus is a common infection in many parts of the world. It can be caught through eating or drinking contaminated food or water. It occurs in the UK, but is more common in countries with poor sanitation. It is usually caught by eating or drinking something that contains the faeces of someone with the virus (perhaps they did not wash their hands before preparing food). The infection is usually mild and clears up quite quickly.

- Hepatitis B is very infectious and the virus can be spread by infected blood through activities such as unprotected sex, sharing contaminated needles, and using non-sterilised equipment for tattooing and body piercing. It is uncommon in the UK. There are vaccinations for hepatitis B.

- Hepatitis C can also be caught through unprotected sex, sharing contaminated needles, and using non-sterilised equipment for tattooing and body piercing. Some infected people may develop liver damage and, in serious cases, it can lead to liver failure.

The symptoms for hepatitis A, B and C are similar, and include flu-like illness, nausea, vomiting, diarrhoea and jaundice (yellow skin and whites of eyes).

The lymphatic system

The lymphatic system is made up of a network of vessels that carry a watery, colourless fluid called lymph.

How is lymph derived?

Blood does not flow into the body tissues, but remains inside the blood vessels. However, plasma from the blood is able to seep through the capillary walls and enter the spaces between the tissues, where it becomes tissue fluid. This fluid provides the cells with nutrients and oxygen. As the fluid leaves the cells it takes cellular waste products with it. Most of this fluid passes back into the capillaries and into the blood system, but about 10 per cent passes into the lymphatic capillaries, and becomes lymph. Lymph is similar to blood plasma but contains more white blood cells.

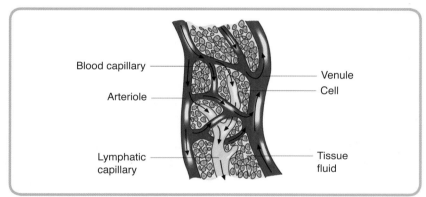

The relationship between blood and lymph

The functions of the lymphatic system

▪ Helps to fight infection. The lymphatic system is an important part of the body's immune system. It produces specialised white blood cells called lymphocytes, which recognise harmful substances and destroy them.

▪ Distributes fluid in the body. Lymphatic vessels drain approximately three litres of excess tissue fluid daily from tissue spaces.

▪ Transport of fats. Carbohydrates and protein, which come from the foods that we eat, are passed from the small intestine directly into the bloodstream. However, fats are passed from the small intestine into lymphatic vessels called lacteals before eventually passing into the bloodstream.

Lymph vessels

Lymph travels around the body in one direction only, towards the heart. It is carried in vessels that begin as lymphatic capillaries. Lymphatic capillaries are blind-ended tubes, situated between cells, and are found throughout the body. The walls of lymphatic capillaries are structured in such a way that tissue fluid can pass into them but not out of them.

Lymphatic capillaries join up and become wider tubes, known as lymphatic vessels. The lymph vessels generally run parallel to the veins. These vessels are similar to veins, as they contain valves, although they generally have thinner walls. The lymph flows around the body through these lymph vessels and passes through a number of lymph nodes to be filtered. Eventually, the lymph will be passed into lymphatic ducts, from where it is returned to the blood circulation.

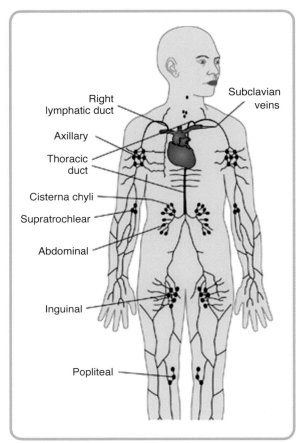

Lymph nodes of the body

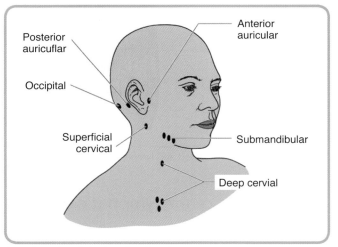

Lymph nodes of the head and neck

Lymph nodes

There are approximately 600 bean-shaped lymph nodes scattered throughout the body. They lie mainly in groups around the groin, breast and armpits, and round the major blood vessels of the abdomen and chest.

As lymph travels through the lymphatic system, it passes through the lymph nodes. They filter out harmful substances from the lymph, such as bacteria, which could cause an infection in the body. They contain specialised white blood cells called monocytes and lymphocytes.

- Monocytes destroy harmful substances by ingesting (eating) them.

- Lymphocytes produce antibodies that stop the growth of bacteria and prevent their harmful action. During an infection there are more bacteria, so the lymph nodes produce more lymphocytes to destroy them. This causes the lymph nodes to enlarge and this is a sign that they are working to fight the infection.

- Important groups of lymph nodes in the head are: the occipital, submandibular, deep cervical and superficial cervical, and anterior auricular and posterior auricular.

- Important groups of lymph nodes in the rest of the body include the axillary, abdominal, inguinal, popliteal and supratrochlear nodes.

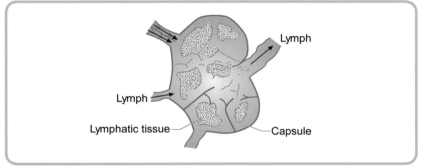

Structure of a lymph node

Lymphatic ducts

The lymphatic ducts are known as the thoracic duct and right lymphatic duct.

- The thoracic duct is approximately 40 cm long. Lymph vessels from the lower body join up to form a large lymph vessel, which leads to the thoracic duct. The thoracic duct is the main collecting duct of the lymphatic system. It receives lymph from the left side of the head, neck and chest, the upper limbs and the whole body beneath the ribs. The thoracic duct drains the lymph directly into the left subclavian vein, so that it is returned back to the blood circulation.

- The right lymphatic duct is about 1.25 cm long, and drains lymph from the upper right hand side of the body. The lymph passes into the right subclavian vein, where it becomes part of the blood circulation.

> **DON'T FORGET**
>
> *While suffering with a sore throat you may be able to feel swollen lymph glands in your neck.*

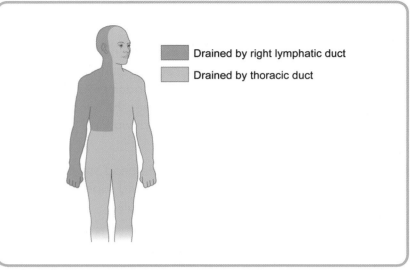

Lymphatic drainage

key terms

Lymphatic circulation: a clever fluid called lymph travels around the body in tube-like verssels. The lymphatic system makes up part of the immune system and so helps protect us from disease.

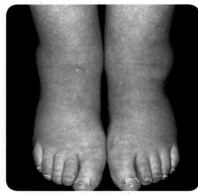

Fluid retention around the ankles

Lymphatic circulation

The lymphatic system does not have a pump like the heart but, like veins, it relies on the movement of the body and the contraction of the skeletal muscles. The squeezing action of the muscles forces the lymph along its vessels. Involuntary actions such as breathing and the heartbeat also help the movement of lymph through the vessels.

Conditions associated with the lymphatic system

Oedema (fluid retention)

Fluid retention is a common problem in which there is a build-up of excess fluid in the body tissues. Depending on the cause, it can either be localised (affecting only a certain part of the body) or generalised (affecting the whole body). Fluid retention causes swelling, which is commonly seen around the ankles. It can be differentiated from other types of swelling by the fact that slight pressure will leave a dent and takes a few seconds to return to normal. It often occurs in women just before a period, and also in the last three months of pregnancy. It can also be a symptom of high blood pressure or injury, and a side-effect of certain drugs.

The nervous system

Millions of nerve impulses (messages) are continually reaching the brain from receptors in, for instance, the skin, and just as many leave the brain and stimulate muscles to move and organs to carry out their work. These messages are in the form of electrical impulses, which pass through neurons (nerve cells). There are billions of neurons within the body and their function is to transmit nerve impulses.

Neurons

A neuron is made up of a cell body, containing a nucleus; a number of short branches that project from the cell body, called dendrites; and a thin tube-like extension of the cell body, called an axon. Dendrites carry nerve impulses from other neurons towards the cell body. These nerve impulses are transmitted away from the cell body, to other neurons (or to muscles or glands), by the axon. Therefore, only impulses move in one direction. Each neuron has only one axon, but this can be anything from one millimetre long to over a metre long.

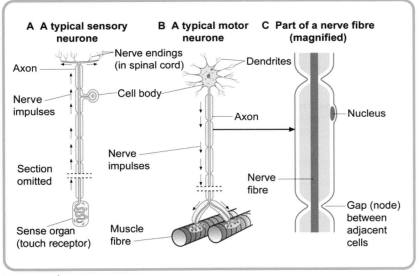

Structure of a neuron

When two neurons meet there is a gap between them called a synapse. The electrical nerve impulse is transferred from one neuron to the next by the release of chemicals, which pass across the synapse. The chemicals then set off a new electrical impulse in the next neuron.

> **DON'T FORGET**
>
> The nervous system can be likened to a telephone network, with messages continually being passed through wires.

> **DON'T FORGET**
>
> There are billions of neurons within the body and their function is to transmit nerve impulses.

> **DON'T FORGET**
>
> The fastest nerve impulses can travel at 250 mph.

There are three types of neurons.

- Motor neurons: these carry nerve impulses from the brain or spinal cord to the muscles and glands, to stimulate them into carrying out their work.

- Sensory neurons: these carry nerve impulses from the skin, sense organs, muscles and joints, to the brain and spinal cord, to make us aware of things like pain, changes in temperature, smells and tastes.

- Interneurons: these carry nerve impulses from sensory neurons to motor neurons, or to other interneurons. They are only found in the brain, eyes and spinal cord.

Nerves

A nerve is a bundle of elongated axons belonging to hundreds or thousands of neurons. A nerve may contain axons from only one type of neuron, or from both sensory and motor neurons. The latter is known as a mixed nerve.

DON'T FORGET

Neurons are rather like electrical wires surrounded by cable.

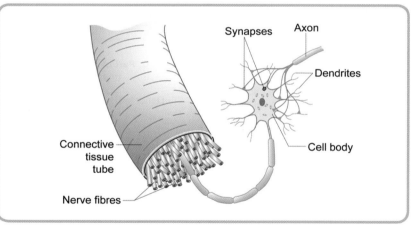

Structure of a nerve

Divisions of the nervous system

The nervous system can be divided into the central and peripheral nervous systems.

Central nervous system (CNS)

The central nervous system consists of the brain and spinal cord.

Brain

The brain is the most important part of the system and contains 100 billion neurons. The brain receives and stores messages as well as transmitting them to all parts of the body.

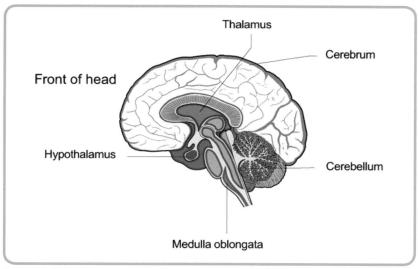

Structures in the brain

Spinal cord

The spinal cord is continuous with the medulla oblongata of the brain extending downwards through the vertebral column. It contains about 100 million neurons. The function of the spinal cord is to provide communication between the brain and all parts of the body.

Peripheral nervous system

The peripheral nervous system consists of the nerves connecting the brain and spinal cord to the rest of the body. It has two divisions: the somatic system and the autonomic system.

Somatic system

The somatic system enables us to consciously react to our environment.

The sensory nerves of the somatic system carry nerve impulses from the skin, sense organs, muscles and joints, to the brain and spinal cord, to make us aware of things like pain changes in temperature, smells and tastes.

The motor nerves of the somatic system carry nerve impulses from the CNS to the skeletal muscles of the body to initiate movement.

Autonomic system

You can blink or move your fingers at will, but you cannot voluntarily control your heart rate or how fast your stomach digests food. The autonomic nervous system controls the involuntary movements of smooth muscle (which is found in the walls of the digestive tract, blood vessels, bladder and other organs) and cardiac (heart) muscle. It also controls the glands.

The autonomic nervous system has two parts: the sympathetic and parasympathetic, which have opposite effects.

- The sympathetic system is activated in times of stress or excitement. It has many effects, including speeding up the heart, increasing breathing rate, increasing blood flow to the skeletal muscles, and slowing digestion. It also activates glands to secrete hormones, such as adrenaline, which further increase arousal. This is known as the 'fight or flight' response as it prepares our body for activity.

- The parasympathetic system has the opposite effect. So, for example, it causes the heart rate to drop, breathing to slow and the digestive system to become active. Its actions are directed towards restoring and maintaining a relaxed state.

Conditions associated with the nervous system

Epilepsy

Epilepsy is a disorder of the brain in which sufferers may experience 'absences' or 'seizures'. An absence is when a person experiences momentary lapses of attention, and perhaps a little abnormal movement. Seizures, or convulsions, are caused by abnormal electrical activity in the brain. Often there is no obvious cause, but in some cases the fits are the result of scars on the brain from surgery or injury. Some sufferers find that flickering fluorescent lights, or television screens, spark off a seizure.

Raynaud's disease

The cause is unknown, but there is an overstimulation of the sympathetic nerves which causes blood vessels to constrict within the fingers and toes. Therefore, blood flow is reduced and the fingers become cold. There is also tingling, burning and numbness in the affected parts.

Anxiety attack

Usually the parasympathetic nerves balance the action of the sympathetic nerves, but when we are stressed the sympathetic nerves dominate. This results in the excess release of adrenaline. Many symptoms can be experienced by a sufferer during an anxiety or panic attack, including difficulty in breathing, churning stomach, dizziness, nausea and racing heart. It can be so distressing that the sufferer may think they are going to die.

How are you doing?

1   Which of the following is **not** a layer of the epidermis?

   a   Horny

   b   Basal

   c   Transparent

   d   Clear

2   Which of the following is **not** part of the structure of the skin?

   a   Arrector pili muscle

   b   Sudiferous gland

   c   Collagen and elastin

   d   Peronychium gland

3   What is the name of the protein found in hair and nails?

   a   Eponychium

   b   Urea

   c   Amino acids

   d   Keratin

4   What is the resting stage of hair growth called?

   a   Catagen

   b   Telogen

   c   Anagen

   d   Datagen

5   Where would you find the tibia?

   a   In the leg

   b   In the shoulder

   c   In the arm

   d   It makes up part of the skull

6   Which of the following is **not** a facial muscle?

   a   Buccinator

   b   Pectoralis major

   c   Orbicularis oculi

   d   Masseter

7   What is the action of the orbicular oris?

   a   Closes the eye

   b   Closes the mouth

   c   Lifts the chin

   d   Raises the eyebrows

8   Which of the following is **not** a vessel that carries blood through the body?

   a   Capillaries

   b   Veins

   c   Lymph

   d   Arteries

9   Where would you find the submandibular lymph nodes?

   a   Near to the lower jaw area

   b   Base of the head

   c   In the neck area

   d   Behind the ears

10 Which of the following is an effect of massage?

   a   Stimulation of the blood and lymphatic circulations

   b   Aids desquamation

   c   Relaxes tense muscles

   d   All of the above

B4 Provide facial skin care treatment

On completion of this unit you will:

1. Be able to use safe and effective methods of working when improving and maintaining facial skin condition

2. Be able to consult, plan and prepare for facials with clients

3. Be able to improve and maintain skin condition

4. Understand organisational and legal requirements

5. Understand how to work safely and effectively when providing facial treatments

6. Understand how to perform client consultation and treatment planning

7. Understand anatomy and physiology that relates to facial skin care treatments

8. Understand contra-indications that affect or restrict facial skin care treatments

9. Understand facial skin care techniques, products and treatment planning

10. Understand the aftercare advice to provide clients for facial care treatments

Introduction

This unit will teach you how to carry out a professional facial treatment that will help to improve and maintain your client's skin condition. You will carry out facials on different types of skin and will use a variety of facial products.

What is a facial?

A facial treatment is one of the most popular, enjoyable and relaxing services available to the salon client. It involves treating the face and neck, and will help to improve the health and appearance of the skin.

A facial treatment lasts for around an hour, depending on which type of facial the client is receiving. During the treatment, a therapist will usually carry out some or all of the following.

- Cleanse

- Tone

- Exfoliation

- Massage

- Mask application

- Moisturise

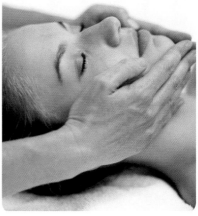
Client receiving facial treatment

A facial warming treatment such as facial steaming may also be carried out as part of a facial. This will generally follow the cleanse.

Benefits of a facial

Benefits of a facial treatment include:

- removal of dirt and impurities from the skin

- stimulation of the blood circulation, which helps to bring oxygen and nutrients to the skin

- stimulation of the lymphatic circulation, which aids the removal of waste products from the area, and helps to drain away excess fluid build-up that can result in puffiness

- **desquamation** of the skin

- making the skin appear fresher and healthier

- adding moisture to the skin, so helping to counteract dryness

- protection of the skin from environmental factors such as sunlight

- relaxing the client and giving a feeling of well-being.

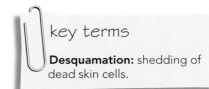
key terms
Desquamation: shedding of dead skin cells.

UNIT OUTCOME 2

Be able to consult, plan and prepare for facials with clients

UNIT OUTCOME 6

Understand how to perform client consultation and treatment planning

UNIT OUTCOME 8

Understand contra-indications that affect or restrict facial skin care treatments

Consultation

DON'T FORGET

Ensure the client record card/consultation form is up to date and accurate.

Before a treatment is carried out, a consultation should be performed, and a record card/consultation form completed. This helps the therapist to find out information such as the client's expectations of the treatment, and if they have any contra-indications to treatment. The therapist can also observe the client's skin, to see its condition, and make notes on the card/form.

Questions can be asked about the client's skin, skin care routine and lifestyle, for example:

- How often do you cleanse, tone and moisturise your skin? What products do you use?
- Do you use soap? (Soap can be drying to the skin.)
- Do any areas of the face feel tight after washing?
- Do you have areas of flaky skin?
- Do any areas of the face feel oily?
- Do you suffer with spots and blemishes?
- Do you regularly have blackheads or whiteheads?
- How much water do you drink each day?
- Do you smoke?
- Do you drink alcohol? If so, how much each week?
- Are you taking any medication?
- Do you spend a lot of time in hot countries?

Also ask the client what she would like to gain from the treatment, for example, would she like help with a particular problem, such as greasy skin.

For more information on the consultation process, see **Unit G20: Ensure responsibility for actions to reduce risks to health and safety**.

Contra-indications

A beauty therapist may not be able to carry out a facial treatment if a client has a contra-indication. However, some contra-indications only restrict treatment, so the affected area is avoided while the facial is carried out. Contra-indications to facial treatment include:

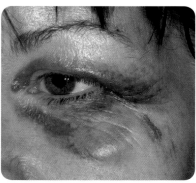

Bruising around the eye

- an infectious skin condition, such as impetigo
- an infectious eye condition, such as conjunctivitis
- bruising
- sunburn
- any bleeding or weeping
- scar tissue less than six months old
- cuts and abrasions
- undiagnosed lumps or swellings
- any injury to the area being treated
- loss of sensation in the face.

You should not carry out a facial warming treatment if the client has any of the following.

- Respiratory disorders such as asthma
- Excessive broken capillaries
- Rosacea
- Skin infections
- Very sensitive skin

Without causing alarm to the client, suggest they seek medical advice regarding a contra-indication, or return for treatment when the contra-indication is no longer present.

DON'T FORGET

Facial steaming is a type of facial warming treatment.

Equipment, materials and products

The following equipment, materials and products will be required to carry out a facial treatment.

- Treatment couch – should be disinfected and covered with either towels or a blanket. Clean couch roll should be placed on top, and place a towel at the head end for the client's head to rest on

- Stool – should ideally be height adjustable and have a backrest

- Trolley – should be disinfected and lined with couch roll

- Magnifying lamp – to help examine the skin. Clues such as spots and blackheads will help you to decide the client's skin type

- Eye make-up remover – removes all traces of eye make-up

- Facial cleanser – there are various types of cleanser to suit different skin types. It usually consists of water and oil and helps to remove grease and dirt from the skin's surface

- Facial toner – there are various types of toner to suit different skin types. It is applied after the skin has been cleansed. It removes any cleanser that remains on the skin and also helps to tighten the pores

- Moisturiser – there are various types of moisturiser to suit different skin types. It protects the skin from the environment and helps the skin retain moisture

- Exfoliator – there are various different types. It is used to remove dead skin cells

- Massage oil/cream – used during massage

- Mask – different types of mask can be used and have various benefits

- Mask brush – to apply face masks

- Gauze – may be used to apply toner, and some masks may be applied over gauze

- Mirror – may be used for consulting with the client before and after the treatment

- Gown – a client may wear a gown to help protect their clothing during the treatment

- Headband – will ensure the hair is kept away from the face and will help prevent products from getting in the hair

- Large bowl – should be filled with warm water

- Small bowls – will be used for items such as cotton pads and to put client's jewellery in

- Spatulas – to remove cream from a pot. The fingers are not used for hygiene reasons

- Sponges – to remove products, such as masks, from the skin

- Cotton wool pads – some products will be applied and removed using cotton wool pads. These are also used to cover the client's eyes during treatment

Face mask

- Cotton buds and orange sticks – may be used to remove mascara

- Facial tissues – there are many uses for tissues, such as blotting the skin after applying toner

- Towels – to cover the client and to dry the hands. Also used to remove some products

- Client record card/consultation form and pen – useful client information is written on the card.

Good practice

If a particular light will be used to assess the skin type, ensure that it is working.

Preparing the client for a facial treatment

- Ask the client to remove any jewellery, such as a necklace and earrings, and place it into a small bowl on the trolley. (If the client wears a necklace during the treatment it could get broken.)

- Check there are pillows and blankets for the client's comfort.

- The client may be given a gown to wear and asked to get on the couch. If the couch is quite high, they may need help getting on it.

Good practice

Wash your hands in front of the client so that they can see you are hygienic.

- A large towel/blanket can be used to cover the client, and a small towel may be placed over the shoulder and chest area.

- A headband can be placed around the client's head to protect the hair. You can also place tissue into the headband, which can be replaced throughout the treatment, if necessary. The tissue helps to prevent the headband from becoming stained and also helps prevent substances getting into the client's hair.

Ensure that your client is comfortable and feels relaxed

Skin analysis

You will need to conduct a skin analysis before carrying out the treatment. A magnifying lamp may be used to look closely at the skin on the face. This will allow you to assess the client's skin type and the condition of their skin.

Skin type

Skin types vary from person to person and can be described as being normal, dry, oily, combination, sensitive, dehydrated or mature.

Normal

This skin type will look healthy, clear and fresh. It is often seen in children, as external factors and ageing have not yet affected the condition of their skin. However, the increased activity of hormones at puberty may cause the skin to become oily. A normal skin type will look neither oily nor dry, and will have a fine, even texture. The pores are small, and the skin's elasticity is good, so it feels soft and firm to the touch. It is usually free of spots and blemishes.

Dry

This skin type may look thin and fine, and broken capillaries can often be seen around the cheek and nose areas. The skin will feel and look dry because little sebum is being produced and the skin is also lacking in moisture (water). This skin type will often tighten after washing, and will not generally contain comedones or visible open pores. This skin type is prone to premature wrinkling, especially around the eyes, mouth and neck.

Oily

This skin type will look shiny and slightly yellowish (sallow) in colour because of the excess sebum production. Oily skin is coarse, thick and will feel greasy. Enlarged pores can be seen and may be caused by the excess production and build-up of sebum. Open pores can let in bacteria, which cause spots and infections. Blocked pores often lead to comedones. Oily skin tends to age more slowly, as the grease absorbs some of the ultraviolet (UV) rays of the sun and so can protect against its damaging effects. The sebum also helps to keep the skin moisturised and prevents drying.

Combination

Most clients will have a combination skin type. With this skin type there will be areas of dry, normal and oily skin. Usually the forehead, nose and chin are oily (this is known as the T-zone). The areas around the eyes and cheeks are usually dry and may be sensitive.

DON'T FORGET

If the client is wearing foundation, carry out a quick cleanse so that you can easily inspect the skin during the skin analysis.

DON'T FORGET

The skin contains natural lipids (fats) called ceramides which help prevent excessive loss of water from the skin.

key terms

Humidity: the amount of moisture (water) in the air.

Sensitive

This skin type is often dry, transparent and reddens easily when touched. Broken capillaries may be present, especially on the cheeks, which gives the face a red colour. Hereditary factors may be a cause of sensitive skin. Certain substances may easily irritate a sensitive skin, so care should be taken when choosing products for this skin type. If a white skin is sensitive to a product, it will show as a reddened area, but on black skin it will show up as a darkened area.

Dehydrated

This skin type lacks moisture (water) and so is dry. The causes include too much sun, illness, medication, dieting, and working in a dry environment with low **humidity**, such as an air-conditioned office. Sebum helps to prevent evaporation of water from the skin, so when insufficient sebum is produced, moisture is lost from the skin. The skin feels and looks dry and tight. There may be flaking and fine lines present on the skin. Broken capillaries are also common with this skin type.

Mature

This skin type is dry, as the sebaceous and sweat glands become less active as we age The skin may be thin and wrinkles will be present. There are usually broken capillaries, often around the nose and cheek areas. The bone structure can become more prominent as the adipose (fat) and supportive tissues become thinner. Muscle tone is often poor, so the contours of the face become slack, causing sagging skin. Because of poor blood circulation, waste products are removed less quickly, so the skin may become puffy and pale in colour. Dark patches known as liver spots may also appear on the face and hands. The cause of this skin type is ageing and altered hormone activity.

Various skin types from teenage to 60s

Other factors that affect the condition of the skin

Sunlight

Of all the factors that cause premature ageing, exposure of the skin to sunlight is the most important. UV radiation from the sun penetrates the dermis of the skin and causes damage. With repeated exposure to the sun, the skin loses the ability to repair itself. This is often termed as photoageing, and is, without doubt, the leading cause of skin ageing. It causes dehydration, breaks down collagen and interferes with the making of new collagen. It also attacks the elastin in the skin so it loses its strength and elasticity, resulting in severe wrinkling and sagging.

Hormones

During the adolescent years, increases in the hormone **testosterone** cause excess sebum production, so many teenagers will suffer with blemishes and acne.

Adults, mostly women, can suffer with adult acne, which is the result of hormonal changes. For women, possible triggers include menstruation (periods) and pregnancy.

An imbalance of hormonal levels during pregnancy can result in oily skin and acne breakouts. Pregnancy can also have other effects on the skin, such as causing dry skin and areas of pigmentation called **chloasma** (also known as melasma).

Taking the contraceptive pill can also cause chloasma, as the pill affects the balance of hormones in the body. In some people, the contraceptive pill can cause acne, although some types of pill can improve acne.

At menopause, a decrease in the hormone **oestrogen** causes a substantial loss of collagen, which makes up most of the skin's supportive structure. Unfortunately this leads to the formation of wrinkles and sagging skin.

Stress

People suffering with stress are more likely to neglect their skin, which can result in it looking unhealthy. Stress can also trigger some skin conditions, or make them worse. Conditions that are particularly sensitive to stress include acne, eczema, psoriasis, hives and cold sores. Chronic stress can also lead to premature ageing of the skin. Tense facial muscles may cause lines and wrinkles to form, and also restrict oxygen and nutrients to the skin. Stress may also lead to excessive alcohol intake and rapid weight loss or gain, resulting in changes to the skin such as dehydration and sagging.

key terms

Testosterone: a hormone produced by the testicles from the start of puberty that is responsible for male characteristics, such as muscle growth, deepened voice and hair growth under the arms. Smaller quantities of testosterone are produced in females and are believed to help maintain muscle and bone strength.

Chloasma: known as the 'mask of pregnancy' when present in pregnant women. Also associated with the contraceptive pill and hormone replacement therapy (HRT) medication. It causes darkened patches on the skin, and is commonly found on the upper cheek, nose, upper lips and forehead.

Oestrogen: a hormone that is produced by the ovaries in women, and is responsible for female sexual characteristics such as pubic hair and breast development.

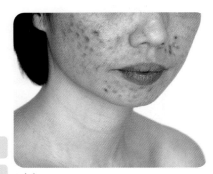

Adult acne

Diet

The best nutritional recommendation for ensuring healthy skin is to eat a well-balanced diet. The Western diet generally contains the essential vitamins and minerals required for a healthy skin. These include vitamins A, C and E.

Vitamin A helps to control the rate of keratinisation in the skin, so deficiency of this vitamin can result in dry skin. Good sources include vegetables, eggs, butter and cheese.

Vitamin C is required by the body to produce collagen, which makes up a large part of the skin. Deficiency can lead to dermatitis, and may cause blood capillaries to become weakened, which leads to bruising. Good sources include fruit and vegetables.

Vitamin E helps to keep the skin hydrated, reduces inflammation, and aids healing. Vitamin E is found in many foods, but good sources include vegetable oils, eggs and meat.

Vitamins A, C and E are all **antioxidants**, which help to prevent premature ageing of the skin.

The eatwell plate

The eatwell plate shows the types and amounts of food we need to eat to have a healthy and well-balanced diet. It is designed for adults. The basic advice is, every day:

- eat plenty of fruit and vegetables, potatoes, bread, rice, pasta and other starchy foods (choose wholegrain types)

- eat some dairy foods, meat, fish, eggs, beans (and other non-dairy sources of protein)

- eat only small amounts of foods and drinks that are high in fat and/or sugar.

> ### key terms
>
> **Antioxidant:** a substance that helps to fight free radicals. Free radicals cause damage to cells, including skin cells.

The eatwell plate

Food Standards Agency
eatwell.gov.uk

Use the eatwell plate to help you get the balance right. It shows how much of what you eat should come from each food group.

Fruit and vegetables

Bread, rice, potatoes, pasta and other starchy foods

Flakes

Meat, fish, eggs, beans and other non-dairy sources of protein

Foods and drinks high in fat and/or sugar

Milk and dairy foods

The eatwell plate

key terms

Carbohydrate: a major class of foods that includes sugars and starches. Carbohydrates provide energy for the body.

Five a day

The 'five a day' rule helps to ensure you get five 80 g portions of fruit and vegetables every day. These provide essential vitamins and minerals for the body. Almost all fruit and vegetables count towards your 'five a day', whether they are fresh, frozen, tinned, juiced or dried. However, potatoes are not included, as they mostly contain starch, which is a type of **carbohydrate**. Any five of the following will give you your five 80 g (approximately) portions of fruit and vegetables for the day.

- One medium fruit, such as an apple, banana or orange.
- Two plums or similar sized fruit.
- Half a grapefruit or avocado.
- One slice of large fruit, such as melon or pineapple.
- One handful of grapes, berries or cherries.
- Three heaped tablespoons of fruit salad.
- Three heaped tablespoons of vegetables.
- One dessert bowl of salad.
- Three heaped tablespoons of beans and pulses (note: beans and pulses only count as one of your 'five a day', however much you eat).
- One heaped tablespoon of dried fruit, such as raisins, sultanas and apricots.
- One small (150 ml) glass of pure fruit juice (note: fruit juice only counts as one of your 'five a day', however much you drink).

Fruit and vegetables

Alcohol

Drinking alcohol in moderation is not harmful to the skin, but large amounts dilate the blood vessels and, over time, may weaken the capillary walls. This can lead to broken capillaries and redness, which can often be seen on the face.

Alcohol also dehydrates the skin, by drawing water from the tissues, and robs the body of vitamins B and C, which are required for a healthy skin.

Caffeine

Caffeine is found in tea, coffee, chocolate and some fizzy soft drinks. If consumed in moderate amounts, it will cause no harm, but in excessive amounts it can interfere with the absorption of vitamins and minerals, which can result in an unhealthy and dry skin.

Smoking

Smoking interferes with cell respiration and slows down the blood circulation, as nicotine is a vasoconstrictor (it causes the blood vessels to become smaller). This makes it harder for nutrients to reach the skin cells and for waste products to be eliminated. Cigarette smoking also releases a chemical that destroys vitamin C. This interferes with the production of collagen and so contributes to premature ageing.

In addition, continual puckering of the lips while smoking can result in wrinkles forming around the mouth. People who have smoked for a long time will generally look older than non-smokers of the same age.

DON'T FORGET

Alcohol can worsen acne rosacea – a skin disorder associated with redness, flushing and pustules.

DON'T FORGET

Some skin care companies add caffeine to their products, as it is an anti-inflammatory and is also beneficial for oily skins.

DON'T FORGET

Botox treatment involves injecting a protein, derived from botulism toxin, underneath the skin to paralyse facial muscles, which helps to minimise frown lines, forehead lines and crows feet. It is also used to treat migraine headaches and excessive underarm sweating.

Dermal filler treatment involves injecting a 'dermal filler' into the skin to help to reduce wrinkles around the eyes and mouth; it can also create fuller lips. The effect lasts between six and nine months.

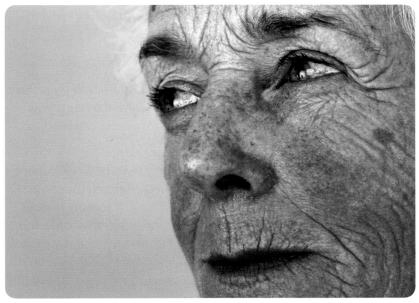

Effects of smoking on the skin

Medical conditions and medications

Some medical conditions can affect the skin. For example, an underactive **thyroid** can cause dry and pale skin, and an over active thyroid can cause oily skin, blemishes, and possibly acne. Thyroid problems can also lead to flushing and increased redness of the skin, and can cause the skin to thicken.

Medications such as antidepressants, antihistamines and antibiotics can also affect the skin.

Antidepressants and antihistamines can cause skin dryness.

Antibiotics may cause temporary drying of the skin, although it will improve after the course of drugs has finished. Antibiotics can also make the skin more photosensitive (sensitive to sunlight), so it is more likely to burn. Some antibiotics can cause hives and flushing of the skin.

Beta blockers are used to treat heart problems, high blood pressure, anxiety and migraine. In some people they may cause the skin to become dry, or lead to the development of hives. Also, the skin may bruise more easily or develop purplish marks.

Steroids are used to treat inflammatory conditions, such as arthritis, asthma and some skin conditions. Taken by mouth they can lead to skin dehydration, fluid retention or swelling of the tissues.

Hydrocortisone creams are a type of steroid that are applied externally and are used to treat skin conditions such as psoriasis and dermatitis. These creams should only be used for short periods of time and in small quantities, otherwise thinning of the skin may result. However, this does depend on the type of hydrocortisone cream used.

Environment

The moisture content of the epidermis can be affected by factors such as central heating, which creates a dry environment. This causes moisture to be lost from the epidermis and can lead to dehydration.

When a person moves between a cold and a warm environment, their capillaries contract (become narrower) or dilate (become wider) to adapt to the change in temperature. If someone does this frequently, for instance if they work outdoors, over time the capillary walls may become weak, leading to permanently dilated capillaries. These are known as broken capillaries or thread veins. These can commonly be seen on the cheeks and nose. There are also many other causes of broken capillaries.

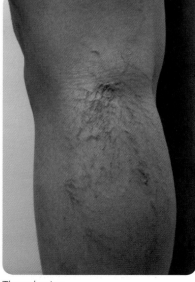

Thread veins

Air pollution, from industry and car fumes, for example, harms the skin and causes dehydration. It can also lead to dirt building up on the skin, resulting in blocked pores.

Ageing

Some ageing of the skin occurs naturally over time, but premature ageing can occur because of various factors, including a person's genetic make up, environment (perhaps working outside in all weathers), inadequate diet, smoking or ill health.

The skin is at its best from birth to the early twenties, when there is good collagen production and the elastin has a lot of 'spring', allowing the skin to easily snap back into place if it is stretched. However, in adolescence, hormonal factors can lead to an overproduction of sebum, resulting in spots and acne.

In the late twenties and thirties, fine lines appear on the skin's surface, especially around the eyes where the skin is thinner. Collagen production slows and the elastin has less spring.

From age 40, hormone activity in the body slows down, so the sebaceous glands produce less sebum and the skin becomes increasingly dry. Lines and wrinkles appear on the surface. Wrinkling is caused by changes in the collagen and elastin fibres of the connective tissue in the dermis. The collagen fibres begin to decrease in number, stiffen and break apart. The elastin fibres lose some of their elasticity and break down, so that if the skin is stretched, it does not immediately snap back into place. Constant movement of the face as we make facial expressions, such as smiling, causes wrinkles, such as crow's feet, which appear at the sides of the eyes.

Crow's feet

In people who are regularly exposed to UV light from the sun, or who smoke, the loss of elasticity of the skin is greatly accelerated (speeded up).

From the late fifties, the blood flow to the skin is reduced and the rate of mitosis (cell division) in the basal layer slows down. The horny layer is therefore thinner, making the skin more fragile. Dilated capillaries appear on the skin, especially on the cheeks and nose.

The sweat glands are less active and the sebaceous glands decrease in size, which leads to dry and cracked skin. The skin of older people heals poorly and becomes more susceptible to infection. Loss of underlying fat leads to hollowed cheeks and eye sockets.

Darkened, flat spots, called lentigines (liver spots), may appear on the skin, because of an increase in the size of some **melanocytes**.

key terms

Melanocytes: melanin- or pigment-producing cells that are found in the basal layer of the epidermis.

Ask Fran

Q: What mainly causes skin changes as we become older?

A: Hereditary factors are important, but most of the skin changes as we age are speeded up by exposure to sunlight. The degree of photoageing that develops depends on a person's skin colour and the amount and intensity of sunlight they have been exposed to.

Sunlight is harmful because UV light triggers the production of free radicals in the skin. These are tiny chemical particles that damage the function of cells, causing the skin to lose resilience and strength, and speeding up the appearance of wrinkles.

Male skin

key terms

Caucasian: refers to a racial group that has white skin, especially a person of European origin.

Liver spots are commonly brown in colour, and are seen on the most sun-exposed areas of the skin, such as around the temple areas of the face and on the backs of the hands.

The cells in our bodies are continually dying and being replaced by new cells. This is known as cell renewal or cell turnover. The appearance of the skin is influenced by the rate at which cell turnover occurs. When we are young, skin cells turn over about every 30 days. As we get older, the cells divide more slowly. At 80 years old, cell turnover takes twice as long as at 30 years old. This causes the top layer of skin to become thinner and more fragile, and the complexion becomes dull because the dead skin cells at the top of the skin slough off more slowly.

Exfoliating treatments increase the rate at which the dead cells are rubbed off. This allows new skin to be brought to the surface more quickly, resulting in cleaner and fresher-looking skin.

Sex

Male skin ages differently from female skin because it doesn't have the same structure. Male skin is 25 per cent thicker than female skin and contains more collagen. Male skin also produces more sebum, which helps to prevents moisture loss and dryness. Therefore, men's skin tends to age more slowly than women's, and is less prone to wrinkles.

Skin colour

Black skin

Black skin contains large amounts of melanin, which provides protection against UV light and so reduces the risk of sunburn and skin cancer. The melanin also helps to protect against the ageing effects of the sun. Black skin also tends to be thicker than **Caucasian** skin, as the dermis contains more collagen, and the collagen and elastin take longer to break down than in other skin types. This helps to slow down the ageing of the skin, keeping it smooth and supple for longer.

Ageing black skin may develop darkened patches because of irregular pigmentation of the skin. Dermatosis papulosis nigra, also called flesh moles, may occur in this skin type and are more common in women. These are dark mole-like markings that often affect the cheeks and may be the result of hereditary factors.

Sweat and sebaceous glands are larger and more numerous in black skins, which may result in an oily skin type. However, this is not always the case.

Black skins are at a higher risk of developing keloid scarring after, for instance, injury, surgery or ear piercing. The scar will be larger than normal and feel hard and rubbery.

Asian skin

Asian skin colouring is often uneven and is based on a yellow undertone. This skin type commonly has dark shadows under the eyes, and scars may lead to pigmentation changes. There is also a tendency towards excess facial hair growth.

Oriental skin

Oriental skin has more of a yellowish tone than other types, and is prone to having areas of uneven pigmentation on the face. The skin contains more melanin than Caucasian skin, which helps to prevent premature wrinkling. This skin type can be prone to excess oil and breakouts.

Caucasian skin

This type of skin is the lightest of all types. Pink or yellow skin tones determine the depth of lightness of the skin. UV rays can penetrate this skin more easily and can damage living cells, leading to dehydration, age spots, and lines and wrinkles.

VTCT expect students to use the following terms for skin tone and skin colour.

- Pallor – skin of African, Asian and Caucasian descent
- Midtone – skin of African, Asian and Caucasian descent
- Tanned to dark – skin of African, Asian and Caucasian descent

Black skin

Asian skin

Caucasian skin

Oriental skin

UNIT OUTCOME 1

Be able to use safe and effective methods of working when improving and maintaining facial skin condition

UNIT OUTCOME 3

Be able to improve and maintain skin condition

UNIT OUTCOME 5

Understand how to work safely and effectively when providing facial treatments

UNIT OUTCOME 9

Understand facial skin care techniques, products and treatment planning

Procedure for a basic facial treatment

Most facials follow a basic facial treatment routine, such as the procedure below.

- Consultation with client
- Skin analysis
- Removal of eye make-up
- Removal of lipstick
- Cleansing the skin
- Skin toning (first)
- Exfoliation
- Massage to the face and neck
- Application of a mask
- Skin toning (second)
- Moisturising the skin

Cleansing the skin

A range of cleansers have been developed to suit different skin types. Cleansers are generally a mix of oils, wax and water. Cleansers designed for dry skin will contain more oil, and

Types of cleansers

cleansers designed for oily skin will contain less oil. The oils in the product will help dissolve make-up and any other substances on the skin surface. Other ingredients are often added to cleansers, such as aromatherapy oils. Types of cleansers include:

- foaming cleansers
- gel cleansers
- liquid cleansers
- cleansing milks
- cleansing lotions
- cleansing oils
- cleansing bars
- antibacterial cleansers
- acne cleansers (these help to remove oil from the surface of the skin, which makes it easier for acne treatments to be absorbed into the skin).

The following table is a guide to skin types and the cleansers used to treat them. However, most cleansers will state which skin type they are useful for on their label. Many are formulated for use on all skin types.

Skin type	Type of cleanser
Normal skin	Use cleansing milks, cleansing lotions or cleansing bars.
Dry skin	Use cleansing milks, cleansing creams or cleansing oils.
Oily skin	Use cleansing bars, facial gels or foaming cleansers, which are water-based and contain little oil.
Combination skin	Use facial gels or foaming cleansers, which are designed to balance the skin.
Sensitive skin	Use cleansing milks.
Oily, acne-prone skin	Use acne cleansers and antibacterial cleansers, which come in the form of liquids, foams, gels and soaps.

Cleansing the skin helps to remove make-up, dirt and grease and increases the effectiveness of other products used during the facial treatment. There are two main types of skin cleansing.

- Superficial cleanse
- Deep cleanse

DON'T FORGET

Use a non-oily eye make-up remover if the client is wearing artificial lashes.

These both involve the use of massage movements to help spread the cleanser over the skin. The cleanser is then removed with damp cotton wool pads, sponges or warm towels.

Superficial cleanse

The facial routine usually begins with a superficial cleanse, which is used to remove any dirt and make-up products. Always treat the eyes and lips first, before moving to the larger areas of the face and neck. This is more hygienic and prevents spreading make-up products over the face. Cleansers can be applied to the back of the hand so they can be easily transferred to the client's face.

A superficial cleanse may be carried out so you can accurately analyse the client's skin.

Good practice

Ensure the client's contact lenses are removed before treatment.

Procedure for a superficial cleanse

1 With the client's eyes closed, apply cleanser or eye make-up remover to the eye area with the ring finger. Spread the cleanser by working in small circles. Treat one eye at a time.

2 Use damp cotton wool pads to wipe the cleanser from the eyes. Use separate pads for each eye. Stroke the pad over the eye, working from the roots of the lashes to the tips, and then sweep out to the side of the eye.

3 To remove any remaining mascara, eye make-up remover can be placed directly onto a cotton wool pad. A tipped orange stick or cotton bud is useful for removing make up from near the base of the lashes.

4 Apply cleanser to the lips using an S shape with the finger to work across them. Use a damp cotton wool pad to wipe the cleanser from the lips.

5 Apply cleanser to the neck and face with the fingers, and gently massage it into the skin using circular movements (pay particular attention to areas where there are creases, such as the sides of the nose and chin).

6 Use damp cotton wool pads, sponges or warm towels to remove the cleanser, using firm upward and outward strokes.

7 Dampen cotton wool pads with a toner and remove any remaining cleanser and oil from the skin. Toners can also be

Superficial cleansing

sprayed onto the face using a vaporiser; ensure you protect the eyes with cotton wool pads before doing so. Another method involves applying toner to a piece of gauze and leaving it on the face for a few minutes before removing it with cotton wool pads.

8 Use facial tissues to blot any excess moisture from the skin. The tissue can either be folded and patted gently onto the skin, or a whole tissue can be placed on the face and a hole made in it to allow for the nose. The tissue is then rolled up the face and removed.

Deep cleanse

The deep cleanse involves choosing a suitable cleansing product for the client's skin type, and ensuring the face and neck are thoroughly cleansed, ready for the rest of the facial treatment.

Examine the skin under a magnifying lamp and analyse it. Decide which products will suit the client's skin type. Now you may carry out a deep cleanse of the skin, which includes the following steps.

- Cleansing the eye area
- Dissolving and removing mascara
- Cleansing the lips
- Cleansing the face and neck
- Removing cleanser
- Applying toner
- Blotting the face with a tissue

As with the superficial cleanse, you should always treat the eyes and mouth first.

The deep cleanse includes massage techniques that help to produce a thorough cleanse. A deep cleanse helps to:

- dissolve and remove dirt and make-up
- stimulate the blood and lymphatic circulations
- relax the skin pores and so help the cleanser penetrate into the hair follicles
- remove dead skin cells, so aiding desquamation
- relax the client.

Procedure for a deep cleanse
Step-by-step guide

1 Apply the cleanser to either side of the neck, and spread it over the neck using alternate hands in a feathery action.

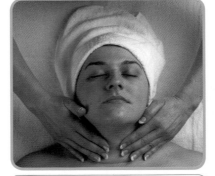

2 With the pads of the fingers of each hand placed either side of the neck, use circular movements to work the cleanser into the neck.

3 Slide fingers up and over the chin, and use circular movements with the pads of the fingers to work the cleanser onto the whole chin and jaw area. Pay particular attention to the crease in the chin.

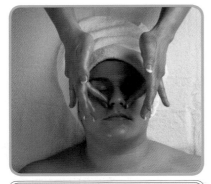

4 Use the ring fingers to work the cleanser into the creases either side of the nose.

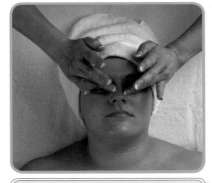

5 Use the ring fingers to gently work the cleanser over the nose.

6 With the pads of the fingers, use circular movements to work the cleanser over the forehead and down on to the temples.

7 With the pads of the fingers, use circular movements to work the cleanser over the cheek and jaw areas and then back towards the temples.

8 Use the ring fingers to circle around the eyes.

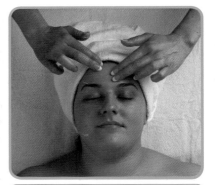

9 Place the index and middle fingers together and create a zigzag movement across the forehead.

10 Stroke the forehead with alternating flat hands.

11 Use damp cotton wool pads, hot towels or facial sponges to remove the cleanser.

Skin toning

After cleansing has taken place, the skin can be toned. There are different types of toning product, which have various effects, including:

- removing oil from the skin – especially toners that contain alcohol

- creating a skin-tightening effect – known as an astringent effect

- helping to cool and refresh the skin.

Skin bracers or fresheners

The mildest toners contain little or no alcohol and so have a gentle effect on the skin. They consist mainly of purified water and floral extracts, such as rose. They are often used on dry, mature and sensitive skin types.

Skin tonics

Skin tonics are slightly stronger toners. They may contain a small amount of alcohol and an astringent substance such as orange flower water, which is a clear, perfumed liquid that comes from the flowers of orange trees. They are often used on normal skin types.

Astringents

Astringents contain a lot of alcohol and so are the strongest toners. They help to dissolve oil, and they may contain antibacterial ingredients that help to treat spots and blemishes. This makes them ideal to use on oily skin types. An example of an astringent is witch hazel.

Skin toner

DON'T FORGET

Rose water is made from rose petals.

Application of toner

Procedure for skin toning

1 Dampen cotton wool pads with a suitable toner and remove any remaining cleanser and oil from the skin.

2 Toners can also be sprayed on to the face using a vaporiser; ensure you protect the eyes with cotton wool pads before doing so. Use two damp cotton wool pads to remove the toner by gently wiping the face in an upward direction.

3 After toning, use facial tissues to blot any excess moisture from the skin. The tissue can either be folded and patted gently onto the skin, or a whole tissue can be placed on the face and a hole made in it to allow for the nose. The tissue is then rolled up the face and removed.

Exfoliation

Exfoliation helps to remove dead skin cells from the top layer of skin. Dead skin cells are naturally shed from the skin's surface by desquamation, but regular use of an exfoliant can help speed up this process. This helps to keep the skin smooth, as a build up of dead skin cells can cause rough and dull-looking skin. The benefits of exfoliation include:

- removes dead skin cells, oil and dirt from the skin's surface
- helps to make dull skin look healthier and fresher
- makes skin feel smoother
- unclogs pores
- stimulates blood circulation, which helps bring oxygen and nutrients to the skin
- allows moisturiser to be more easily absorbed into the skin.

Exfoliation can be carried out using:

- exfoliating scrubs
- enzyme peels
- microdermabrasion
- hydroxy acids.

Exfoliating scrubs

These are products that contain abrasive particles. Most are a combination of **emollients**, in a cream or gel base, mixed with some slightly abrasive particles such as tiny beads. They are particularly good at stimulating blood circulation.

Exfoliation products

key terms

Emollients: these fill in the spaces between the cells in the skin, helping replace lipids (fats) and helping to smooth and moisturise dry skin. They also help to prevent water loss from the skin.

Enzyme peels

These are products that contain enzymes, often in a gel base. The enzymes usually come from plant sources, such as papaya, pomegranate or pineapple. They exfoliate the skin by dissolving the dead skin cells.

Microdermabrasion

This is a treatment that helps to reduce fine lines and wrinkles on the face, and is safe for most skin types. It involves gentle 'brushing' of the face with crystals or other abrasive materials. This removes the stratum corneum (dead skin layer) and stimulates the production of collagen and new skin cells.

Hydroxy acids

Products that contain **alpha hydroxy acids** (AHAs) and **beta hydroxy acids** (BHAs) come in various forms, including creams, gels and lotions. They can be used for all skin types. They help to remove dead cells at the skin's surface, providing room for the growth of new, healthy skin. They are also good for stimulating the blood circulation.

AHAs and BHAs are only effective as exfoliants at certain concentrations. Most AHA products range from 1 per cent or less, BHAs up to about 15 per cent. For an effective exfoliation treatment you need a product with a minimum of 4 per cent. A product that contains 8 per cent to 15 per cent will be more effective at desquamation, but is more likely to irritate the skin as well.

There are different types of AHAs, which are derived from different sources. For example:

- citric acid comes from citrus fruits, like oranges and grapefruits
- glycolic acid comes from sugar
- lactic acid comes from sour milk.

The most common BHAs are a group of acids found in flowering plants and herbs. These include salicylic acid.

Procedure for exfoliation

Apply some exfoliating scrub to your finger pads, then rub the fingers of both hands together and apply to the client's face; the product will usually work better if your fingers are wet. Be careful to avoid the eye area, and pay particular attention to the creases of the nose and chin. Use damp facial sponges or towels to remove the product.

key terms

Alpha hydroxy acid and beta hydroxy acid: products that contain acids, such as alpha hydroxy acids (AHAs) and beta hydroxy acids (BHAs), are used to slough off dead skin cells from the skin's surface. They come in various forms, including creams, gels and lotions, and can be used for all skin types.

DON'T FORGET

AHAs can be found in cleansers, toners, face masks and even shampoos.

Exfoliation

Aftercare advice

Clients can be encouraged to use exfoliants as part of their homecare facial routine. Inform your client that exfoliation should be carried out after cleansing and toning but before the application of moisturiser. The product should be applied to the skin and massaged in using the tips of the fingers. It can then be rinsed off with water. The skin can then be toned again and moisturised.

Good practice

If the client has oily skin, recommend they exfoliate twice a week. For any other skin type only once a week is required.

Massage to face and neck

A facial massage is generally given before the mask treatment. However, facial treatment procedures can vary. The client usually lies flat on the beauty couch for a facial massage treatment.

The massage is one of the most relaxing parts of the facial. There are numerous benefits of massage, both physical and emotional. These include the following.

- Improves the condition of the skin
- Relaxes the mind and body
- Encourages deeper and relaxed breathing
- Helps to induce feelings of calmness
- Encourages sleep
- Increases the blood and lymphatic circulation, which helps to bring oxygen and nutrients to the part being massaged. It also helps to remove waste products, which may be responsible for muscle stiffness, aches and pains
- Relaxes tight muscles
- Relieves stiff joints
- Creates a feeling of well-being.

Massage movements and their effects

While carrying out the facial massage routine you will use different types of massage movements called effleurage, petrissage, tapotement and vibrations.

Effleurage

Effleurage involves using one or both hands to lightly stroke a body part. Effleurage always begins and ends the massage on each area. It is also usually performed after tapotement massage movements to soothe the area. The effleurage movement can be superficial (using light pressure) or deep (using slightly deeper pressure). These movements must always follow the direction of venous return (blood in the veins) back to the heart, and should also be in the direction of a group of lymph nodes, such as those in the neck. The hands stay in contact with the body during the return stroke, but using almost no pressure.

Uses of effleurage

- To distribute the massage medium (cream or oil) so that the whole area is lubricated

- To introduce the therapist's hands

- To warm up the area so deeper massage movements can be used

- To link massage movements together, so that the massage flows

- To relax the client

Effects of effleurage

- Improves the blood and lymphatic circulation

- Aids desquamation, so the skin will look healthier and feel smoother

- Soothes nerve endings, which helps to induce relaxation

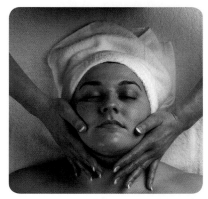

Effleurage

Petrissage

Petrissage movements are deeper movements in which soft tissues, such as muscle, are compressed. Petrissage involves either picking up or kneading muscle tissue.

- Picking up – the muscle is picked up and lifted away from the bone and then released. One or both hands can be used.

- Kneading – the muscle is pressed on to the bone using firm movements. This movement can be performed with the palm of one hand or both, or with the pads of the fingers or thumbs.

Uses of petrissage

- To stimulate sluggish blood circulation

- To aid lymphatic drainage

- To improve the condition of the skin

- To ease muscular tension

Petrissage

Tapotement

Vibration

Effects of petrissage

- Blood and lymphatic circulation is increased, encouraging the delivery of fresh oxygen and nutrients to the tissues and the removal of waste products from the tissues
- Erythema (redness) is produced
- The elimination of toxins is speeded up
- Sebum secretion is increased, which helps to moisturise the skin

There are different types of petrissage movement that are used during a facial massage routine; these include knuckling, zigzag, pinching and scissor movements.

Knuckling

Knuckling is a technique used throughout the massage routine. It involves making a loose fist with each hand, the fingers and knuckles slightly apart. Circular massage movements are created with the fist, using the parts of the fingers about 2.5 cm down from the nail and keeping the wrists loose.

Tapotement

Tapotement movements are also known as percussion movements. Tapotement movements used during the facial massage routine include tapping the client's face with the fingers.

Uses of tapotement

- To increase blood circulation to the area
- To warm the area
- To tone the muscles

Effects of tapotement

- Stimulates muscle fibres so muscle tone is improved
- Increases circulation to the area so that erythema is produced

Vibration

The hands or fingers of one hand are vibrated so that a fine tremor is produced in the tissues. The tremor is produced by the contraction of the forearm muscles.

Uses of vibration

- Stimulates sluggish lymphatic drainage
- Relieves tension and so induces relaxation

Effects of vibration

- Soothes nerves, and so promotes relaxation in the muscles worked
- Relieves tiredness and fatigue
- Relieves pain

Procedure for massage to the face and neck

Choose a suitable medium, either oil or cream, and apply it to your hands – not directly on to the client's skin.

Step-by-step guide

1 Effleurage to the sides of the neck, sweep across the upper chest and work round to the upper back, then glide fingers back towards the neck. Repeat 6 times.

2 Thumb or finger kneading to the upper back. Use the pads of the thumbs or fingers to make circular movements. (Do not massage directly over bony areas.)

3 Link effleurage to the chest area. Then finger knead to the upper chest (use the pads of the fingers to carry out circular movements).

4 Knuckling to the deltoid muscles (the thick triangular muscles that cap the shoulders).

5 Knuckling to the upper back.

6 Effleurage to the sides of the neck, sweep across the upper chest and upper back, then stroke fingers back to the neck. Repeat 4 times.

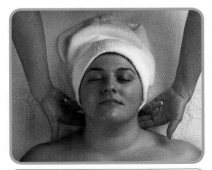

7 Vibrations to the back of the neck. Place the index and middle fingers of each hand either side of the spine. Create fine tremors with the fingers and slowly work up the neck. Repeat 4 times.

8 Place one hand on top of the other and gently stroke up one side of the neck, then across the chin, then down the other side of the neck. Then work back the opposite way. Repeat 6 times.

9 Knuckling to either side of the neck (if the neck is large enough, if not, use finger circles instead).

10 Link effleurage to the chin.

11 Thumb knead to the chin. Create circular movements with the pads of the thumbs over the chin area.

12 Finger knead to the lower jaw. Use the pads of the fingers to create circular movements to either side of the lower jaw, working from the chin towards the ear.

13 Knuckling to the lower jaw.

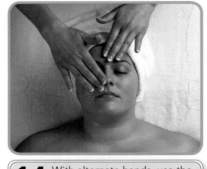

14 With alternate hands, use the fingers to stroke up the nose. Repeat 2 times.

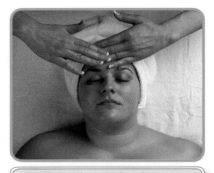

15 Use alternate hands to stroke the forehead. Work across the forehead from the eyebrows to the hair line. Repeat 8 times.

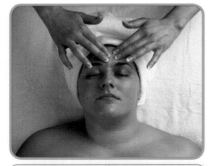

16 Finger kneading to the forehead. Use the pads of the fingers to make slow circular movements over the whole forehead.

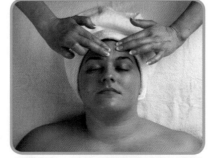

17 Zigzag to the forehead. Put the index and middle fingers together and create a zigzag action across the forehead. If the forehead is small, use only the index fingers.

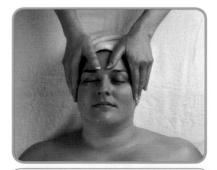

18 Thumb strokes to the forehead. Stroke across the forehead with the sides of the thumbs, working from the centre of the forehead to the temples. Repeat 4 times.

19 Eye circles. Use the ring finger of each hand to stroke slowly around the eyes. Repeat 4 times.

20 Finger circles to the cheeks, chin and temples. Use the pads of the fingers to create circular movements to the cheeks, chin and temples.

21 Cheek lift. Use alternate hands in an upward direction to slowly effleurage the cheek area and then repeat with the other cheek. Repeat 4 times to each cheek.

22 Tapping to the face. Link the thumbs together and use the middle and ring fingers to carry out a tapping movement to the face.

23 Tapping under the chin. Link the thumbs together and use the middle and ring fingers to carry out tapping beneath the chin.

24 Light tapping to the cheeks using alternate hands. Hands roll over each other during this movement. Work on both sides of the face.

25 Link effleurage to the eyebrows.

26 Scissor movement to the eyebrows. Use the index and middle fingers of each hand to create a scissor-like action to the eyebrows. Work from the bridge of the nose towards the outside of the face. Repeat 4 times.

27 Pinching to the eyebrows. Use the index finger and thumb of each hand to pinch the eyebrows. Work from the bridge of the nose towards the outside of the face. Repeat 4 times.

28 Use your ring fingers to gently tap around the eyes. Repeat 6 times.

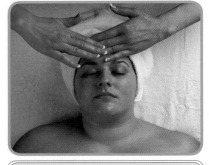

29 Alternate stroking to the forehead. Repeat 8 times.

30 Carefully position and hold the client's head to one side then, with your other hand, stroke down the side of the neck, over the deltoid, the upper back area and then up the neck. Repeat 6 times to each side.

31 Effleurage to the face, neck, upper chest and upper back area. Begin at the temple areas and stroke the hands down the cheeks, neck, over the upper chest and then over the deltoids to the upper back. Slide the fingers gently up the neck and return them to the temples. Repeat 6 times.

32 Prayer effleurage. With hands in a prayer position over the chin, pull the hands down over the chin to effleurage the jaw area, then lift the hands back into a prayer position. Then slide the hands off the chin and towards the forehead to effleurage the temple and cheek areas. Repeat 4 times.

33 Place the hands either side of the face to complete the massage.

Application of a mask

Face masks contain different ingredients that have various actions on the skin. The results of a skin analysis will help you to decide which mask to use on the client's face.

There are two main types of mask: setting masks and non-setting masks.

Setting masks

Setting masks are applied to the face and neck in a thin layer and allowed to dry out. The effects of the mask depend on its ingredients and the length of time it is left on the skin. Setting masks include clay and peel off masks and paraffin wax.

DON'T FORGET

Excess cream or oil can be removed from the face with a facial tissue.

Clay masks

These contain natural earth ingredients and help to draw out dirt and impurities from the skin. The masks are applied to the neck and face in a thin layer.

Different types of clay mask include:

- calamine (pink powder) – ideal for sensitive skin, as it gives a gentle action on the skin and also helps to soothe and calm it

- magnesium carbonate (white powder) – useful for normal to dry skin types, and can be mixed with calamine for sensitive skin types. It has a gentle action and helps to tighten the pores and soften the skin

- kaolin (white powder) – useful for congested and oily skin with spots or blackheads. It has a deep cleansing effect and removes impurities from the skin. It stimulates the blood and lymphatic circulations

- fuller's earth (grey/green powder) – useful for oily, congested skins, but not suitable for sensitive skins. It has a very deep cleansing action and stimulates the blood and lymphatic circulations

- flowers of sulphur (yellow powder) – useful for treating **pustules** and **papules** because of its drying action.

key terms

Pustules and **papules:** a pustule is a spot containing pus and a papule (pimple) is an inflamed, raised, irritated spot.

Good practice

A mixture of clay masks can be used on a combination skin type.

The clay mask is mixed with a liquid, often flower water, until it becomes a paste. Rose water may be used for dry skin types and witch hazel for oily skins. For sensitive skins, vegetable oil can be used.

DON'T FORGET

Some salons offer a volcanic ash clay mask treatment.

Step-by-step guide to applying a clay mask

1 Apply the mask to the face and neck with a mask brush, working in an upwards direction from the neck, and ensuring you leave the mouth, eyes and nostrils uncovered.

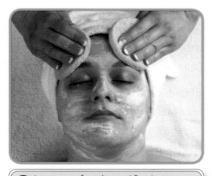

2 Leave on for about 10 minutes, then remove using damp sponges or towels that have been soaked in warm water.

3 Remove the mask gently and do not drag the skin.

153

Peel-off masks

Peel-off masks may be made of gel or latex.

- Gel masks contain starches, gums or gelatine. As soon as the mask is applied to the skin it starts to dry. When it has completely dried, it can be pulled off the skin in one piece. Gel masks may contain different ingredients to suit different skin types.

- A latex mask consists of latex and water. The mask is applied and the water evaporates leaving a rubber layer on the skin. It helps to firm and tighten the skin and is particularly useful on dry and mature skin types.

Paraffin wax

Paraffin wax is suitable for dry skin types and has a stimulating action on the skin. It is not recommended for oily and very sensitive skin types. Paraffin wax is heated to a temperature of 44 °C inside a heater.

Procedure for applying paraffin wax as a mask

1 Pour some paraffin wax into a bowl lined with tin foil.

2 Check the temperature on yourself, then check it is comfortable for the client.

3 Apply some damp cotton wool pads to the client's eyes.

4 Use a brush to apply the paraffin wax. It can be applied over gauze or directly to the face and neck.

5 Leave it on for about 10 minutes, or until it begins to cool.

6 After the wax has cooled, remove the eye pads, then slide the fingers under the gauze or edges of the mask and pull up gently to release it from the skin.

Non-setting masks

Non-setting masks are masks that do not set on the skin. They commonly consist of cream, oil and plant extracts. Each mask is designed to treat different skin conditions, depending on its ingredients. Non-setting masks include biological and warm oil masks.

Biological masks

Biological masks can be made of fruit, plants, herbs, or foods such as yogurt, honey and oatmeal. They have a gentle action on the skin.

Procedure for applying a biological mask

1   Use a mask brush to apply the mask directly on to the skin or over gauze. Start at the neck and move in an upwards direction. The whole face should be covered, except for the eyes, nostrils, lips and hair line. Be careful not to put the mask too close to the eyes.

2   Place two dampened cotton wool pads over the eyes.

3   After 10 minutes, remove the cotton wool pads from the eyes. Then pick up two damp sponges and press them down on to the mask. Leave for a few seconds as the dampness will help to loosen the mask and make it easier to remove.

4   Use upward and outward strokes to remove the mask.

5   Next, tone the skin to help remove any remaining bits of mask.

Warm oil masks

Warm oil masks are beneficial for dry, mature and dehydrated skin.

Mask being applied over gauze

Procedure for applying warm oil as a mask

1   Place damp cotton wool pads over the eyes.

2   Soak a gauze in warm vegetable oil, such as almond or olive oil, and position it on the face, making sure the eyes and mouth are left uncovered.

3   An infrared lamp can be used to direct heat on to the client's face. This will help the skin to absorb nutrients from the oil and any further products used during the facial treatment.

4   After 10–20 minutes, turn off the infrared lamp and massage the oil into the client's face and neck.

Good practice

Apply the mask quite thinly. There is no need to apply it thickly as the result will be the same. You will waste the mask product and also it will require a longer time to remove it from the skin.

Good practice

If a client complains of a burning sensation while a product is on the face, remove the product immediately.

After the mask treatment the skin should be toned again and moisturised.

Moisturising products

key terms

Humectants: substances that help to increase the water content of the skin. Useful for moisturising dry skin and softening thickened or scaly skin.

Lanolin: a thick oil that comes from the wool of animals, such as sheep, where it helps to make the wool waterproof. When used in cosmetics, it makes an effective moisturiser, but some people are allergic to it.

Moisturising the skin

The skin produces its own natural moisturiser, called sebum, which helps to keep it soft and supple, and also helps to prevent loss of water from its surface. Unfortunately, factors such as the environment, hormonal changes and ageing can reduce the amount of sebum that is produced by the skin.

Moisturisers help to put moisture into the skin and reduce moisture loss. They are mostly made up of water and oil. The water helps to return moisture to the skin and the oil helps to stop loss of moisture from the surface of the skin. A moisturiser plumps out the skin with moisture, which helps to reduce the appearance of fine lines. It also softens the skin, which helps to improve its feel (texture) and appearance.

Moisturisers also help to create a barrier between the skin and its environment, therefore protecting the skin from sun, wind, cold and air pollution. Many moisturisers contain SPF and UVA protection, which help protect the skin from the damaging effects of the sun's UV rays.

There are two main types of moisturiser: creams and lotions. Moisturising creams have a thicker consistency than moisturising lotions and also contain more oil. They are therefore particularly useful for dry, mature and dehydrated skin types.

Moisturisers commonly contain a mixture of emollients, **humectants**, fragrances (perfumes) and preservatives.

Emollients
Including **lanolin** and mineral oil.

These ingredients fill in the spaces between the cells in the skin, helping replace lipids (fats) and helping to smooth and moisturise dry skin. They also help to prevent water loss from the epidermis by covering it with a protective film. Emollients are either oil based, which means they contain a small amount of water dissolved in oil; or water-based, which means they are mostly water and have a light, non-oily feel. Oil-based creams leave a slight film on the skin and stay on longer than water-based creams.

Lanolin is sheep sebum and helps to waterproof sheep's wool. It is a mixture of semi-solid oils, fats, and waxes, and may cause skin irritation.

Humectants
Including glycerine and alpha hydroxy acids.

These are substances that absorb water from the air when there is high humidity (lots of moisture in the environment) and help to increase the water content of the skin. Humectants also attract water from the dermis into the epidermis to help hydrate it. Humectants are useful for moisturising dry skin and softening thickened or scaly skin. They also help to desquamate the skin and act as a barrier against chemicals in the environment that may come into contact with the skin.

Fragrances (perfumes)

Most moisturisers contain fragrances. These give the product a pleasant smell and cover up the smell of other ingredients. However, fragrances in skin care products are the most common cause of skin irritations or skin allergies.

Preservatives

Products that include water and oil must contain one or more preservatives to help prevent bacterial contamination after the product is opened – otherwise the product would deteriorate. Most products contain many preservatives, and these can sometimes cause skin allergies or other unwanted reactions.

Parabens are a group of preservatives that are used widely in moisturisers, and other cosmetics, to make the products last longer. They can cause skin irritation in some people, but are considered less irritating than some other preservatives. However, some experts believe that parabens can affect certain hormones in the body and increase the risk of breast cancer. Therefore, many cosmetic companies now offer products that are 'paraben-free'.

Moisturisers may also include other beneficial ingredients, such as vitamins, minerals, plant extracts and sunscreens. They may also contain stabilising ingredients, such as emulsifiers and thickeners, to help to prevent the oil and water from separating or deteriorating.

Procedure for moisturising the skin

1 Use a spatula to remove moisturiser from its pot. Put some moisturiser on the back of your hand and use the free hand to apply it to the face.

2 Spread the moisturiser over the skin using similar strokes to those used during the cleansing process. Begin at the neck area and work in an upward direction until you reach the forehead.

3 Blot excess moisturiser from the skin using a facial tissue.

Application of moisturiser

DON'T FORGET

A tinted moisturiser is a moisturiser that gives light coverage and adds a little colour to the face to make it look fresh and healthy.

DON'T FORGET

DON'T FORGET

There are moisturising products that will both tan and moisturise the skin. The ingredient that will tan the skin is a type of sugar called dihydroxyacetone (DHA), which interacts with the dead skin cells found in the stratum corneum and causes a colour change. As the dead cells are shed, the tan will fade.

Ask Fran

Q: Would you give the same facial treatment to a man?

A: The treatment is the same. However, if they have facial hair, especially stubble, you will find the cotton wool pads drag across the skin and fibres stick to the hairs; ensure you use downward strokes working in the direction of your client's hair growth. It is advised to ask your client to shave before coming for treatment. There are facial products that are designed for men and have a masculine smell.

Moisturising products that can be recommended to clients

These may be used during the facial treatment and recommended for purchase and home use.

- Eye creams – the skin around the eyes is thin and prone to wrinkling, therefore eye creams can be recommended to help plump out the skin and reduce fine lines. Use the ring finger to stroke them around the eye.

- Eye gels – these have a slightly astringent (tightening) effect. This is because of their active ingredients and the fact that water evaporates from them when they are applied to the skin. Use the ring finger to stroke them around the eye.

- Neck creams – the neck is particularly prone to becoming wrinkled, so a good moisturising cream can be recommended to the client to help protect this area.

- Lip creams – lips need protection from sunlight, as they do not contain melanin, and also from the harsh conditions of winter. Lip creams can help to soften and protect the lips.

- Ampoules – an ampoule is a small sealed vial that is used to contain and preserve whatever is inside it. Beauty therapists often use them during facial treatments, as they contain concentrated, highly active ingredients such as botanical extracts, vitamins and enzymes. Ampoules can also be applied alone, and are useful to help a variety of skin conditions, including skin redness, sun sensitivity, dehydration and ageing.

Warming the skin

Warming of the skin, using facial steaming or hot towels, may be carried out as part of a facial treatment. This is particularly useful for clients who require comedone (blackhead) or milia (whitehead) extraction. Skin warming would normally be carried out after cleansing.

The benefits include:

- stimulating the blood and lymphatic circulations

- opening the pores

- softening the stratum corneum, which helps to free any dead skin cells (desquamation), dirt, bacteria, etc.

- allowing products to be more easily absorbed into the skin

- allowing easier removal of skin blockages such as comedones and milia

- helping to hydrate the skin

- leaving the skin feeling fully cleansed and refreshed.

Preparation for a skin warming treatment
- Make sure everything is clean and tidy.

- Make sure the room is not too hot or cold, stuffy or smelly.

- Make sure there are enough pillows and bedding for the client's comfort.

- Make sure there is a clean gown for the client to put on.

- Make sure there is couch roll on the couch.

- Make sure the trolley contains everything needed to carry out the treatment.

- Make sure items such as comedone extractors are sterilised.

- Make sure there is a clean bin nearby.

- Make sure there are enough towels, position them correctly and fold them neatly.

- If using a facial steamer, fill the water container of the steamer (vapour unit) with **distilled water** and switch it on.

Equipment, materials and products
The following additional equipment, materials and products will be required for a skin warming treatment.

- Steamer – to apply steam to the face, which helps to cleanse and improve blood flow to the skin

- Towels – for hot towels treatment

- Bowl – to be filled with very warm (not hot) water

- Comedone extractor – a metal tool used to remove comedones (blackheads)

- Disposable needle (will be pre-packed and sterilised) – to remove milia spots (whiteheads)

- Tape measure – to measure the distance from the steamer to the client's face

- Petroleum jelly – to protect sensitive areas of the face during steaming

- Antiseptic lotion and soothing lotion – to clean and soothe skin after blockage removal

- Disposable gloves – to wear when removing skin blockages

> **key terms**
>
> **Distilled water:** water that has been cleaned to remove substances such as mineral deposits.

Comedone extractor

- Medical antiseptic swabs – to clean the comedone extractor after use
- Sharps box – for disposal of needles

> ### Good practice
> Never overfill a steamer as this may cause the machine to spit water on to a client or therapist, which could result in scalding.

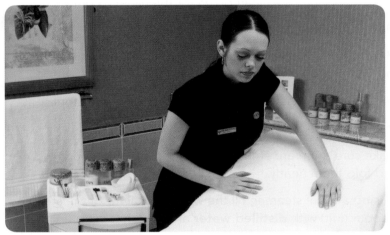

Prepared treatment room

Procedure for a facial steaming treatment

Inside a vapour steaming unit is a heating element that usually takes about 10 minutes to boil water. When ready, it produces a jet of steam from a nozzle or other outlet, which can be used to treat the face or other parts of the body, such as the back.

> ### Good practice
> When warming up a steamer, make sure it is directed away from the client.

Before carrying out a steam treatment on a client, ensure you discuss with them how long the treatment will take and the benefits to their skin. Do not leave the treatment room while carrying out this treatment in case there is a problem.

1 Ensure the back of the couch is lifted, so the client is in a semi-reclined position.

2 Before applying steam to the face, place some damp cotton wool pads on the client's eyes to protect them from the steam.

3 Petroleum jelly can be applied to areas with dilated capillaries, or other sensitive areas.

4 Use a tape measure to ensure the steam outlet is positioned 30–35 cm from the client's skin.

5 To allow the steam to cover the face evenly, the unit may need to be adjusted and moved to the correct position.

6 The treatment will take about 10 minutes, although oily skin types can be treated for longer periods of time than drier types. Sensitive skins will have the shortest treatment times.

7 Some steamers also produce vapour ozone by passing oxygen from the steam over a UV bulb. Ozone has an antibacterial effect so is useful for acne-prone skin and, if required, is used towards the end of the steam treatment. When ozone is used, the steam will change to a bluish-white colour.

8 After the steam treatment, blot the skin dry using a facial tissue to remove any moisture. The skin is now ready for removal of any blockages, such as comedones and milia.

Facial steaming

Good practice

Remember to follow the manufacturer's instructions when using a facial steamer.

Good practice

When you have finished, don't forget to switch off the steamer, tie up any trailing leads, and place it in a safe position to avoid anyone tripping over it as they walk by.

DON'T FORGET

The timing of the treatment can be adjusted to suit a client's skin type.

Procedure for a hot towels treatment

Another method of skin warming involves applying very warm towels (not hot) to the skin.

1 Place towels into a bowl or container with very warm water.

2 Remove a towel from the water and wring it out.

3 Ensure the towel is at a comfortable temperature for the client, then position it on their face so that their nose and mouth are visible.

4 Gently press the towel on to the face until it cools, then replace it with another warm towel.

5 Repeat this process for about 10 minutes.

6 Blot the skin using a facial tissue. It is now ready for removal of any blockages.

Procedure for removal of skin blockages

Warming the skin will help to soften the skin and open the pores, allowing an easier removal of skin blockages such as comedones and milia. Afterwards, cleanse the treated area with antiseptic lotion and also soothing lotion.

Hot towels

> **DON'T FORGET**
>
> *Special heaters, rather like microwaves, can be used to store and heat towels.*

> **Good practice** ✓
>
> All waste created during skin blockage treatment will be regarded as contaminated, so it must be disposed of carefully.

> **Good practice** ✓
>
> Clean the comedone extractor with antiseptic and then sterilise it in the autoclave. It can be stored in the UV cabinet.

Comedones

The comedone extractor is often made of stainless steel and is looped at either one end or both ends. Wearing disposable gloves, apply the looped end around the comedone and apply a little pressure. This should release the contents, which can be collected on a tissue. Another method involves wrapping tissue around the tips of your index fingers and gently rolling the skin around the comedone to help release its contents.

Removal of cometones

Milia

The milia can be pierced with a sterilised needle, which will allow it to be released and collected on a tissue. The needle should be disposed of in a sharps box. Disposable gloves should be worn while carrying out this treatment.

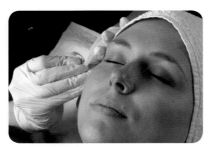
Removal of milia

> **UNIT OUTCOME 10**
>
> **Understand the aftercare advice to provide clients for facial care treatments**

Aftercare advice

The aftercare advice ensures the client gets the most from their facial treatment, and helps them to maintain a healthy and fresh-looking skin after they leave the salon.

Provide the following aftercare advice to your client.

- Avoid applying make-up for 12 hours, except light mascara and lipstick.

- Avoid swimming and sunbathing for 12 hours.

- No depilation (hair removal) should be carried out on the face for 24 hours.

- Advise the client what they should do if they experience a contra-action. For example, if the skin should become red and slightly irritated they should apply a cool compress.

Advise the client when to return for further treatment, and recommend other treatments that could help to improve their skin condition. A client should aim to have a facial treatment every four weeks. However, if you are targeting a specific problem they can be encouraged to attend more regularly; perhaps once each week for six weeks, or until the skin condition has improved.

Aftercare advice

Also, discuss the client's homecare routine and suggest how they could improve it. Tell them what products have been used during the treatment and their benefits. They may then decide they would like to purchase these products to take home.

UNIT OUTCOME 4

Understand organisational and legal requirements

See **Unit G20: Ensure responsibility for actions to reduce risks to health and safety**, for details of legislation relating to beauty therapy.

UNIT OUTCOME 7

Understand anatomy and physiology that relates to facial skin care treatments

To carry out a professional facial treatment, the therapist must have knowledge of the structure and functions of the skin. For information about the structure and functions of the skin see the **Anatomy and physiology** unit.

How are you doing?

1 Which of the following is **not** a contra-indication to facial treatment?

   a Scar tissue less than six months old

   b Cuts and abrasions

   c Vitiligo

   d Sunburn

2 What is an AHA?

   a Alpha hydro advice

   b Alpha hydroxy acid

   c After hydration application

   d Azulene hydro acid

3 Spots and comedones are often associated with which skin type?

   a Dry

   b Mature

   c Sensitive

   d Oily

4 Which of the following is **not** a type of skin toner?

   a Skin lifter

   b Skin bracer

   c Skin tonic

   d Astringent

5 Which of the following describes desquamation?

   a The mitosis of skin cells

   b The shedding of dead skin cells

   c The action of a cleanser

   d Stimulation of the blood circulation

6 Which of the following is an effect of massage?

   a Desquamation of the skin

   b Stimulation of the blood circulation

   c Relaxation of tight muscles

   d All of the above

7 Which of the following is not carried out during a facial treatment?

   a Cleansing

   b Toning

   c Buffing

   d Steaming

8 Which of the following would be a contra-action to facial treatment?

   a Free radicals

   b Comedones

   c Skin irritation

   d Milia

9 Which of the following describes the main action of a moisturiser?

   a To protect and add moisture to the skin

   b To remove oil from the skin

   c To help remove dead skin cells from the skin surface

   d To create erythema

10 Facial steaming is usually carried out after which of the following?

   a Cleansing

   b Exfoliation

   c Mask application

   d Moisturisation

are you ready for assessment?

The evidence for this unit must be gathered in the workplace (salon) or realistic working environment (training centre).

Simulation (role play) is not allowed for any performance evidence within this unit.

You must practically demonstrate in your everyday work that you have met the required standard for this unit.

All outcomes, assessment criteria and range statements must be achieved.

Knowledge and understanding in this unit will be assessed by a mandatory (compulsory) written question paper. These questions are set and marked by VTCT.

Assessing your practical work

Your assessor will observe your performance of a practical task, such as a facial treatment.

Your assessor will sign off an outcome when all criteria have been competently achieved.

On occasions, some assessment criteria may not naturally occur during a practical observation. In such instances you will be asked questions to demonstrate your knowledge in this area. Your assessor will document the criteria that have been achieved through oral questioning.

In this unit you must demonstrate competent performance of all practical outcomes on at least **three** occasions, each involving a different client.

Testing your knowledge and understanding

You will be guided by your tutor and assessor on the evidence that needs to be produced.

Your knowledge and understanding will be assessed using the assessment tools listed below.

- Mandatory (compulsory) written question paper
- Oral questioning
- Portfolio of evidence

B5 Enhance the appearance of eyebrows and eyelashes

UNIT OUTCOMES

On completion of this unit you will:

1. Be able to use safe and effective methods of working when providing eyebrow and eyelash treatments

2. Be able to consult, plan and prepare for the treatment with clients

3. Be able to shape eyebrows

4. Be able to tint the eyebrows and lashes

5. Be able to apply artificial lashes

6. Understand organisational and legal requirements

7. Understand how to work safely and effectively when providing eyebrow and eyelash treatments

8. Understand how to perform client consultation, treatment planning and preparation

9. Understand how to shape the eyebrows

10. Understand how to tint the eyebrows and lashes

11. Understand how to apply artificial lashes

12. Understand the contra-indications and contra-actions that affect or restrict eyebrow and eyelash treatments

13. Know the equipment, materials and products to use when carrying out eyebrow and eyelash treatments

Introduction

As a beauty therapist, you will be expected to carry out a range of eyelash and eyebrow treatments, which help to enhance the eyes and so make a face look more attractive. These popular salon treatments include eyebrow shaping, eyelash and eyebrow tinting, and application of artificial lashes.

UNIT OUTCOME 2

Be able to consult, plan and prepare for the treatment with clients

UNIT OUTCOME 8

Understand how to perform client consultation, treatment planning and preparation

UNIT OUTCOME 12

Understand the contra-indications and contra-actions that affect or restrict eyebrow and eyelash treatments

Enhanced eyelashes

Consultation

Before you begin the treatment, you should carry out a consultation to explain the treatment to your client and discuss their expectations of the treatment. You should also find out if they have any contra-indications to treatment. For eyelash and eyebrow tinting, and for artificial lash application, you will also need to carry out a skin sensitivity test.

Remember to fill out a record card/consultation form and ensure the client signs it.

For more information on the consultation process, see **Unit G20: Ensure responsibility for actions to reduce risks to health and safety**.

key terms

Flare lashes: flare lashes are small bundles of single lashes connected at the end in a little knot. 'Flare' describes the way in which the eyelash is shaped.

Strip lashes: strip lashes are a strip containing many lashes. These generally cover the whole width of the eye.

Service times

The table shows the types of treatment you will carry out and the recommended service time for each.

Treatment	Time
Eyebrow tidy	15 minutes
Eyebrow shape	15 minutes
Eyebrow tint	10 minutes
Eyelash tint	20 minutes
Apply a full set of artificial **flare lashes**	20 minutes
Apply a full set of artificial **strip lashes**	10 minutes
Apply a partial set of artificial flare lashes	10 minutes
Apply a partial set of artificial strip lashes	10 minutes

Eyebrow shape

Eyebrows help to protect the eyes from sweat and dust. They also frame the eyes and, when correctly shaped, can improve the appearance of the eyes and face. There are two types of eyebrow shaping generally offered in salons: an eyebrow reshape and an eyebrow tidy. An eyebrow reshape can take up to 30 minutes and involves creating a new eyebrow shape. An eyebrow tidy will only take about 15 minutes, as the shape is already there but some stray hairs need to be removed to make the eyebrows look tidy.

As the eyebrows frame the eyes, having a neat and appropriate, balanced shape can do a lot to accentuate them. If an eyebrow reshape is required, it is important to discuss the client's expectations of the treatment so that they are pleased with the final result. They may have unrealistic expectations about the shape of their eyebrows; however, you can give them professional advice regarding which shape would suit them best.

Contra-indications

Eyebrow shaping should not be carried out if the client has any of the following around the eye area.

- Inflamed skin
- Bruising or swelling
- Eye infections
- Skin infections

Nicely shaped eyebrows

- Cuts or abrasions

- Scar tissue under six months old

- Any skin disorder that may be irritated and cause discomfort if touched

Without causing alarm to the client, suggest they seek medical advice regarding a contra-indication, or return for treatment when the contra-indication is no longer present.

Eyebrow tint

An eyebrow tint is useful for people who would like their eyebrows to be more defined; perhaps the client has fair coloured hair, or has few hairs on the brow area. The tint colours commonly used are grey (light brown) or brown. The longer the tint is left on the darker the hairs will become.

When discussing the tinting treatment with your client, ensure the colour chosen will meet with their expectations. If a client has fair eyebrows, they may find it shocking if you colour them dark brown!

Contra-indications

Eyebrow tinting should not be carried out if the client has any of the following.

- Inflammation or swelling around the eye area

- Bruising around the eye area

- Eye infections such as conjunctivitis

- Skin infections around the eye area

- Cuts and abrasions around the eye area

- Extremely sensitive skin

- Recent scar tissue

- Any skin disorder that may be irritated and cause discomfort if touched

- A positive reaction to the sensitivity test

Without causing alarm to the client, suggest they seek medical advice regarding a contra-indication, or return for treatment when the contra-indication is no longer present.

> **DON'T FORGET**
>
> The grey tint doesn't provide a grey colour to the hair, but a light brown colour. It is a good choice for fair- or white-haired people.

Eyelash tint

Tinting the eyelashes will make them look darker, longer and thicker. This is useful for the following reasons.

- It is ideal for clients who have allergies to make-up.
- It is useful for clients with light coloured lashes and eyebrows.
- It is ideal for clients who are going on holiday.
- It is useful for clients who do a lot of physical exercise, such as swimming.
- Less time is required for the client to apply make-up.
- Clients who wear glasses or contact lenses may find it tricky to apply mascara.
- Clients who work or live in a hot environment may be concerned about the heat causing their mascara to smudge or run.

There is a range of permanent tints available, including jelly, liquid, and cream tints. The most commonly used is cream tint, as it is thicker in consistency and is easy to work with. The various colours of eyelash tint include brown, grey, blue and black.

Tinting the eyelashes makes them look darker, longer and thicker

Good practice

Ask your client to remove their contact lenses before having an eyelash tint treatment.

Eyelash tinting usually takes around 15 minutes, but it can take longer if the client is wearing thick mascara that needs to be removed. Ask them to come to the salon wearing no eye make-up, if possible.

Contra-indications

Eyelash tinting should not be carried out if the client has any of the following.

- Inflammation or swelling around the eye area
- Eye infections such as conjunctivitis
- Skin infections around the eye area
- Cuts and abrasions around the eye area
- Extremely sensitive skin

- Contact lenses – these need to be removed

- Clients who are unable to keep their eyes fully closed and blink a lot – this will allow tint to enter the eyes

- Highly nervous clients – in case tint gets in the eyes

- A positive reaction to the sensitivity test

Without causing alarm to the client, suggest they seek medical advice regarding a contra-indication, or return for treatment when the contra-indication is no longer present.

Skin sensitivity test

This must be carried out at least 24 hours before an eyebrow or eyelash tint.

Eyelash/eyebrow tints contain vegetable dyes so are generally safe to use. However, if a client suffers an allergic reaction it can be quite severe. It can cause the eyelids to swell, which results in the person not being able to see, and can also be painful. If this happens the client will need to go to a hospital.

Items required for a skin sensitivity test
- Small amount of eyelash/eyebrow tint

- Hydrogen peroxide – 3 per cent (10 vol.)

- Cotton bud

- Non-metallic dish for mixing the tint (tint dishes are usually made from glass)

Good practice ✓

Never let a client talk you into giving an eyelash or eyebrow tint without having a skin test first.

Good practice ✓

The hydrogen peroxide used during an eyelash/eyebrow treatment must not have a higher strength than 3 per cent (or 10 volume) hydrogen peroxide, otherwise irritation and minor burning may result.

Procedure for carrying out a skin sensitivity test
1 Mix a small amount of tint and hydrogen peroxide according to the manufacturer's instructions.

2 Cleanse a patch of the client's skin, either behind the ear or on the inside of the arm where the arm bends.

Skin sensitivity test

Artificial lashes applied

DON'T FORGET

Some artificial lashes are made from 100 per cent mink fur.

3 Use a cotton bud to apply a blob of the mixed tint.

4 Leave the tint on the skin for five minutes.

5 Wipe off any excess tint with cotton wool.

6 Ask the client to leave the remainder of the tint on the skin for at least 24 hours before washing it off.

7 There will either be a positive or negative reaction. Fortunately, most people have a negative reaction.

8 Record the information about the sensitivity test on the client's record card/consultation form, including the date, and ensure the client has signed the card/form.

Positive reaction

A positive reaction means that the client's skin had an unwanted reaction to the products applied to it. This will probably show itself as redness, itching and swelling. The client must **not** have an eyelash/eyebrow tint treatment.

Negative reaction

A negative reaction means the skin has responded well to the tint and so it should be safe to continue with the treatment.

Artificial lashes

Artificial lashes give a glamorous look as they make the lashes appear thicker and longer. They are ideal for clients having evening make-up, or for photographic shoots. They are available in different lengths, thicknesses and colours, and some even contain small coloured stones, ideal for a party effect. They can be applied in whole strips, in sections, or individually. They are usually made from threads of nylon, but expensive ones can be made from real animal fur or human hair. However, real hair or fur lashes will not hold their curl as long as synthetic ones. The two main types of artificial lashes are:

- strip lashes

- individual flare lashes.

Strip lashes are basically a strip containing many lashes. Individual flare lashes contain two or more lashes from one bulb (knot).

Contra-indications

- Inflammation or swelling around the eye area

- Eye infections such as conjunctivitis

- Skin infections around the eye area

- Cuts and abrasions around the eye area

- Extremely sensitive skin

- Contact lenses – these should be removed while the lashes are being applied

- Highly nervous clients – in case adhesive gets into the eyes

- Clients who blink a lot

- A positive reaction to the sensitivity test

DON'T FORGET

Artificial lashes are useful for people with sparse hairs on the lashline, as it makes the lashes appear thicker and fuller.

Skin sensitivity test

Carry out this test for both the individual and strip lashes. Clients *must* have a sensitivity test 24 hours before treatment can take place, in case there is an allergic reaction to the adhesive (glue).

1 Cleanse a patch of the client's skin, either behind the ear or on the inside of the arm where the arm bends.

2 Use a cotton bud to apply a small amount of adhesive.

3 Ask the client to leave it on for 24 hours.

4 Record the information about the sensitivity test on the client's record card/consultation form, including the date, and ensure the client has signed the card/form.

Positive reaction
A positive reaction means that the client's skin had an unwanted reaction to the products applied to it. This will probably show itself as redness, itching and swelling. The client must *not* have an individual and strip lashes treatment.

Negative reaction
A negative reaction means the skin has responded well to the tint and so it should be safe to continue with the treatment.

UNIT OUTCOME 13

Know the equipment, materials and products to use when carrying out eyebrow and eyelash treatments

Equipment, materials and products

Check that you have all the necessary equipment, materials and products close to hand, and that they meet with legal, hygiene and industry requirements for eyebrow and eyelash treatment services.

key terms

Manual tweezers: these types of tweezers have two ends, which vary in shape (although the slanted ends are preferable) and that should meet together at the bottom to make them effective at pulling out hairs. They are ideal for removing stray hairs and creating the final shape.

Automatic tweezers: these types of tweezers have a spring-loaded action, so they can work very quickly to remove hairs. They are useful for removing a lot of hair at one time.

Automatic tweezers

Manual tweezers

DON'T FORGET

Disposable mascara wands are useful for brushing the eyebrow hairs into shape during an eyebrow shaping treatment.

Eyebrow shape

Tiny molecules of pigment and hydrogen peroxide mix together, and then enter the cuticles of the hair.

- Treatment couch – this should be disinfected and covered with either towels or a blanket. Clean couch roll should be placed on top, and place a towel at the head end for the client's head to rest on
- Stool – should ideally be height adjustable and have a backrest
- Trolley – should be disinfected and lined with couch roll
- Sterilised **tweezers** – either **manual or automatic**
- Cleanser or eye make-up remover – to cleanse the eyebrow area
- Orange sticks – to measure the eyebrows and help ensure a correct shape is achieved
- Scissors – to trim long hairs
- Eyebrow brush or disposable mascara wand – to brush the eyebrow hairs into shape
- Hand mirror – for the client to see the result
- Headband – to hold the client's hair back, if necessary
- Disposable gloves – to help prevent cross-infection
- Surgical spirit – for wiping the tweezers during treatment
- Antiseptic lotion or cream and soothing lotion – to be used after treatment
- Disinfectant – to clean the tweezers before sterilising them
- Barbicide in a jar – to store the tweezers
- Cotton wool – to cleanse the skin and clean the tweezers
- Tissues – to wipe tools, the skin and protect clothing
- Bowl – to store cotton wool and the client's jewellery
- Towels – to protect clothing and for wiping hands
- Client record card/consultation form and pen – important information about the client and their treatment is written on the card/form.

Good practice

The tweezers with slanted ends are usually preferable when carrying out an eyebrow shaping treatment.

Good practice

Store the sterilised tweezers in the ultraviolet (UV) cabinet when not in use.

Eyelash tint and eyebrow tint

- Treatment couch – this should be disinfected and covered with either towels or a blanket. Clean couch roll should be placed on top, and place a towel at the head end for the client's head to rest on
- Stool – should ideally be height adjustable and have a backrest
- Trolley – should be disinfected and lined with couch roll
- Variety of eyelash and eyebrow tints
- Hydrogen peroxide – 3 per cent (10 vol.)
- Non-oily cleansing lotion, or eye make-up remover, and toner – to cleanse the eye area
- Non-metallic bowl – for mixing tint (glass bowls are often used)
- Petroleum jelly – to protect the skin
- Skin stain remover – to remove tint from the skin
- Headband – to hold the client's hair back, if necessary
- Eyeshields (either paper or made from round cotton wool pads) – to place beneath the eyes to protect the skin
- Eyebrow brush or disposable mascara wand – to separate eyebrow hairs
- Tint brush, disposable brush or orange stick – to apply the tint
- Disposable brush or cotton bud – to apply the petroleum jelly
- Hand mirror – to show the client the result
- Towels – to protect the client's clothing.
- Cotton wool – to apply and remove products
- Disposable spatulas – used to remove products, such as petroleum jelly from containers
- Tissues – to wipe tools, the skin and protect clothing
- Bowls – to store cotton wool and the client's jewellery
- Client record card/consultation form and pen – important informtion about the client and their treatment is written in the card/form.

Good practice

After using the hydrogen peroxide, quickly put the top back on the bottle, otherwise the product will lose its strength owing to **oxidation**.

Good practice

Heat can make the eyelash tint less effective, so ensure you store the tint in a cool, dark place.

key terms

Oxidation: the chemical reation caused by the combination of a substance with oxygen.

How does tinting work?

Eyelash tint and hydrogen peroxide are mixed together, applied to the hairs and left to develop. During this time, the tiny molecules of pigment (toluenediamine) enter the cuticles of the hairs. The hydrogen peroxide contains oxygen, and as the tint oxidises (combines with oxygen to make a chemical reaction) the molecules of pigment get bigger, join together, and become trapped in the cortex layer of the hair, resulting in colour. The hair will be permanently coloured until it falls out and a new one grows in its place.

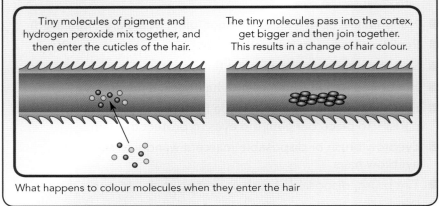

Tiny molecules of pigment and hydrogen peroxide mix together, and then enter the cuticles of the hair.

The tiny molecules pass into the cortex, get bigger and then join together. This results in a change of hair colour.

What happens to colour molecules when they enter the hair

Artificial lashes

- Treatment couch – this should be disinfected and covered with either towels or a blanket. Clean couch roll should be placed on top, and place a towel at the head end for the client's head to rest on

- Stool – should ideally be height adjustable and have a backrest

- Trolley – should be disinfected and lined with couch roll

- Strip lashes

- Individual flare lashes

- Lash adhesive (glue) – to attach artificial lashes to the eyelids. There are different types of glue for strip lashes and flare lashes

- Non-oily eye make-up remover – to cleanse eyelashes

- Tweezers – to apply lashes

- Scissors – to trim the lashes

- Disposable mascara wand or mascara comb – to separate eyelashes

- Container for adhesive
- Orange sticks – to apply the adhesive
- Hand mirror – to show the client the result
- Surgical spirit – to clean the adhesive off the tweezers
- Solvent – to remove lashes, if necessary
- Headband – to hold the client's hair back, if necessary
- Eyeliner – to fill the gap between the artificial lashes and the natural lashes
- Mascara – to apply after the treatment
- Disposable spatulas – used to remove products from containers and to temporarily store substances such as glue
- Cotton wool – to cleanse eyelashes
- Cotton wool buds – to wipe away glue from the skin
- Towels – to protect clothing and for wiping hands
- Tissues – to wipe tools, the skin and protect clothing
- Client record card/consultation form and pen – important information about the client and their treatment is written on the card.

UNIT OUTCOME 1

Be able to use safe and effective methods of working when providing eyebrow and eyelash treatments

UNIT OUTCOME 3

Be able to shape eyebrows

UNIT OUTCOME 7

Understand how to work safely and effectively when providing eyebrow and eyelash treatments

UNIT OUTCOME 9

Understand how to shape the eyebrows

Procedure for an eyebrow shape treatment

Step-by-step guide

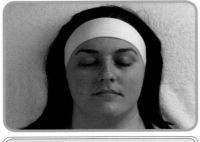

1 If required, secure a headband to keep hair away from the face.

2 Cleanse the eyebrow area with a cleanser or eye make-up remover and use damp cotton wool pads to remove it.

3 Blot the area with a facial tissue.

4 Brush the eyebrows into shape using a disposable mascara wand or eyebrow brush.

5 Brush the hairs in an upward direction and trim any long hairs using small scissors.

6 Measure the eyebrows with an orange stick.

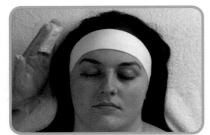

7 Place some surgical spirit on a piece of cotton wool and place it over your index finger or near to the client's head – this is used for collecting the hairs.

8 If required, put on disposable gloves (check with your assessor). Lightly stretch the skin with your thumb and index finger, and begin tweezing.

9 During shaping, allow your client to see their eyebrows in a mirror to ensure they are happy with the progress. Finish the treatment by wiping the eyebrows with an antiseptic lotion or cream (apply it with a cotton wool pad).

10 Soothing lotion may be applied to the eyebrow area if the skin is very red and slightly swollen. Show the client the results in the mirror and write down details of the treatment on the client's record card/consultation form.

Sienna's Beauty Salon — Client record card

Surname: .... Forename: .... Date of Birth: ....

Address: ....

.... Postcode: ....

Telephone (Home): .... Work: ....

GP: .... Name: ....

Address: ....

.... Telephone: ....

Statistics   Height: .... Weight: .... Chest: .... Waist: .... Hips: ....

Prescribed Medication ☐ No ☐ Yes   Details: ....

Surgery ☐ No ☐ Yes   Details: ....

Ailments ☐ No ☐ Yes   Details: ....

Skin Analysis ☐ Dry ☐ Combination ☐ Oily ☐ Sensitive ☐ Fair ☐ Dark

Any Known Allergies ☐ No ☐ Yes   Details: ....

Sample record card/consultation form

Good practice

Ensure you have sufficient lighting so that you can see all the hairs that need to be removed.

Good practice

Regularly wipe the tweezers with a cotton wool pad containing surgical spirit.

To ensure an effective and more comfortable treatment

- Make sure the skin is sufficiently stretched by using the index and middle fingers on the area to be worked. This will help to make the removal of hairs easier, and make the treatment less uncomfortable for the client.

- Regularly brush the brow hairs into shape to ensure you are creating the correct shape as you tweeze.

- Pluck out hairs in the direction in which they are growing; pulling them out in the opposite direction will make them harder to remove, and will be more painful for the client. The hairs will also be more likely to break.

- Tweeze hairs as near to the base as possible; removing hair by the tip will be more painful for the client and may result in hair breakage.

- At the end of the treatment, wipe over the brow with an antiseptic soothing agent to help reduce redness.

DON'T FORGET

If there are any bald areas within the eyebrows, you can use an eyebrow pencil to disguise them.

Ask Fran

Q: I have a client with very long hairs scattered throughout her eyebrows. What should I do?

A: If the client has some stray long hairs in her eyebrows, simply brush the hairs in an upward direction with an eyebrow brush, to help define them, and then trim them using small scissors. If you try to pluck them out, you may find you remove others at the same time and create bald spots.

DON'T FORGET

Why not ask your client if they would like to consider having an eyelash or eyebrow tint? You could give a sensitivity test at the end of the eyebrow shaping treatment.

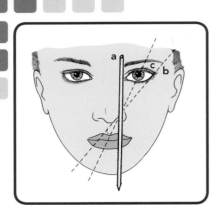

Measuring for eyebrow shaping

key terms

Iris: the circular, coloured part of the eye.

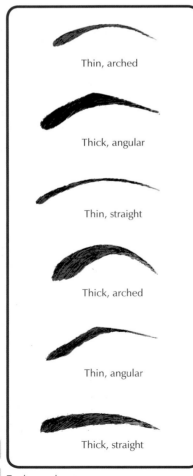

Thin, arched

Thick, angular

Thin, straight

Thick, arched

Thin, angular

Thick, straight

Eyebrow shapes

- Brush the eyebrows into shape, and then raise the couch so the client can see the finished result in the mirror.

Good practice

Ensure you hold the skin taut when tweezing, as this will help to avoid the skin being nipped and possibly bleeding.

To ensure correct eyebrow shape

1 Place an orange stick beside the nose and the inner part of the eye (a). Remove any hairs from the inner side (near the bridge of the nose).

2 Place an orange stick so it lies at the outer corner of the eye and also by the side of the nostril (b). Any hairs found outside this line should be removed.

3 Now place the orange stick so that it lies beside the nostril and is in line with outer edge of the **iris** – ensure the client is looking forward (c). This will help to show you where the highest point of the arch should be.

This method of measuring eyebrows works well unless someone has a very wide nose. In this case, use the tear duct as a guide and remove all hairs between the tear duct and the bridge of the nose.

Face shape and eyebrow shape

Certain shaped faces suit different shaped eyebrows. Of course, sometimes it can be difficult to create an arch in a straight eyebrow and vice versa; however, the following is a guide.

- An oval face suits a brow shape that has a soft angle.
- A heart face shape can be softened by creating rounded eyebrows.
- A wide or round face requires a more angular and distinct strong arch. (Create as high an arch as you can.)
- A thin face needs a softer arch with more of a curve than a sharp arch.
- A long face can look shorter by creating horizontal shaped eyebrows.
- A square face can be softened by creating eyebrows with soft arches.

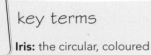

Gently tapered arched brows enhance an oval face

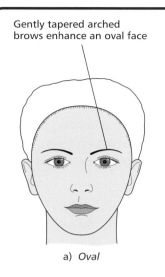

a) *Oval*

Eyebrows quite thick at the inner edge, tapering to a high angular arch to draw attention away from fullness of the face and help create illusion of extra length

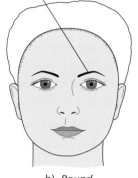

b) *Round*

Smooth tapering arch softens the effect of an angular face shape

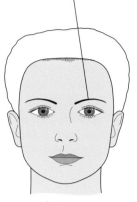

c) *Square*

Tapered eyebrows, not too thin, help enhance the deeper and wider upper part of the face without drawing attention to the widest points of the head

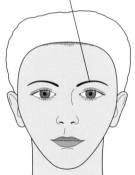

d) *Heart-shaped*

Well-defined angular arch helps to create balance with the widest part of face

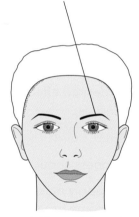

e) *Diamond-shaped*

Brows of medium thickness kept almost straight help to divide the length of face and draw attention across its width

f) *Oblong*

Angular brows with high arch at outer corners help to widen the forehead and provide balance with the heavier bone structure in the lower part of the face

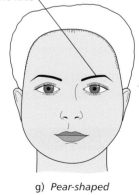

g) *Pear-shaped*

Eye positioning and eyebrows

DON'T FORGET

Thick eyebrows often maker a person look older, but very thin eyebrows can give a harsh look to the face.

HAVE A GO

Browse through magazines and study the eyebrow shapes of the models.

Eye positioning and eyebrow shape

If a client's eyes are either too close together or too wide apart, the eyebrows can be altered to help create the impression of width between the eyes, or reduce the space between them.

Eyes too close together

If the eyes are less than one eye's width apart, you need to give the illusion that there is a little more space between them. To achieve this, pluck a few extra hairs between the eyebrows so that the space is widened.

Eyes too wide apart

If the eyes are more than one eye's width apart, you can give the illusion that they are closer together. Therefore, do not remove hairs from the inner corner of the eyebrows. This will mean the brows extend more towards the bridge of the nose, and gives the impression there is less space between them.

Good practice

Generally, only hairs growing under the eyebrows should be removed, but stray hairs above the eyebrows can be tweezed to give the desired effect.

Aftercare advice

- Any redness should disappear quite quickly.

- Do not apply make-up to the area for 12 hours, as the follicles may become irritated by the make-up product.

- Do not touch, especially scratch, the treated area, as this can allow bacteria from the fingers and nails to enter the empty hair follicles and infect them.

- Recommend the client use an eyebrow pencil or powder if the hairs are sparse.

- If the eyebrow hairs are thick and messy, recommend using some gel to help them lie flat.

- Recommend your client to come back every two weeks for an eyebrow tidy, or four to six weeks for an eyebrow shape.

Good practice

Empty hair follicles can allow bacteria to enter and infect them, perhaps causing a spot to form, so ensure you inform the client not to touch the area after treatment.

Good practice

Inform the client that there will be hairs just underneath the skin, which will appear shortly. This accounts for around 20 per cent of hairs at any time.

Good practice

If the client has very thick eyebrows, it may be too uncomfortable for them to have all the hairs removed during one treatment, so encourage them to have a few separate treatments instead.

UNIT OUTCOME 4

Be able to tint the eyebrows and lashes

UNIT OUTCOME 10

Understand how to tint the eyebrows and lashes

Procedure for an eyebrow tint treatment

Step-by-step guide

DON'T FORGET

Eyebrow hair will tint quicker than eyelash hair, so do not leave tint on the eyebrows for too long.

DON'T FORGET

Brushes are difficult to clean thoroughly, so use disposable brushes to apply products such as petroleum jelly.

DON'T FORGET

Fair eyebrows will tint quickly, so ensure you do not leave the tint on for too long, or they will probably look too dark. Red and grey hairs are more resistant to the tint, so they may take longer to develop colour.

1 Ensure the client did not have a positive reaction to the skin sensitivity test. Cleanse and tone the eyebrow areas.

2 Use a clean eyebrow brush or disposable mascara wand to separate the eyebrow hairs. This makes them easier to tint.

3 Use a cotton bud or disposable brush to apply petroleum jelly around the eyebrows. Keep as close to the hairs as possible, but make sure it does not get on the hairs. Following the manufacturer's instructions, mix the tint and hydrogen peroxide in a glass dish.

4 Use a tint brush or orange stick tipped with cotton wool to apply the tint to one eyebrow. Ensure the hairs are covered evenly from the base to the tips. Now apply tint to the other eyebrow.

5 After a minute, check the inner part of the eyebrow to see how the colour is developing. Eyebrows will rarely need longer than two minutes to tint.

6 When the correct colour has been achieved, remove the tint and petroleum jelly with damp cotton wool pads. Provide the client with a mirror to make sure they are pleased with the final result. Write down the details of the treatment on the client's record card/consultation form.

DON'T FORGET

As long as there are no contra-actions, you can repeat the eyebrow tint treatment, if necessary, to achieve the desired colour.

Good practice

If you are also doing an eyebrow shape, ensure you tint the eyebrow hairs before tweezing them. Otherwise, the open follicles may react with the tint, causing irritation.

Aftercare advice

- If a contra-action occurs, such as soreness and redness, recommend the client applies a cool compress to the area.
- If there is still a problem after 24 hours, the client should return to the salon and any reactions should be recorded on the client record card/consultation form.
- Advise the client to return for an eyebrow tint every three to four weeks.

DON'T FORGET

Professional skin staining removers can be purchased which are designed to remove tint from the skin.

Procedure for an eyelash tint treatment

Step-by-step guide

1 Ensure the client did not have a positive reaction to the skin sensitivity test. Ensure the back of the couch is slightly raised, because there is an increased likelihood that the tint will enter the eyes if the couch is in a flat position.

2 If required, secure a headband and use towels to protect the client's clothing.

3 Use a non-oily cleanser, on a damp cotton wool pad, to remove any make-up from the eye area, then blot the eyelashes with a clean facial tissue. Look out for any contra-indications.

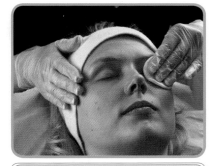

4 A mild toner can be applied to the eyes, using cotton wool pads, to help to remove any oil. Remove any remaining moisture with a tissue.

5 Place some petroleum jelly under the eyes using a cotton bud (ask the client to look upwards to make it easier to apply). Be careful not to get it on the lashes as it will prevent the tint from penetrating into the hair.

6 Apply the eyeshields under both eyes. Either use pre-formed paper ones, or make them by splitting damp cotton wool pads, then cutting them into half moon shapes to fit neatly under the lower lashes.

7 Following the instructions found on the product container, mix the correct amounts of tint and hydrogen peroxide in a glass or plastic dish, until they form a smooth paste. Usually around three drops of hydrogen peroxide and about five millimetres of lash tint are used.

8 Ask the client to close their eyes and then apply petroleum jelly to the upper lids.

9 Load a tint brush or disposable brush with tint, then wipe away any excess on the side of the bowl. Apply tint from the base to the tips of the lashes in a thin, even layer. Wipe off any tint that accidentally touches the skin with a moist cotton bud.

10 When you have done both eyes, the tint can be left to develop for about five to ten minutes, depending on the manufacturer's instructions and the depth of colour required.

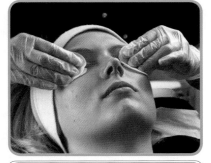

11 Now place damp eye pads on the eyes and wipe away the eyeshields. Use clean damp eye pads to remove the tint, working from the root area down to the tips of the lashes.

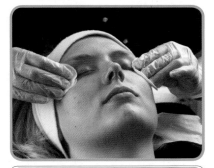

12 The client's eyes must remain closed until the last trace of tint has been removed from the lashes. Provide the client with a mirror to make sure they are pleased with the final result. Write down the details of the treatment on the client's record card/ consultation form.

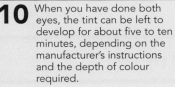

DON'T FORGET

Eyelash tints are made from a plant and vegetable base, so are generally safe to use.

Ask Fran

Q: I carried out an eyelash tint but the result was disappointing: the eyelashes didn't seem to take the colour. Where did I go wrong?

A: Are your products old, or have they been exposed to air for too long? If so, they may have lost their strength. Did you cleanse the area thoroughly with a suitable product? If not, grease or make-up could have acted as a barrier to the tint. Did you mix the correct amount of tint and/or hydrogen peroxide?

DON'T FORGET

The longer the eyelash tint is left on to develop, the darker the eyelashes will be.

Good practice

Place a towel across the client's chest to protect their clothing.

Good practice

Stay with your client at all times during the tinting treatment, in case tint gets into their eyes.

Good practice

If you put too much tint on the eyelashes, there is a good chance it will enter the eye and cause discomfort. Apply just enough to fully cover the lashes.

Good practice

Use a cotton bud soaked in cleanser or stain remover to take away any remaining tint from the skin around the eye.

Aftercare advice

- If the eyes become irritated after the tinting treatment, recommend that the client applies a cold compress to them. If necessary, they should seek medical advice.

- Don't forget to note any contra-actions on the client's record card/consultation form.

- Advise the client to return for treatment in four to six weeks. However, if the client is going on holiday, bright sunlight may cause the colour to fade more quickly.

UNIT OUTCOME 5

Be able to apply artificial lashes

UNIT OUTCOME 11

Understand how to apply artificial eyelashes

Procedure for artificial lashes treatment

Strip lashes

These artificial lashes are attached to a strip and can be cut to the correct length so they cover the whole width of the eyelashes, from the inner corner to the outer corner of the eye. Unlike individual lashes, strip lashes are only worn for a day.

Ask Fran

Q: I've noticed there is a grey eyelash tint colour – who would want to dye their lashes grey?

A: The grey tint will give a light brown colour to the eyelashes, so is ideal to use on grey or fair hairs.

Step-by-step guide

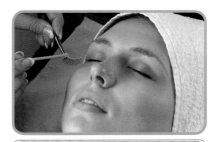

1 Discuss with your client the required outcome of the treatment and choose the lashes to be applied. Remove the client's eye make-up.

2 Measure the lashes by holding them against the client's eyelid (without glue), ensuring the strip does not reach either end of the corner of the eye; instead leave a small gap each side. Use small scissors to cut them to the correct size. If necessary, trim the lashes of the strip too.

3 Use a mascara wand to comb and separate the client's eyelashes.

4 Place some adhesive into a container, then use an orange stick to apply it evenly along the bottom of the strip lash. The adhesive is white, but when it dries it becomes colourless.

5 Gently stretch the eyelid with your fingers to make it easier to place the strip lashes.

6 Using tweezers, place the lash strip on the skin as close as possible to the base of the eyelashes.

7 Beginning from the inner corner of the eye, use an orange stick or your fingertips to gently press on the strip until you reach the outer corner of the eye.

8 Check to make sure the strip is located in the correct place. It will take three to five minutes for the adhesive to dry.

9 Eyeliner and mascara can then be applied. Now you are ready, with the help of a mirror, to show the client the final result. Write down your client's comments on the record card/consultation form.

To ensure an effective strip lash application

- Each eyelash strip is made to fit either the left or right eye – don't mix them up!
- As the eyes may water while applying strip lashes, it is advisable to apply any eye make-up afterwards.
- Do not cut the lashes of the strip lashes straight across; this will give a harsh and unnatural look. Instead, lightly cut hairs to different lengths. The shorter lashes should be near to the inner corner of the eye, and they should gradually get longer as they reach the outer corner.
- Placing a section of the strip lashes around the centre of the eye will help to give a widening effect. Placing them on the outer side will give the illusion of lengthening the eyes.
- Don't apply too much adhesive, as it may cause irritation to the eyelid.
- If the natural lashes are blonde, put on mascara first, or advise your client to have an eyelash tint around 48 hours before applying the eyelash strip.

How to remove strip lashes

Step-by-step guide

1 Place a finger on the temple and gently pull the skin to help stretch the eye area.

2 Use the finger and thumb of the other hand to gently peel the strip lashes from the outer corner of the eye towards the inner corner.

3 Then, using tweezers, gently remove the adhesive from the strip, being careful not to stretch the lash out of shape.

How to recurl strip lashes

This method of recurling the strip lashes is not carried out in the salon, but is advice given to the client to ensure she keeps her strip lashes in a curled shape.

The strip lashes should be cleaned in warm, soapy water and then left to dry. Roll a facial tissue around a pencil or similarly shaped item and place the eyelashes side by side on the tissue.

> **DON'T FORGET**
>
> *To clean strip lashes, place them in soapy water for a few minutes and then rinse them in warm water.*

> **DON'T FORGET**
>
> *Ensure you don't attach lashes that are too long as it may give an unnatural look.*

The lashes can now be rolled around the pencil with the facial tissue and be secured with an elastic band. This will help them to keep their shape. When the eyelashes are recurled they can be placed back into their box.

Individual flare lashes

These types of lashes help to make the eyelashes look longer and thicker. The client can choose to have only a few applied, or may require lots for a dramatic effect. Flare lashes last longer than strip lashes, but may be lost as individual natural eyelashes fall out.

Good practice

Avoid applying glitter-type artificial lashes, as the glitter can enter the client's eyes and cause irritation.

DON'T FORGET

Use surgical spirit on a cotton wool pad to clean any adhesive from the ends of the tweezers.

DON'T FORGET

An older client will probably require artificial lashes that are lighter coloured and medium length. Dark, long lashes may look too harsh for an older face.

Step-by-step guide

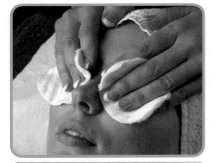

1 Cleanse the eyes with an oil-free product. If required, trim the artificial lashes. Make the ones you apply towards the outer corner of the eye a little longer, to give a natural look.

2 Using tweezers, dip the root into the adhesive and place the lashes as close as possible to the base of the client's eyelashes (you may find it easier to stand behind the client).

3 Use a stroking movement to apply the root of the artificial lash to the client's eyelash.

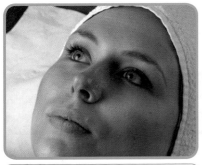

4 Ask the client to open their eyes so you can check the lashes are correctly positioned.

5 After the adhesive has dried, use a mascara comb to comb through the natural and artificial lashes.

6 If required, use eyeliner to fill the visible gaps between the natural lashline and the artificial lashes.

DON'T FORGET

Lashes applied to the lower eyelid are usually shorter than those chosen for the upper lid.

DON'T FORGET

Placing just a few individual lashes at the outer corners of the eyes can help to lengthen them.

DON'T FORGET

There are mascaras that are made to be worn with individual flare lashes and can be easily removed.

DON'T FORGET

Lower individual flare lashes will remain on the client for around a week.

DON'T FORGET

Eyelashes naturally fall out, so individual flare lashes may be lost as a result. Make sure your client is aware of this.

A client can be recommended to return weekly to have individual flare lashes replaced if necessary.

How to remove individual flare lashes

1. Cleanse the eye area.
2. Place an eyeshield under the lower lashes and ask the client to close their eyes.
3. Use a solvent applied to a cotton bud and roll it across the base of the lashes until the adhesive dissolves.
4. Gently attempt to pull away the eyelashes (ensure the upper eyelid is supported) and place them on a facial tissue. If they do not remove easily, apply more solvent.
5. Gently wipe the eyes with damp cotton wool pads to soothe them.

Aftercare advice

The following advice will help to ensure the client's artificial lashes stay on for as long as possible and look their best.

- Use oil-free eye make-up remover, because oil will cause the artificial lashes to separate from the natural lashes.
- The client may apply make-up over the artificial lashes.
- Try not to touch or fiddle with the lashes, as this could lead to them falling off.
- Do not shower or go swimming directly after having the treatment – it is advised to wait several hours.
- Do not use a sauna as the hot temperature could cause the hairs to loosen and may make the lashes become frizzy.

Eye shapes and artificial lash application

The following diagrams show how artificial lashes can be used to enhance various different eye shapes and give them a more proportioned look.

UNIT OUTCOME 12

Understand the contra-indications and contra-actions that affect or restrict eyebrow and eyelash treatments

Contra-actions

Eyebrow shape treatment

Erythema will probably occur after an eyebrow shape treatment because of stimulation of the blood supply in this area; however, the redness usually goes away fairly quickly. If there is swelling too, a cool compress and a soothing lotion or cream may be applied. Record any contra-actions and any action taken on the client's record card/consultation form.

Eyebrows that have been plucked for many years may not grow back, especially if the client is older. You can recommend using an eyebrow powder or pencil, or even semi-permanent make-up. Other treatments include applying false individual eyebrow hairs, and even hair transplants!

Eyebrow tint treatment

Erythema may occur after the eyebrow tint treatment. This may be the result of rubbing to the area. The redness usually goes away fairly quickly. If there is swelling too, a cool compress and a soothing lotion or cream may be applied. Record any contra-actions and any action taken on the client's record card/consultation form.

Eyelash tint treatment

Occasionally, a little bit of tint may enter the eye; perhaps you applied too much tint or the client's eyes were blinking a lot during treatment. This will cause discomfort. If this should happen, quickly remove the tint with damp cotton wool pads. The eyes can then be flushed with clean water and cool pads can be placed on the eyes to help soothe them. Another treatment can be given if the eyes do not feel sensitive and the client agrees to it. Record any contra-actions and any action taken on the client's record card/consultation form.

DON'T FORGET

Did you know you can purchase eyebrow wigs that come with glue? The range is made out of human hair and includes soft angled eyebrow wigs, round eyebrow wigs, and men's eyebrow wigs.

Good practice

Using dye products other than those intended for eyelash tinting can cause serious problems, and may even lead to blindness.

Artificial lashes

Eyes may begin to water during treatment if the lashes irritate the eyes. Tears may cause the adhesive to form white crystals, which will spoil the final look of the lashes. Wipe away any tears using tissues.

Use a solvent to remove any lashes that cause irritation during or after treatment.

UNIT OUTCOME 6

Understand organisational and legal requirements

For information about health and safety regulations relating to beauty treatments, see **Unit G20: Ensure responsibility for actions to reduce risks to health and safety.**

Pre-16 restrictions

A beauty therapy student who is under the age of 16 (pre-16) is not allowed to use any of the following equipment or products.

- Eyelash curlers
- Automatic tweezers
- Eyelash tint
- Perm lotion
- Individual lash adhesive (glue)

How are you doing?

1 Which of the following is **not** a contra-indication to eye treatments?

a Paronychia

b Inflammation

c Eye infection

d Bruising

2 What is the usual service time for an eyebrow shape treatment?

a 5 minutes

b 15 minutes

c 30 minutes

d 45 minutes

3 What are the two types of tweezers commonly used to carry out an eyebrow shaping treatment?

a Electronic and manual

b Autonomic and handheld

c Manual and automatic

d Automated and spring-action

4 Where should sterilised tweezers be stored when not in use?

a In a drawer

b On a window ledge

c In a plastic bag

d In a UV cabinet

5 Which of the following are you **not** recommended to do during an eyebrow shape?

a Gently stretch the skin

b Remove hairs from their base

c Pull out two hairs at a time to the make the treatment quicker

d Pluck out the hairs in the direction of the hair growth

6 What should the therapist do if the client has very long eyebrow hairs?

a Trim them with small scissors

b Pluck them all out

c Apply petroleum jelly to flatten them

d Brush them flat

7 Which of the following is needed for an eyelash tinting treatment?

a Tweezers

b Glue

c Individual flare lashes

d Eyeshields

8 What is the purpose of a skin sensitivity test?

a To see which tint colour best suits the client

b To find out if a client may be allergic to products used during treatment

c To make sure the tint will be effective at colouring the hairs

d To ensure erythema will not occur after treatment

9 What could happen as a result of not carrying out a skin sensitivity test?

a Your salon could be sued

b You could cause unnecessary discomfort to a client

c It could affect the reputation of your salon

d All of the above

10 Which of the following is **not** aftercare advice for artificial lashes?

a Use an oily eye make-up remover to remove eye make-up

b Do not fiddle with the artificial lashes

c Mascara may be applied to the artificial lashes

d Do not use a sauna

are you ready *for* assessment?

The evidence for this unit must be gathered in the workplace (salon) or realistic working environment (training centre).

Simulation (role play) is not allowed for any performance evidence within this unit.

You must practically demonstrate in your everyday work that you have met the required standard for this unit.

All outcomes, assessment criteria and range statements must be achieved.

Knowledge and understanding in this unit will be assessed by a mandatory (compulsory) written question paper. These questions are set and marked by VTCT.

Assessing your practical work

Your assessor will observe your performance of a practical task, such as an eyelash tint.

Your assessor will sign off an outcome when all criteria have been competently achieved.

On occasions, some assessment criteria may not naturally occur during a practical observation. In such instances you will be asked questions to demonstrate your knowledge in this area. Your assessor will document the criteria that have been achieved through oral questioning.

In this unit you must demonstrate competent performance of all practical outcomes on at least **three** occasions, involving **three** different clients. The assessor will want to see you applying a partial set of artificial lashes and tinting eyebrows and eyelashes.

Testing your knowledge and understanding

You will be guided by your tutor and assessor on the evidence that needs to be produced.

Your knowledge and understanding will be assessed using the assessment tools listed below.

- Mandatory written question paper
- Oral questioning
- Portfolio of evidence

Provide make-up and instruct clients in the use of skin care products and make-up

B8 & B9

UNIT OUTCOMES B8

On completion of this unit you will:

1. Be able to use safe and effective working methods when providing make-up services

2. Be able to consult, plan and prepare for make-up

3. Be able to apply make-up products

4. Know the organisational and legal requirements related to make-up application

5. Know how to work safely and effectively when providing make-up services

6. Know how to use client consultation, treatment planning and preparation for make-up services

7. Know anatomy and physiology related to make-up

8. Know the contra-indications and contra-actions of make-up

9. Know how to apply make-up

10. Know how to provide aftercare advice for clients following make-up services

Keep up-to-date with make-up trends

UNIT OUTCOMES B9

On completion of this unit you will:

1. Be able to use safe and effective working methods when providing skin care and make-up instruction

2. Be able to prepare and plan for skin care and make-up instruction

3. Be able to deliver skin care and make-up instruction

4. Be able to evaluate the success of skin care and make-up instruction

5. Know the organisational and legal requirements of skin care and make-up instruction

6. Know how to work safely and effectively when providing skin care and make-up instruction

7. Know how to use client consultation, treatment planning and preparation for skin care and make-up instruction

8. Know about the use of skills for instructing on skin care and make-up

9. Know how to plan and prepare for skin care and make-up instruction

10. Know how to evaluate skin care and make-up instruction activities

Introduction

Make-up has been used for thousands of years. The ancient Egyptians used make-up as a way of beautifying themselves, and it was an important part of their culture. They used natural ingredients such as kohl (a black powder) and soot for eye make-up. Ancient records show that they also used substances made from berries, tree bark, leaves, herbs, minerals and insects. Nowadays, many other materials are used to produce make-up, and there has never been so much choice and such a variety of colour, shade and texture.

Make-up trends, like fashions in clothing, undergo constant change, so it is important for a beauty therapist to regularly read trade magazines and attend beauty shows to keep up to date with these trends.

The application of make-up helps to make the face look more attractive, by accentuating good features and helping to disguise less attractive features. Well-applied make-up can help a person feel a lot more confident about the way they look.

Make-up accentuates good features

Consultation

Before providing a make-up service, you will need to carry out a consultation. This will help you to find out what your client's expectations of the service are, and if they have any contra-indications to treatment.

The following questions will help you to fully understand your client's needs and so provide an excellent make-up treatment.

- Do you have a skin care routine?

- Do you often wear make-up?

- What products do you use?

- What are your colour preferences?

- Would you like a natural-looking make-up?

- How long do you usually take to apply make-up?

- Are you happy for me to work around the eyes?

- Are there features of your face that you particularly like or dislike?

- Has your skin ever been sensitive to any cosmetics?

- If the make-up is for a special occasion, what colour clothing and accessories will you be wearing?

- What are your expectations regarding this treatment?

- Do you have any questions regarding this treatment?

The consultation will also allow you to do a visual assessment of your client's face.

Record all of this information on the client's record card/consultation form, and devise a suitable treatment plan, including the products and application methods that you recommend for the client. At the end of the treatment this information will help you to sell retail products to the client.

DON'T FORGET

The term 'cosmetics' or 'cosmetology' derives from the Greek word kosmeetin, *which means to decorate.*

A thorough consultation will allow you to choose the correct products for your client

UNIT OUTCOME 2

Be able to consult, plan and prepare for make-up

UNIT OUTCOME 6

Know how to use client consultation, treatment planning and preparation for make-up services

UNIT OUTCOME 8

Know the contra-indications and contra-actions of make-up

Evening make-up

key terms

Contouring: using shaders, highlighters and blushers to help disguise the less attractive features of the face, and accentuate the more attractive features.

Good practice

Don't forget to ensure that your client signs and dates the record card/consultation form.

Good practice

If the client is under the age of 16, you will need to get permission from their parent/guardian in order to carry out the make-up treatment. The parent/guardian will also need to be present while the treatment is being carried out and sign the record card/consultation form.

For more information on the consultation process, see **Unit G20: Ensure responsibility for actions to reduce risks to health and safety.**

Service times

The table below gives some examples of different types of make-up service a client may require, along with recommended service times.

Type of make-up service	What is it?	Time to book out on appointment page
Day make-up	A natural-looking make-up, ideal for normal daytime wear.	45 minutes
Evening make-up	The client may have an evening function to attend, such as a party. Evening make-up tends to be heavier than daytime make-up.	45 minutes to an hour
Special occasion make-up	The client may be attending a special occasion, such as a wedding.	45 minutes to an hour
Bridal make-up	Wedding make-up for a bride. Ensure the client is booked in for a trial make-up before the wedding day, so you can be sure that you have chosen the correct products and application. This will help to ensure she is happy with the final result.	One hour for the trial make-up One hour for the wedding day
Make-up lesson	The client is taught how to choose suitable products and apply make-up.	One hour and 15 minutes
Remedial make-up	The client is taught how to use camouflage creams to cover up blemishes, such as birthmarks, or **contouring** techniques using highlighters and shaders.	Depends on the client's needs

Contra-indications

A make-up treatment should not be carried out if the client has any of the following:

- Eye infections or disorders
- Cuts or abrasions
- Any painful areas
- Any infectious conditions such as a cold sore
- Any area that is weeping or bleeding
- Swelling and inflammation
- Recent scar tissue
- Recent **haemorrhage**
- Any allergies to cosmetics

Without causing alarm to the client, suggest they seek medical advice regarding a contra-indication, or return for treatment when the contra-indication is no longer present.

Good practice

Never tell a client they may have a nasty skin disease! It's best to refer them to a doctor for diagnosis.

Skin sensitivity test

Some ingredients, such as perfumes, lanolin and parabens, which are found in cosmetics, may cause allergic reactions in some people, though this is rare. If your client thinks there is a good chance her skin will react to a product, you can carry out a sensitivity test.

Place a small amount of the product behind the client's ear or on the inside of the arm. Unwanted reactions often occur quite quickly, but you should wait 24 hours to see if anything happens before using the product. Selecting **hypoallergenic** products for a client with sensitive skin should help to reduce the chances of any reaction occurring.

DON'T FORGET

Most contra-indications will only restrict treatment, so make-up can still be applied to the unaffected skin.

DON'T FORGET

Some people are allergic to parabens. These are chemicals that have antiseptic properties and are used as a preservative in facial cosmetics. They keep products free from bacteria, moulds and fungi that would spoil the product and could be harmful.

key terms

Haemorrhage: an excessive loss of blood.

Hypoallergenic: unlikely to cause an allergic reaction.

DON'T FORGET

Lanolin is commonly added to cosmetics as an emollient (skin softener) but some people are allergic to it.

Preparation for a make-up treatment

Setting up the treatment room

Adequate and flattering lighting is crucial during the consultation and while applying make-up. Make sure the client's face is evenly lit, without dark shadows. If you are applying a daytime make-up, try to work close to a window with daylight coming through it, as this will help to ensure a natural look. If natural daylight is not possible, warm, white fluorescent light will make a good alternative.

Treatment room for make-up treatment

Good practice

Disposable make-up applicators are an excellent way to prevent cross-infection, as they can be thrown away after use.

If you are fully prepared before the arrival of a client, this will help the treatment run more smoothly. Make sure that all the make-up equipment and products that you need are close to hand and laid out neatly. Also ensure that everything is clean. This will help prevent cross-infection, which can occur as a result of contaminated products and dirty equipment.

Equipment, materials and products

The following equipment, materials and products are required during a make-up treatment.

- Treatment couch – this should be disinfected and covered with either towels or a blanket. Clean couch roll should be placed on top, and place a towel at the head end for the client's head to rest on

- Stool – should ideally be height adjustable and have a backrest

- Trolley – should be disinfected and lined with couch roll
- Make-up brushes – to apply make-up such as eyeshadow and blusher to the face
- Make-up palette – cosmetics are transferred to the palette from their container for hygiene reasons
- Sponges – to apply make-up, such as foundation, to the face
- Disposable applicators – to apply make-up such as eyeshadow. These can be thrown away after use
- Eyebrow brush – to brush eyebrow hairs to give a nice shape
- Eyelash curlers – these help to make the lashes appear longer
- Eyelash separator – to separate eyelashes after applying mascara
- Cleanser/toner/moisturiser – to prepare the skin before make-up application
- Concealer – to help conceal blemishes, for example, dark circles around the eyes
- Foundation – to help give an even colour to the whole face
- Face powder – to set foundation and absorb oil
- Blusher – to help emphasise the cheekbones and add colour to the face
- Bronzer – to give a healthy, tanned look to the face
- Shader – to help draw attention away from an area
- Highlighter – to help draw attention towards an area
- Eyeshadow – to bring out the eye colour
- Eyeliner – to accentuate the eyes
- Eyebrow pencil – to make the eyebrows more defined, especially if the hairs are fair
- Mascara – to make the eyelashes look longer and thicker
- Lipstick/lip gloss – to draw attention to the lips
- Lip pencil – outlines the shape of the lips and can make them appear fuller
- Headband – to protect the client's hair
- Gown – to protect the client's clothing
- Mirror – so that the client can see the completed make-up treatment

Make-up products and equipment

- Pencil sharpener – to sharpen make-up pencils
- Spatulas – to remove products from pots
- Orange sticks – orange sticks may be tipped with cotton wool and used to remove excess make-up from around the eyes
- Cotton buds – to remove eye make-up, apply concealer and smudge eyeliner
- Cotton wool pads – to remove make-up or other products from the skin
- Tissues – many uses
- Record card/consultation form and make-up chart – to record information such as the products and make-up chosen.

Brushes

It is important to have the right tools to achieve a professional make-up. Good quality brushes can last for years and may prove to be your best investment, so always ask to try them out before you buy. The best brushes are soft to the touch and do not shed hairs when you use them. Professional brushes are made of natural animal hair. Natural fibres, such as sable hairs, are usually preferable to synthetic (man-made) fibres, as they can be put through a **sanitisation** process more easily. Brushes made from synthetic fibres can damage make-up products in compacted powder form, and they quickly lose their shape as the fibres become splayed.

Good make-up brushes are shaped according to the part of the face they are used on, and there are many different types. The table describes some of the different brushes that are available.

> **Good practice**
>
> Small, dome-shaped brushes are used for applying eyeshadows. Remember to use a separate brush for each of the eyeshadows used.

Brush hygiene

To prevent cross-contamination, ensure the brushes are cleaned well after each use. If the brushes are not kept clean, harmful microorganisms, such as bacteria, can live in the bristles and cause infections and skin rashes. Brushes should first be cleaned in hot, soapy water – make sure the fibres are splayed to ensure thorough cleaning – then placed into a brush cleaner, which contains mild alcohols and will dissolve grease and any residue of cosmetics on the bristles. Brush cleaner will clean, disinfect and help condition the brush fibres. Follow the manufacturer's

DON'T FORGET

Make-up brushes are sometimes made from the hair of animals such as camels, ponies and squirrels!

key terms

Sanitisation: a method that helps to kill germs and make an environment more hygienic.

Selection of brushes

Type of brush	Description and use
Small contour brush	This brush has a soft, rounded dome tip that is used to apply, blend or contour powder products.
Blusher brush	This brush is used for shading and highlighting the cheeks and face with blusher. The fibres are soft and form a full, rounded shape. Make sure you select a brush in which the fibres are not all cut to the same length but graduate gently, with shorter fibres on the outsides and longer fibres at the middle. This will ensure an even delivery of blusher across the cheek, and help you avoid giving a blotchy look.
Powder brush	A brush that has a fluffed, rounded tip. It is designed for application of powder to the face or body.
Tapered face brush	A domed brush that has a slightly pointed tip with round chiselled sides. It is ideal for contouring and shaping. The chiselled side is for contour shaping of facial planes; the pointed tip is for applying and blending powder blush, highlighter or face powder.
Large angled contour brush	The shape of this brush is ideal for the application of powder to contour the cheeks.
Foundation brush	This brush is designed to create an even finish when applying foundation, and can be used to apply, distribute, and blend foundation into all areas of the face.
Square foundation brush	A large, flat, square-shaped brush with a fine, firm edge. For spreading and blending of liquid, emulsion or cream foundation products on the face or body.
Concealer brush	A firm, flat, slightly tapered brush. It is specially designed for covering small areas and for precise application. It is ideal for blending over dark shadows under the eyes and for covering spots.
Angled brow brush	The angled shape of this brush makes it ideal for applying colour to the brow. It can be used to apply powder, liquid or cream products.
Eyeliner brush	The extra-fine tip of this brush helps to provide a firm, even stroke when applying eyeliner to the eyes.
Fluff brush	The thick bundles of fibres are arranged in a rounded shape, which makes it ideal for applying eyeshadow to the lid area.
Short shader brush	This brush is a short, rounded, double-chiselled brush that can be used with shadow to line and smudge around the lashline, and is very effective for densely shading the lids.
Pencil brush	The soft, smooth fibres of this brush are gathered into a pencil-shaped top, which makes it useful for shading onto the lid, in the eye crease or along the lashline.
Eye shader brush	The tapered, rounded edge has smooth, firm, fine fibres, making it ideal for building intense colour on the eyelid.
Small angled brush	This brush is flat shaped with an angled tip and helps to spread colour over the lid and into the corners. It is useful for lining, shading or shaping the eye or eyebrow.
Angled shading brush	This brush is ideal for applying and blending eye shadow, owing to its soft, smooth fibres and angled design.
Flat eyeshadow brush	The fibre tips of this brush end in a straight line, which make it is useful for blending away hard edges of eyeshadow colour. This brush should not be dipped into the eyeshadow – its job is just to blend. Patchy areas can result if this brush is used to apply eyeshadow.
Lip brush	A lip brush has small, flat, firm fibres and a tapered tip, making it useful for applying lipstick. Brushes made of sable hair are generally best.

instructions on how to use the brush cleaner. Brushes can be left to dry naturally in a clean environment. Once dry, the brushes should be stored away so they are safe and remain free from dust – ideally inside an ultraviolet (UV) cabinet.

Sponges

Make-up sponges, which are commonly made from latex, will be part of your make-up toolkit. Latex sponges can be used to apply cream or powder foundations, and to blend concealer. They can also be used to blend other make-up products and are available in various shapes and sizes. The wedge shape is ideal for blending close to the eyes, as well as into the creases at the side of the nose. Depending on your preference, they can be used dry or wet.

Natural sea sponges can also be used to apply foundation. If they are used damp they do not absorb the foundation as much as a latex sponge would, so less is wasted. After wetting the sponge, squeeze out any water, then place the sponge inside a tissue and squeeze it again – it is now ready to use.

Sponge hygiene

After use, sponges need to be cleaned in hot, soapy water, and then soaked for about an hour in disinfectant. They can then be rinsed in water and left to dry. Placing them into a UV cabinet, and exposing each side for 20 minutes, will ensure they are thoroughly sanitised. When the sponges begin to crumble it is time to throw them away.

Palettes

Palettes are usually made from plastic, and are used to hold make-up products while carrying out a make-up treatment. Applying make-up directly from the container would be unhygienic and could cause cross-infection.

After use, wash the palette in soapy water and then dry it thoroughly. It can then be stored inside a UV cabinet.

> **DON'T FORGET**
>
> *Stipple sponges are used to create textured effects; they can be fine or coarse.*

Different types of sponges

> **DON'T FORGET**
>
> *There are large make-up cases with wheels available, which are ideal to use if you intend to carry out a mobile make-up service.*

Good practice

Always use a clean spatula to remove products from their containers during a make-up treatment.

Preparing the client

When you have discussed your treatment plan with your client, and are clear about her expectations, you are then ready to cleanse, tone and moisturise the skin.

Carry out a visual assessment of your client's face. Observe her face shape, features and colouring and consider the following questions.

- Are there big features that need to be made to look smaller, or vice versa?

- Does the client have attractive features such as high, prominent cheek bones?

- What colours would complement the client's features, such as her blue eyes?

- Which areas need contouring (shading and highlighting)?

See **Unit B4: Provide facial skin care treatment**, for further information about cleansing, toning and moisturising.

Facial primers

A facial primer is a product, often in a gel-like formula, which is applied after the moisturiser but before the foundation. It creates a smooth base for foundation and also helps make-up to stay on for a longer time. It can help improve the skin's appearance by minimising open pores and reducing the appearance of fine lines.

Primers are especially useful for combination to oily skin types, as they absorb oil and control excess shine, but are also beneficial for dry skin types because of their moisturising effects.

DON'T FORGET

The skin should be cleansed, toned and moisturised before the application of make-up.

DON'T FORGET

Use a facial tissue to blot off any excess moisturiser.

DON'T FORGET

To remove stubborn eyeliner from your client's eyes, dip a cotton bud in eye make-up remover, and gently stroke and roll it from the outer corner of the eye, along the lashline, towards the nose.

UNIT OUTCOME 1

Be able to use safe and effective working methods when providing make-up services

UNIT OUTCOME 3

Be able to apply make-up products

UNIT OUTCOME 5

Know how to work safely and effectively when providing make-up services

UNIT OUTCOME 9

Know how to apply make-up

Make-up application

Order of make-up application

1 Apply concealer.

2 Apply foundation.

3 Use cream/liquid products to contour the face.

4 Apply face powder.

5 Use powder products to contour the face.

6 Apply blusher/bronzing products.

7 Apply eyeshadow.

8 Apply eyeliner.

9 Apply mascara.

10 Apply eyebrow pencil.

11 Apply lip liner.

12 Apply lipstick.

13 Apply powder to set lipstick.

This is only a suggested order; some make-up artists prefer to apply blusher towards the end of the treatment.

Concealer

Concealers are mostly used to hide flaws on the skin – in other words, to conceal. They can provide coverage for spots, age spots, broken capillaries and dark circles under the eyes.

Ideally, the concealer should be one or two shades lighter in colour than the foundation and the client's natural skin tone. If the right concealer is used, the result should be a flawless and natural look.

DON'T FORGET

If required, concealers can be mixed together to get the correct colour.

DON'T FORGET

Asian people often require concealer underneath the eyes, as their skin tends to be darker in this area.

Concealer

DON'T FORGET

Spots can be concealed using a wax-based, skin-coloured concealer on a cotton bud to cover the redness (fingers will spread the product too much).

Good practice

The skin around the eyes is delicate, so use concealers that are light in texture and so are easily applied.

Good practice

Spots should never be picked immediately before applying make-up, as any weeping or bleeding will spread bacteria across the skin and may contaminate the therapist's hands and tools.

There are various types of concealer, which each have different uses.

Cream concealer

Cream concealer is the type most commonly used by make-up artists, because it covers well and is easy to blend. It is ideal for covering all blemishes, including spots, **birthmarks**, pigmentation and dark circles under the eyes.

Liquid concealer

Liquid concealer is useful for older skin types, as cream or stick concealers tend to clog into lines and wrinkles and draw attention to them. Also, liquid concealer blends softly and easily, so the skin is not pulled as it is applied. This also makes it ideal for use around the delicate eye area. However, because of its thin consistency, this type of concealer isn't good for completely covering blemishes.

Stick concealer

Stick concealers are useful for covering small blemishes, such as spots. However, it is difficult to blend this type of concealer without pulling the skin, so it shouldn't be used close to the eyes.

Medicated stick concealer

As the name implies, these concealers contain antiseptics and drying substances. They are good for covering spots, as they can help to heal them at the same time.

Colour corrective concealer

These are useful for helping to even out skin tone on the face. Different coloured concealers are used for different purposes.

- Green is used to hide redness on the face.

- Lilac helps to brighten a sallow (yellowy) skin colour.

- A peach colour is helpful for concealing blue veins and pigmentation.

- Yellow helps to hide the appearance of dark circles under the eyes.

Notice how the green and red, orange and blue, and yellow and mauve colours are opposite each other on the colour wheel.

How to apply concealer

1 Transfer a small amount of concealer to a make-up palette.

2 Use a cotton bud or concealer brush to apply the concealer to the skin, then dab it with a dry sponge to blend it in.

3 The concealer can be sealed with powder, to help set it and blend it into the foundation.

> **key terms**
>
> **Birthmarks:** birthmarks may be flat or raised and can have different shades of colouring, commonly brown to red. The two main types of birthmarks are: red, vascular birthmarks, such as port-wine stains and strawberry naevus; and pigmented birthmarks, such as moles and dark brown pigmented areas.

DON'T FORGET

Colour corrective foundations are also available, including green tone foundation, for skin that is prone to redness. These can be worn underneath a normal foundation to help improve the skin tone.

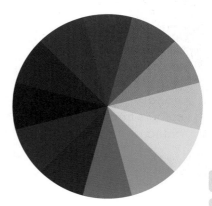

Colour wheel

Even if your client does not have any blemishes or other imperfections, applying concealer underneath the eyes will give them a brighter and more vibrant look.

Foundation

Foundation helps to create an even skin tone, and smoothes the skin texture to give a flawless finish. It also provides a base for other make-up products, which helps them to blend well and to last longer on the face. Foundations can also help to protect the skin by providing a barrier against the damaging effects of sunlight.

Foundation is useful for the following reasons.

- It creates an even skin tone.
- It creates a smooth finish.
- It covers up minor blemishes.
- It helps to minimise the look of fine lines and wrinkles.
- It brightens the skin.
- It provides a base for other make-up products.
- It helps to protect the skin.

There are many different types of foundation available, including liquid, cream, oil-free, powder, cake, stick, stay-on, hypoallergenic, cream to powder, **non-comedogenic** and camouflage foundations. Foundations will either contain a lot of water, so are called water-based, or a lot of oil, so are called oil-based. Pigments are added to provide colour, and there are a range of colours available to suit different skin tones.

The main types of foundation include:

- liquid
- cream
- cake and pancake
- gel
- medicated
- mousse
- mineral.

DON'T FORGET

Some foundations contain anti-ageing ingredients, such as vitamins A, C and E, which help to destroy free radicals. Free radicals play an important part in skin ageing, including the formation of lines and wrinkles.

key terms

Non-comedogenic: does not cause blocked pores or blackheads.

DON'T FORGET

Foundation colours can be mixed to form the correct shade for your client's skin colour. However, ensure you mix colours from the same brand.

Liquid foundation

Liquid foundations are good for all skin types. They are available in water-based and oil-based formulas, but generally contain a higher quantity of water. Oil-based formulas are ideal for dry, mature skin types and water-based formulas are useful for normal to oily skin types. Both oil-based and water-based formulas can be used on combination skins.

They usually offer light to medium coverage and have the most natural look. They are easy to apply – though oil-based liquids spread easier than water-based ones – and don't feel as heavy as some foundations. They also come in the widest range of colours.

Cream foundation

Cream foundations are traditionally the main choice of make-up artists, as they can provide a creamy flawless finish and are easy to apply. They are usually available in compacts or sticks, provide very good coverage and blend easily on the skin.

They contain wax, powder and a humectant (a product that helps to trap water in the skin, such as **glycerol**).

They are oil-based, so are useful for drier complexions, but because they are heavier, they may emphasise fine lines around the eyes.

Cake/stick foundation

These are solid in form and may contain an oil, wax or powder base. They give a **matt** coverage and are best suited for an oily skin. Because of their heavy texture they can also be used as concealers, and are useful for covering blemishes and scars. They are a popular choice for photographic work.

Pancake foundation

Pancake make-up is a thick, full-coverage foundation used to cover skin problems such as skin discolouration, scars and tattoos. It also helps to give the skin a flawless finish in film, television and photographic work.

Gel foundation

Gel foundations give a sheer, oil-free coverage and a matt finish. They are particularly useful for black skin types and tanned skin.

Medicated foundation

These foundations contain ingredients such as salicylic acid to help prevent and treat spots. This makes them useful for oily, blemished, acne-prone skin.

DON'T FORGET

Liquid foundations are made up of water, oil, powder, humectants, pigments and additives.

Liquid foundation

Cream foundation

key terms

Glycerol: a colourless, odourless liquid that comes from fats and oils.

Matt: doesn't reflect light, so isn't shiny.

Mousse foundation

Mousse foundation is a liquid make-up with air whipped into it, making it light and smooth.

It is good for all skin types, but is particularly useful for older skin because it doesn't collect in fine lines and wrinkles and, because it is easy to apply, there is no pulling of the skin.

Mineral foundation

Mineral foundations contain pure crushed minerals and have been used for cosmetic purposes for thousands of years.

These foundations suit all skin types, but are particularly useful for sensitive skin and for covering pimples and acne. This is because they contain zinc oxides, which have anti-inflammatory properties.

Mineral foundation usually comes in the form of a loose powder, which can be applied dry or wet. It can be messy to use, but it is safe for use on sensitive skin, won't clog pores and provides some sun protection.

Choosing the foundation colour

Always try to choose a foundation that matches your client's skin colour exactly. Skin is usually described as being light, medium or dark, but there are many different shades within these categories.

You may need to mix a couple of different foundations to get the correct colour, but it is worth taking the time to get it right. When you are happy with the colour, apply it to the client's jawline. If the foundation blends into the skin, so that you cannot see it, then you know you have the right colour.

When you apply the foundation over the face, it must be fully blended into the skin; if there is even one small area that is not blended, it will be noticeable in the sunlight. Pay particular attention to the jawline, as this is where lines tend to appear.

How to apply foundation

1 Transfer some foundation onto a clean make-up palette.
2 Use a foundation brush or cosmetic sponge to apply the foundation to the skin.
3 Apply foundation using a stroking movement to one area at a time.
4 Blend the foundation carefully into the hair line and across the jawline.
5 Use a small soft brush or the angular edge of a cosmetic sponge to work around the eyes.
6 Apply foundation to the whole face, including the eyelids and lips, but avoid the neck as the foundation may stain the client's clothes at the neck line.

DON'T FORGET

Mineral foundation often contains titanium dioxide, an ingredient used in cosmetics for its sun protection factor (SPF).

DON'T FORGET

If you use a product containing titanium dioxide on a black skin, it may give the skin a chalky appearance.

DON'T FORGET

Mineral make-up can be applied directly after giving a facial treatment, as its formulation allows the skin to function normally without clogging pores.

DON'T FORGET

Therapists can purchase spray foundation that is contained in an aerosol and can be sprayed on a sponge or directly on the skin.

Face powder

Face powder can be loose or pressed. It is applied on top of foundation and helps it to set and last longer.

Face powder will help to:

- ensure the foundation stays in place
- set the make-up to help it last longer
- reduce shiny areas on the face
- give an even, matt finish, to make the face look fresh
- make the pores look smaller and so improve skin texture
- remove any stickiness created by the foundation or concealer.

Face powder contains various ingredients, including:

- talc – to help it spread smoothly onto the skin
- chalk or kaolin – to help absorb moisture from sweat and sebum
- magnesium stearate – to help it adhere to the foundation
- zinc oxide and titanium oxide – to help ensure the skin is thoroughly covered
- pigments – to give colour.

Some types of face powder contain extra ingredients for added benefits, such as SPF ingredients to help protect the skin from the sunlight.

Loose powder

Loose powder is a fine, translucent powder that spreads easily and gives a natural, fresh look to the face. It also helps to conceal blemishes on the skin. It is extremely light, and if too much is applied the excess can easily be removed with a soft brush. Translucent powder should not add colour to the skin, but should blend with the client's skin tone.

For dry skin, light-reflecting, moisture-infused loose powder is preferable, as the moisture in the powder will help to moisturise the skin. For oily and combination skin, talc-based loose powder is preferable, as the talc will help to absorb oil.

How to apply loose powder

1 Place some powder onto a make-up palette or into a bowl.

2 Use a powder brush, cosmetic sponge or cotton wool to apply the powder to the face. Work in a downwards movement, ensuring you cover all of the face, and then blend.

3 Remove any excess powder with a powder brush.

DON'T FORGET

Light-diffusing foundations are ideal for mature skin, as they contain hundreds of tiny light-reflective particles that bounce light away from the skin. This helps to reduce the appearance of fine lines, blemishes and wrinkles.

DON'T FORGET

Pick the shade that is closest to the skin tone and try it on the jawline. If the shade disappears into the skin, it is the right match.

DON'T FORGET

If the cosmetic sponge is dry, there will be a heavier coverage. If the cosmetic sponge is damp, coverage will be light and sheer.

DON'T FORGET

Most people have skin with yellow tones, so become familiar with your yellow-toned foundations.

Face powder

Pressed powder

Pressed powder is made into a block shape and then inserted into a compact. It offers more coverage than loose powder and helps to given an even tone to the skin. It helps to cover blemishes and control oil, so will make an oily face appear less shiny. Pressed powders come in different colours and you should choose one that blends with the client's skin tone. This type of powder is ideal for the client to use at home.

How to apply pressed powder

Pat lightly onto the face with a cosmetic sponge, using gentle downward strokes.

Contouring cosmetics

The following products are commonly used as contouring cosmetics.

- Blushers and bronzers
- Highlighters and shaders

Blusher and bronzer

The main purpose of blusher is to add colour, warmth and depth to the skin. However, it can also be used to enhance the shape of the face by contouring and creating visual illusions. There are different types of blushers, including powders, creams, gels and mineral-based products.

Powder blusher

Powder blushers are the most popular type, because they are the easiest to control and blend, and there is a huge choice available. They are particularly good for use on oily and combination skins.

Powder blusher should be applied over foundation and under face powder, as it will stay on longer if 'sandwiched' between them. However, some make-up artists prefer to apply powder blusher after they have applied face powder.

Mineral-based powder blusher is made from pure earth-based minerals, so does not contain any synthetic (man-made) chemicals such as additives and preservatives. Owing to ingredients such as titanium dioxide, it provides a natural SPF and has anti-inflammatory properties. It is ideal for sensitive and blemish-prone skins.

How to apply powder blusher

1 Transfer some powder blusher onto a make-up palette.

2 Dip a blusher brush into the powder and then tap off the excess.

3 Start at the 'apples' of the cheeks and apply upwards in long strokes to the top of the cheekbone towards the hair line (ask the client to smile to help you find the 'apple' of the cheek).

Good practice

Build up the blusher slowly on the skin. If you apply too much, use some loose face powder to tone it down.

Cream blusher

This type of blusher is good for dry and sun-damaged skin because of its moisturising ingredients, however, it may be too harsh for sensitive skins. A cream or wax base helps to hold the pigment (colour) in place, and silicone is added to make it easier to apply to the skin. It can be applied with a sponge or brush and is easy to blend.

Good practice

Always apply less blusher than you think is necessary. When the client goes out in the daylight, the blusher always appears darker.

Gel blusher

Gel blusher offers the sheerest form of colour because it is transparent. It gives a natural-looking glow and so is perfect for the summer months. Gel should normally be applied over moisturiser, not foundation, which makes it glide on more smoothly. If it is worn over foundation, it should first be mixed with a small amount of foundation to ease blending of the products.

This type of blusher works best on normal to oily skin, as it does not spread easily and is fast drying on the skin.

How to apply cream and gel blushers

1 Transfer some gel/cream blusher onto a make-up palette.

2 Use the fingertips to dab a small amount of cream/gel blusher onto the apples of the cheeks.

3 Blend up towards the hair line.

4 Loose powder can be applied over cream blusher to help set it.

Good practice

Always ensure blusher is blended well to avoid harsh edges.

DON'T FORGET

Talc is the main ingredient in most powders. However, substitutes such as light-reflecting mica are becoming more popular.

Mica is the name given to a group of minerals that are widely used in eyeshadows, face powder, lipstick and nail polish – they help to give these products a pearlised look.

DON'T FORGET

Powder blusher is best for oily and combination skins; gel is good for oily skins; and cream is ideal for dry skins.

DON'T FORGET

Cream blusher will give a dewy look to the face.

Choosing the blusher colour

The table below shows the blusher colours that are recommended for different skin tones.

Blusher colours

Skin tone	Recommended blusher colour
Fair	Fair-skinned women should not have strong colours applied to their cheeks. Instead choose colours with beige, tawny and pink tones. Ideal colours include shimmery peach or light pink.
Pink	Pink skin tones may not need blusher at all, if the cheeks are already pink or if the client tends to blush easily. Peach tones can help to tone down the colour of the cheeks if they are too rosy.
Medium	Medium skin tones suit warm peaches or warm pinks.
Olive/yellow	Olive/yellow skin tones will suit warm brown, peach, almond and copper shades.
Dark olive	Dark olive skin tones look best with shades of terracotta, brown and deep bronze and russet pinks.
Tanned and redheaded	Redheads suit apricot, peach and coral shades. These also look good on anyone with a tan.
Black	Black skin tones need brown shades to enhance the skin colour. Avoid bright pinks, as these look unnatural.

Bronzers

Bronzing products give a suntanned look to the skin, and can have a matt or shimmery effect.

Bronzing powder can be dusted around the hair line, on the nose and chin, and across the cheekbones, to give a healthy, tanned look. Ensure you don't use too much bronzer, or pick too dark a tone, as it could make the client's face look dirty.

To ensure an even coverage of bronzing powder, apply it with a wide, fluffy brush, first working over the cheek areas, then moving on to the nose, chin and neck.

Bronzers also come as liquids, sticks, gels and beads. Experiment with the different types and choose one that you enjoy working with.

Bronzing powder

DON'T FORGET

Powder and liquid bronzer is suitable for all skin types; gel bronzer is good for dry and mature skin types.

Highlighters and shaders

Highlighters and shaders can be used for corrective make-up techniques, to help make the face shape and the features appear more proportioned.

- A highlighter is lighter than the skin colour and will help to highlight certain features of the face. Highlighters can be used to create an illusion of extra width and length to the face. Highlighters may be white, cream or other very light colours.

- A shader is darker than the skin colour and is used to shade areas of the face. This helps to disguise flaws and irregularities and to make facial features look smaller.

Highlighters and shaders are available in powder, liquid and cream forms. Powders can be applied with a large angled contour brush or a small contour brush. Liquids and creams can be applied with a sponge.

Corrective make-up techniques for different face shapes

Face shapes can be categorised as oval, round, square, long/oblong, heart shaped and diamond shaped. The perfect face shape is considered to be an oval, which means that the forehead and the chin area are of equal proportion. Corrective make-up techniques can be used to make other shaped faces appear more oval.

Some people's faces are a combination of two or more shapes, so it is not always easy to assess the shape. When looking at the face, consider the size of the forehead in relation to the chin. Does the forehead or chin make a subtle pointed shape? Is the jawline square in shape? Is the face padded with quite a lot of fat, or does it have prominent cheekbones? All these questions will help you to work out which areas need highlighting and which need shading.

Oval shape

The shape and proportions of the oval face form the basis for modifying all other face shapes. Model Elle Macpherson has an oval-shaped face.

As this face shape is considered ideal, it is only necessary to add blusher to the cheek areas.

DON'T FORGET

Think about where the sunlight hits the face and tans the skin; these are the areas that should be brushed with bronzing powder.

DON'T FORGET

Light colours make features appear larger or more prominent; dark colours make features seem smaller and less noticeable.

DON'T FORGET

It can be very tricky to determine a person's face shape, as many people's faces are a combination of shapes.

When you look at your client's face, try to imagine how you could make it look like a perfect oval shape – think about which areas you need to highlight and shade.

Round shape

A round face has a rounded shape, and is wider in proportion to its length than the oval face. This shape has soft, rounded, non-angular features, and tends not to have prominent cheekbones. Reality TV star Kelly Osbourne has a round face.

The focus of corrective make-up should be to make the face look thinner and longer, which will make it appear more oval shaped. Use shader at the sides of the face to make it appear thinner, and highlighter down the centre of the face to give an illusion of length. To make the cheekbones appear more prominent, apply a neutral shade of brown directly under the cheekbones and a white or cream highlighter on top of the cheekbones to help to 'pull' the cheeks forward.

Square shape

This face shape has a wide forehead and square jawline. Actresses Jennifer Aniston and Demi Moore have square-shaped faces.

Apply shader to the angles of the jawbone and the outer corners of the forehead. This will help to soften the four angular corners of the face. Highlight the chin to help lengthen the face.

Heart shape

This shape has a wide forehead and a narrow, pointed chin. Models Claudia Schiffer and Naomi Campbell have heart-shaped faces.

Apply shader to the tip of the chin, to make it appear less pointed, and also to the sides of the forehead, to reduce its width. Apply highlighter to the jawline to make it appear wider.

Diamond shape

This face shape has a narrow forehead and chin, and has the greatest width across the cheekbones. Supermodel Linda Evangelista and actress Elizabeth Hurley have diamond–shaped faces.

To reduce length, apply shader to the top of the forehead and the tip of the chin. Highlight the sides of the temples and the lower jaw to make them appear wider.

Long/oblong shape

This face shape has greater length in proportion to its width than the oval face. It is basically long and narrow. Actress Sarah Jessica Parker has this face shape.

Long faces need width, so apply highlighter at the angles of the jawbone and at the temples. Apply shader at the hair line and to the tip of the chin to make the face appear shorter.

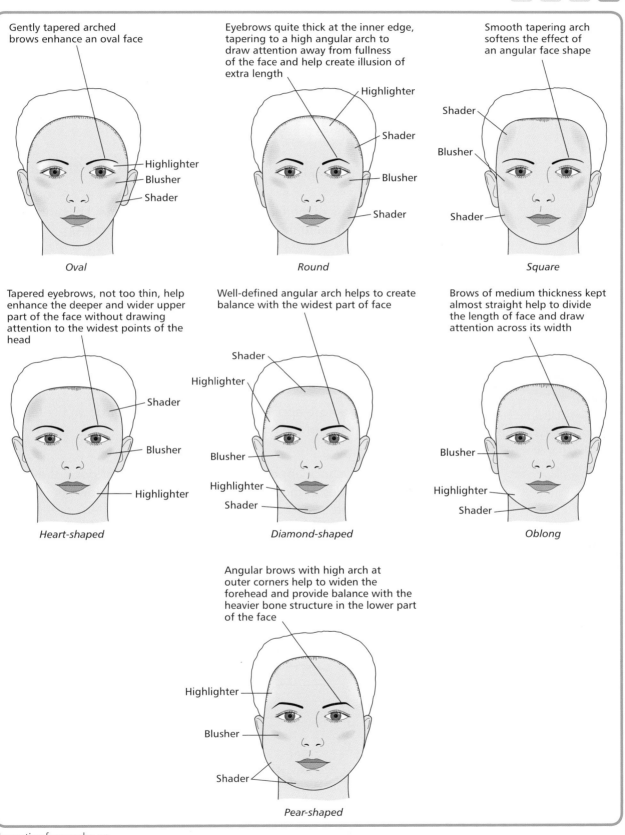

Gently tapered arched brows enhance an oval face

Highlighter
Blusher
Shader

Oval

Eyebrows quite thick at the inner edge, tapering to a high angular arch to draw attention away from fullness of the face and help create illusion of extra length

Highlighter
Shader
Blusher
Shader

Round

Smooth tapering arch softens the effect of an angular face shape

Shader
Blusher
Shader

Square

Tapered eyebrows, not too thin, help enhance the deeper and wider upper part of the face without drawing attention to the widest points of the head

Shader
Blusher
Highlighter

Heart-shaped

Well-defined angular arch helps to create balance with the widest part of face

Shader
Highlighter
Blusher
Highlighter
Shader

Diamond-shaped

Brows of medium thickness kept almost straight help to divide the length of face and draw attention across its width

Blusher
Highlighter
Shader

Oblong

Angular brows with high arch at outer corners help to widen the forehead and provide balance with the heavier bone structure in the lower part of the face

Highlighter
Blusher
Shader

Pear-shaped

Corrective face make-up

Pear shape

The pear-shaped face is wider at the cheeks and jawline and becomes narrower at the forehead. Hollywood actress Bette Midler and British actress Billie Piper have pear-shaped faces.

Apply highlighter to the sides of the forehead to give the illusion of added width. Apply shader to the sides of the jawline and chin to make these areas appear narrower.

Corrective make-up techniques for other areas of the face

Other areas of the face, such as the nose, jawline, chin and neck, may also require the application of corrective make-up.

Nose
Long nose

To make a nose appear shorter, apply a shader just below the nose and over the tip of the nose.

Short nose

To make a nose appear longer, use a highlighter just below the nose and under the tip of the nose.

Thin nose

To make a nose appear wider, use a highlighter down the length of both sides of the nose.

Broad nose

To make a nose appear narrower, apply a shader down the length of both sides of the nose, and use a highlighter down the centre of the nose.

Large or protruding nose

Use a colour that is one or two shades darker than the client's natural skin colour to shade the nose. To make the nose appear thinner and more defined, use the darker shade down the length of both sides of the nose leaving a lighter vertical strip down the centre.

DON'T FORGET

Always blend highlighters and shaders thoroughly to achieve a natural look.

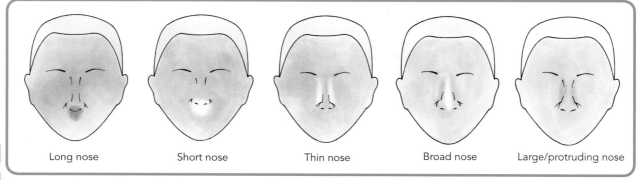

| Long nose | Short nose | Thin nose | Broad nose | Large/protruding nose |

Corrective make-up techniques for the nose

Jawline

Broad jaw
Use a shader at the sides of the jawline to make it appear smaller.

Narrow jaw
Use a highlighter at the sides of the jawline to make it appear wider.

Square jaw
Use shader at the angular edges of the jawline to help minimise this area; apply highlighter in a narrow strip down the centre of the chin, to help draw attention there and away from the angular edges.

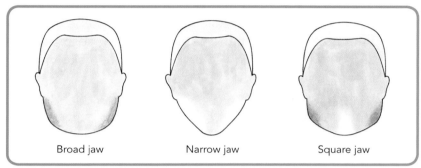

| Broad jaw | Narrow jaw | Square jaw |

Corrective make-up techniques for the jawline

Chin and neck

Prominent chin
Shade over the prominent area of the chin.

Receding chin
Highlight the centre of the chin.

Double chin
Apply shader to the fullest area of the double chin.

Thin neck
Apply highlighter down either side of the neck.

Thick neck
Apply shader down either side of the neck.

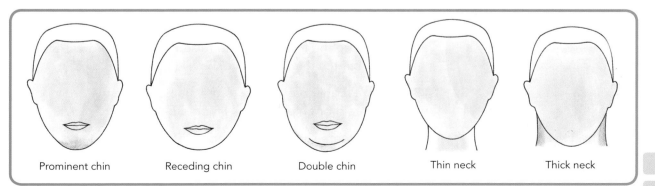

| Prominent chin | Receding chin | Double chin | Thin neck | Thick neck |

Corrective make-up techniques for the chin and neck

Eyeshadow colours

Soft pink is a good shade for fair skin

Deep purple is a good shade for dark skin

Eye make-up

Eyeshadow

Eyeshadow is used around the eyes to draw attention to them and to enhance their natural shape and colour. Eyeshadows come in the form of pressed and loose powders and as creams. They can be matt, frosted, satin, or iridescent (shimmering). There is a vast range of different shades available.

Powder eyeshadow

Powder eyeshadows contain talc mixed with oils to help the product spread easily onto the skin. Other substances, such as nylon powder and a mineral called silica, may also be added, to help the powder blend more easily. Silica also absorbs sweat and oil on the skin and so helps to ensure make-up stays on for longer.

Cream eyeshadow

Cream eyeshadows have a velvety smooth texture and often contain wax, oil and silica. They can be used alone, or applied as a base and covered with powder eyeshadow. This helps the eyeshadow stay on for longer. They are easy to apply and come in range of bright and exciting colours.

Choosing eyeshadow colour

When choosing eyeshadows, it is important to choose colours that work well with each other and that will suit the client's skin tone and eye colour.

For a fair-skinned client you will want to choose colours with soft undertones, such as pink, light purple, light brown and soft white. For a dark-skinned client, it is best to choose shades with dark undertones, such as dark brown, deep pink or deep purple.

Different colours of eyeshadow can help to enhance different eye colours. The pictures below show some examples of eyeshadows that suit specific eye colours.

How to apply eyeshadow

1 Transfer some eyeshadow onto a palette.

2 Gently use the index finger to raise the client's brow. This will lightly stretch the skin above the eye.

3 Apply a highlighter shade to the area beneath the brow bone, to create a brightening and lifting effect.

4 With a dome-shaped brush, apply a medium shade of eyeshadow to the eyelid area above the upper lashes.

5 Starting at the outer corner of the eye, apply a darker colour to the socket area (crease of the eyelid).

6 Use a blending brush to blend the eyeshadow and get rid of any harsh lines.

7 With the aid of a mirror, discuss the effect with your client.

Eyeliner

Eyeliner helps to accentuate the eyes. It can be used on both the top and bottom lids to create a frame around them. It can also be used to create illusions around the eyes, making them appear larger, or more elongated, for example. Eyeliner pencils are the most popular type, but eyeliners also come in liquid and cake form.

Pencil eyeliner

Pencil liner is the most common type of eyeliner and is the easiest to use. It looks like an ordinary pencil and can be sharpened with an eyeliner sharpener. Some pencil liners are encased in plastic tubes and don't require sharpening. Eyeliner pencils are available in soft and hard textures and in various sizes; for instance, Kohl pencils are thick and very soft. A pencil is easier to control than a liquid liner and gives a softer look.

1 Eyes look rounder when the line is deeper in the middle

2 A softened, upwardly tapered line provides a more youthful 'lift' to the eye

3 A dramatic sweep above and below the eye makes the eye look larger, provided that he lines do not meet and 'close up' the eye

4 The upper and lower line are softened with a clean damp brush – providing more subtle emphasis

5 Fifties 'flick' for a fashionable effect

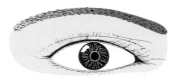

6 A fine tapered line to provide 'natural' enhancement

Different eye-lining effects

HAVE A GO

Flick through some magazines and look at the eye make-up of the models. Cut out models with blue eyes, green eyes and brown eyes and notice what colours are used and how the eyeshadow is applied.

Applying eyeshadow

DON'T FORGET

You can use eyeshadow instead of, or in combination with, your client's chosen liner. Try adding a very thin line of eyeshadow near to the client's lower lashes and then draw the liner on top of it. This can really enhance your client's look.

Pencil eyeliner

Liquid eyeliner

How to apply eyeliner

Kohl eyeliner

Kohl eyeliner is traditional in Asia and the Middle East, including Egypt and India, and its use goes back to the Bronze Age. It generally comes in pencil form and glides on easily.

Liquid eyeliner

Liquid eyeliner usually comes in a bottle with a small brush. It may require some practice to become good at applying it, but it will give the eyes a more dramatic effect than pencil, and does not smudge so easily. Liquid eyeliner is usually waterproof and is available in many colours.

Cake eyeliner

Cake eyeliner comes in a compact or container. It can be applied using a moistened eyeliner brush.

Choosing an eyeliner colour

When choosing an eyeliner colour, it is important to consider your client's skin tone, age, eye colour and style.

If a client has very fair skin, they should stay away from very dark eyeliners and use more subtle browns or greys. If they have medium to dark skin, a dark brown or medium black should be used.

If the client has light-coloured eyes, such as light blue or green, you should consider using brown, navy or charcoal-coloured liner. For a dark-eyed client, use brown or black.

Use lighter colours on an older client, as dark colours can be too harsh.

Lighter colours are generally more suitable for daytime wear, while darker and more dramatic colours can be used for an evening make-up.

How to apply eyeliner

1 Firstly, to avoid smudging the client's foundation, you may wish to place a clean, folded piece of tissue on their face, to rest your hand upon.

2 Gently lift the brow to stretch the skin of the eyelid slightly. This makes it easier to apply the eyeliner.

3 Begin at the outer corner of the eye, and apply the eyeliner very close to the edge of the upper lashes. Then apply it underneath the lower lashes.

4 If using a pencil, a cotton bud can be used to lightly smudge the eyeliner and soften the line.

5 You may use a mirror to ensure the client is satisfied with the application and colour of the eyeliner.

Liquid mascara

Mascara

Mascara makes eyelashes look darker, thicker and longer, which helps to enhance the colour and shape of the eyes. Mascara comes in a range of shades including brown, black, charcoal grey and blue. Clear, colourless mascara is also available. Some mascaras contain glitters or pearls. Mascara comes in liquid, cake and cream forms.

Mascaras contain waxes that provide adhesion and help to thicken the lashes. They also contain polymers, which provide a flexible non-flaking film that helps to prevent the mascara from smudging, and silicones, which improve water resistance and make the mascara more permanent. Pigments are also added to provide the colour.

Liquid mascara
Liquid mascara is by far the most popular form, and comes in a tube with its own brush (or wand) in the cap. There are many different types available, including waterproof formulas that contain resins to prevent them from smudging.

Cake mascara
Mascara was originally created in the form of a pressed cake, which came in a small block and was applied with a dampened brush. The main ingredients for cake mascara were soap and black pigments, in equal amounts. Cake mascaras are still available today, but now they often contain mineral oil, waxes and lanolin.

Cream mascara
In cream mascaras the colour pigment is suspended in a mixture of oil and water. These mascaras help to condition the lashes. They come in a toothpaste-style tube with a separate brush.

How to apply mascara
1 Eyelash curlers may be used before applying mascara to give the eyes a more dramatic look.

2 Use a disposable mascara brush to prevent cross-infection. Hold the mascara brush parallel to the client's eyelashes.

3 Lift the eyebrow and ask the client to look downwards. Apply mascara to the top side of the upper lashes, working from the base to the tips.

> **DON'T FORGET**
>
> *Apply one coat of mascara for a subtle look, or two or three coats for a more dramatic look.*

> **DON'T FORGET**
>
> *If you borrow a friend's mascara, you are also borrowing their dead skin cells, parasites and eye secretions!*

How to apply mascara

4 Ask the client to look upwards, and apply mascara to the underside of the upper lashes, working upwards from the base to the tips, but using a side-to-side motion as well.

5 Always apply mascara to the upper lashes, but only put mascara on the lower lashes for a heavier, more dramatic look. Use a side-to-side motion to apply mascara to the lower lashes.

6 Use an eyelash separator to remove any blobs of mascara from the lashes. A cotton bud is useful to remove any unwanted dots of mascara from the face.

7 You may use a mirror to ensure the client is pleased with the result.

Good practice

Do not pump the mascara wand in and out of its container, as this will allow air to get in and dry out the product.

Eyebrow pencil

Eyebrow pencils are used to define and darken the eyebrows. They are particularly useful for people who have few hairs on the brow area, as they can create an illusion of even hair growth throughout the length of the eyebrows, which makes them look thicker. If the eyebrow hairs are fair, an eyebrow pencil can make them darker and more noticeable, so that they frame the eyes better. Eyebrow pencils are generally available in black, dark brown, light brown and grey. Other eyebrow products include eyebrow powder, eyebrow mascara and liquid eyebrow.

How to apply eyebrow pencil

1 If required, place a clean, folded piece of tissue at the side of the client's forehead on which to rest your hand.

2 Use an eyebrow brush to brush the hairs into the correct shape.

3 Use your pencil or other eyebrow product to create fine strokes over the eyebrow until the desired result has been achieved.

DON'T FORGET

Make-up normally has a shelf life of about two years. However, mascara only lasts about six months.

DON'T FORGET

If your client has very light hair, choose an eyebrow pencil that is one or two shades darker than their natural hair colour. If the colour is too dark it will give an unnatural look.

How to apply eyebrow pencil

DON'T FORGET

Products containing wax or gel can be used to help eyebrow powder stick to the eyebrow hairs.

Corrective make-up techniques for different eye shapes

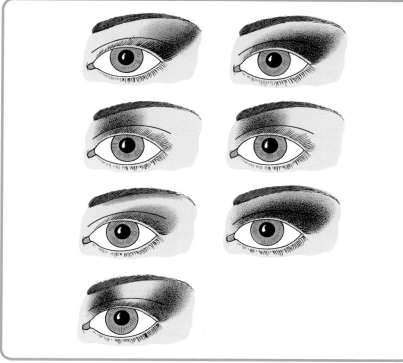

Some eyeshadow effects

Small eyes

Small eyes have a short distance between the upper and lower lashes.

Use light eyeshadow colours around the eyes, and highlight under the brow, as this will help to open up the eye area. Apply eyeliner along the entire top lashline, and extend the line slightly at the corners of the eyes to make them appear wider. Do not use dark eyeliner on the bottom lashline as this would make the eyes appear smaller. Applying white or beige eyeliner to the lower inner rim of the eye will help to make the eyes look bigger. Curling the eyelashes and applying mascara will also help the eyes look larger and enhance their shape.

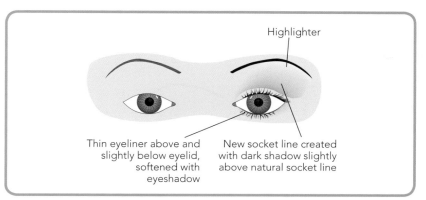

Highlighter

Thin eyeliner above and slightly below eyelid, softened with eyeshadow

New socket line created with dark shadow slightly above natural socket line

Corrective make-up for small eyes

Prominent eyes

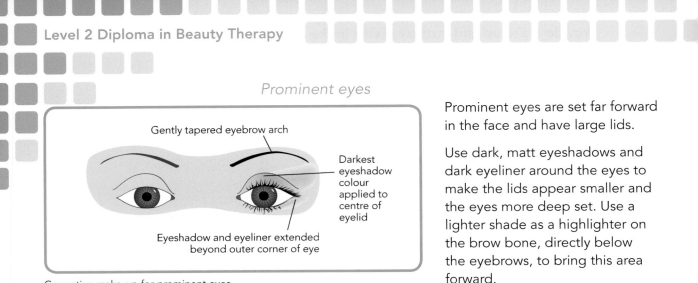

Gently tapered eyebrow arch

Darkest eyeshadow colour applied to centre of eyelid

Eyeshadow and eyeliner extended beyond outer corner of eye

Corrective make-up for prominent eyes

Prominent eyes are set far forward in the face and have large lids.

Use dark, matt eyeshadows and dark eyeliner around the eyes to make the lids appear smaller and the eyes more deep set. Use a lighter shade as a highlighter on the brow bone, directly below the eyebrows, to bring this area forward.

Round eyes

To lengthen round eyes, apply a medium shade eyeshadow along the crease of the eyelid, and apply a dark shadow to the centre part of the lid. If using eyeliner, make the line thicker at the outer and inner corners of the eye. This will help to emphasise the horizontal line of the eye and give the illusion of width.

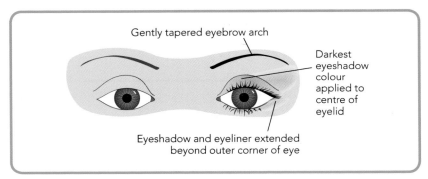

Gently tapered eyebrow arch

Darkest eyeshadow colour applied to centre of eyelid

Eyeshadow and eyeliner extended beyond outer corner of eye

Corrective make-up for round eyes

Deep-set eyes

Deep-set eyes are set far back in the face, which makes the brow area more prominent.

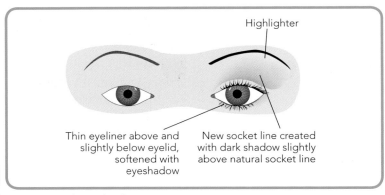

Highlighter

Thin eyeliner above and slightly below eyelid, softened with eyeshadow

New socket line created with dark shadow slightly above natural socket line

Corrective make-up for deep-set eyes

To bring the eyes forward, apply a light shade of eyeshadow from the lashline to the brow, then sweep a slightly darker shade right above the crease of the lid. Use an eyeliner to make a thin line, which thickens on the outer two-thirds of the eye, along both the upper and lower lashlines. Smudge the eyeliner gently to avoid a hard line and finish with a generous coat of mascara.

Close-set eyes

Close-set eyes are eyes that are less than one eye width apart.

Apply a light shade of eyeshadow from the lashline to the brow, then apply a medium shade to the outer half of the lid. Use a darker eyeshadow at the outer corners of the eyes to make them look further apart. Use a highlighter on the brow bone area and at the inner corners of the eyes. When applying mascara, concentrate it on the outer half of lashes.

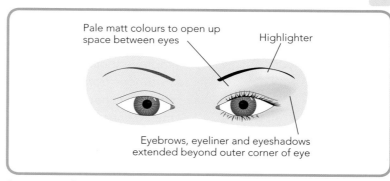

Pale matt colours to open up space between eyes

Highlighter

Eyebrows, eyeliner and eyeshadows extended beyond outer corner of eye

Corrective make-up for close-set eyes

Wide-set eyes

Wide-set eyes are spaced more than one eye width apart. The aim is to bring the eyes closer together so they look more in proportion.

Apply a light shade of eyeshadow from the lashline to the brow, then sweep a medium shade onto the inner half of the lid. Use a darker shade to deepen the inner half of the crease. Then use an eyeliner to line the eyes from the inner corner to the middle of the lid, softening the line as you blend outwards. When you apply mascara, concentrate it on the inner half of the lashes.

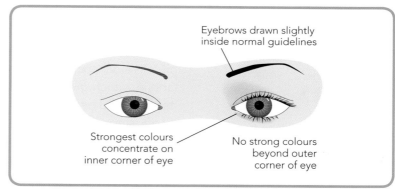

Eyebrows drawn slightly inside normal guidelines

Strongest colours concentrate on inner corner of eye

No strong colours beyond outer corner of eye

Corrective make-up for wide-set eyes

Droopy eyelids

Apply a light, natural-coloured eyeshadow over the whole lid to open up the eye area. Do not use shimmery shadows, as they will make the area look worse. A smoky eye pencil can be used around the eye.

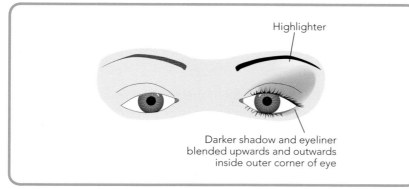

Highlighter

Darker shadow and eyeliner blended upwards and outwards inside outer corner of eye

Corrective make-up for droopy eyelids

DON'T FORGET

Matt colours are most complementary to mature skin types, as they can reduce the appearance of lines and wrinkles.

Lip products

Lip liner

Lip liner generally comes in the form of a pencil. It is applied to the outer edges of the lips, and is used to give them more definition. It can also make the lips look bigger and fuller and improve their shape. There is a wide choice of lip liner colours to choose from, and choosing the right one is important. Try to choose a shade that matches the lipstick you are using, otherwise the lip liner will be too noticeable and so will look unnatural.

Lipstick

Lipstick usually comes in the form of a tube. It helps to accentuate the lips, draw attention to a smile and add colour to the face. It also helps prevent the lips from drying out. Lipsticks are available in a variety of different formulas, including cream, sheer and frosted, and in a wide range of colours.

Lipsticks are made from a blend of waxes, emollients and pigments. They also contain oils, such as mineral oil, castor oil, olive oil, cocoa butter and lanolin, which give the product its shine and help provide a soft, smooth coverage.

Lipsticks

Moisturising substances such as vitamin E and aloe vera may also be added to help keep the lips soft.

How to apply lipstick

1. Outline the lips with a sharpened lip pencil.
2. Place some lipstick onto a palette or spatula.
3. Use a disposable lip brush to apply the lipstick.
4. Ask the client to open their mouth slightly to help make the application easier.
5. Apply one coat of lipstick and then blot gently with a facial tissue – this removes excess lipstick and sets the colour.
6. Apply some powder to the lips to help seal in the first coat.
7. Apply the second coat.
8. Use a mirror to show the client the finished result and to ensure she is satisfied with the lipstick colour and application.

Lip gloss

Lip gloss is available in tinted or colourless forms, and can be used alone or over lipstick. It is not recommended for use on mature skin, as it tends to bleed into any little lines around the lips.

DON'T FORGET

Lipsticks contain a high wax content, commonly beeswax and carnauba wax. The wax gives lipstick its shape and makes it easy to apply.

DON'T FORGET

Lips naturally thin with age because of changes in collagen and fat levels; sun damage and smoking can also play a part.

How to apply lipstick

DON'T FORGET

Lip stains contain oils that dry and set to create a tough, shiny film on the lips.

DON'T FORGET

Some lipsticks now contain UV filters to help protect the lips against sun damage.

If the client has very fair skin do not use deep reds and purples; instead choose more subtle tones, such as peach, warm pink and clear. If a client has a medium skin tone, use warmer colours such as medium pink and light red. If your client has a dark skin tone most colours of lip gloss will suit them.

Corrective make-up techniques for different lip shapes

Thin lips

Using a lip liner that matches the client's lip colour, outline the lips slightly outside their natural line. Use bright coloured, pearlised lipsticks to help accentuate the mouth. Dark, matt colours will make the lips look smaller.

Full or thick lips

Use darker coloured, matt lipsticks to make the lips appear smaller. Avoid using bright, pearlised or glossy lipsticks.

Uneven lips

You can balance uneven lips by using a liner to outline just outside the thinner part of the lip. Pink lipsticks work well for uneven lips, so choose shades of pink that blend well with your client's skin tone.

Droopy mouth

Similar to thin lips, but aim to redraw a lip line lifting the corners of the mouth.

Narrow mouth

To make the mouth appear wider, slightly extend the lip liner and lipstick outside the corners of the lips.

DON'T FORGET

Lip glosses contain more oils and fewer waxes than lipsticks, which makes them more liquid and glossy.

DON'T FORGET

Always apply powder to the lips before carrying out corrective work.

Q: How do lip plumpers work?
A: Lip plumpers are products that make the lips appear fuller. These products can be worn alone, or under or over lipstick.

Some lip plumpers contain ingredients such as cinnamon oil, capsaicin (the spicy chemical in chilli peppers) and ginger, which irritate the sensitive skin of the lips and so may produce a slight tingle when applied. These work by stimulating the blood circulation to the lips, which instantly plumps the lips and enhances their natural colour.

Lip plumpers may also contain a gel-like substance called hyaluronic acid, which works by absorbing moisture from the skin, and collagen, which helps to plump out fine lines.

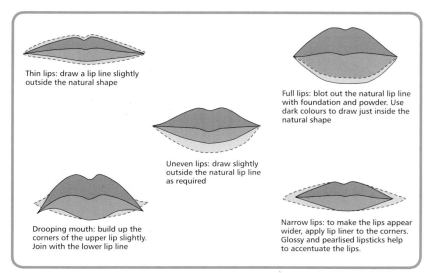

Thin lips: draw a lip line slightly outside the natural shape

Full lips: blot out the natural lip line with foundation and powder. Use dark colours to draw just inside the natural shape

Uneven lips: draw slightly outside the natural lip line as required

Drooping mouth: build up the corners of the upper lip slightly. Join with the lower lip line

Narrow lips: to make the lips appear wider, apply lip liner to the corners. Glossy and pearlised lipsticks help to accentuate the lips.

Corrective lip make-up

Make-up for different client groups

1 The skin is cleansed, toned and moisturised in preparation for the make-up application.

2 Concealer is applied to cover blemishes and help lessen the appearance of dark circles under the eyes.

3 Foundation and face powder are applied to help eliminate shine and give a flawless appearance to the skin. The foundation should match the client's skin colour.

4 Blusher is applied to help highlight the cheekbones.

5 Eyeshadows are applied to help emphasise the eyes.

6 Mascara, eyeliner and eyebrow powder is applied.

7 Lip liner, lipstick and lip gloss is applied to help define the lips.

8 The client now has a glamorous evening make-up.

1 The skin is cleansed, toned and moisturised in preparation for the make-up application.

2 Concealer is applied to cover blemishes and help lessen the appearance of dark circles under the eyes.

3 Foundation and face powder are applied to help eliminate shine and give a flawless appearance to the skin. The foundation should match the client's skin colour.

4 Blusher is applied to help highlight the cheekbones.

5 Eyeshadows are applied to help emphasise the eyes.

6 Mascara, eyeliner and eyebrow powder is applied.

7 Lip liner, lipstick and lip gloss is applied to help define the lips.

8 The client now has a glamorous evening make-up.

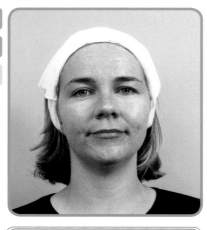

1 The skin is cleansed, toned and moisturised in preparation for the make-up application.

2 Concealer is applied to cover blemishes and help lessen the appearance of dark circles under the eyes.

3 Foundation and face powder are applied to help eliminate shine and give a flawless appearance to the skin. The foundation should match the client's skin colour.

4 Blusher is applied to help highlight the cheekbones.

5 Eyeshadows are applied to help emphasise the eyes.

6 Mascara, eyeliner and eyebrow powder is applied.

7 Lip liner, lipstick and lip gloss is applied to help define the lips.

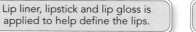

8 The client now has a glamorous evening make-up.

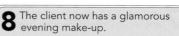

1 The skin is cleansed, toned and moisturised in preparation for the make-up application.

2 Concealer is applied to cover blemishes and help lessen the appearance of dark circles under the eyes.

3 Foundation and face powder are applied to help eliminate shine and give a flawless appearance to the skin. The foundation should match the client's skin colour.

4 Blusher is applied to help highlight the cheekbones.

5 Eyeshadows are applied to help emphasise the eyes.

6 Mascara, eyeliner and eyebrow powder is applied.

7 Lip liner, lipstick and lip gloss is applied to help define the lips.

8 The client now has a glamorous evening make-up.

Make-up for different occasions

Day make-up

Daylight will show up every mark and imperfection on the face, so consider the following points when carrying out a day make-up.

Day make-up

- If possible, carry out the make-up treatment near to a window that lets in natural light – it's surprising how different a make-up can look in artificial light.

- A day make-up should be as natural as possible, so use neutral shades rather than bright ones.

- Foundation should be the same colour as the skin tone and set with a translucent powder.

- Do not apply too much blusher, and be aware the blusher may look darker when the client leaves the salon and goes outdoors.

- If the client is fair, use brown or grey eyeliner rather than black.

- Do not apply mascara or eyebrow pencil too thickly.

- Ensure the lipstick and lip liner are a good match.

Evening make-up

An evening make-up can be more dramatic than a day make-up. Consider the following points when applying an evening make-up.

- If possible, try to apply make-up in a similar light to the one the client will be wearing it in.

- Use brighter and more shimmery colours than for day make-up – perhaps even metallic colours.

- Use a warm, vibrant blusher.

- Pay attention to the eyebrows – maybe use a slightly darker shade of pencil than for day make-up.

- Use eyelash curlers before applying mascara, or apply artificial lashes to help provide a more glamorous look.

- Add lip gloss on top of lipstick to accentuate the mouth.

Evening make-up

Special occasion make-up

This type of make-up applies to a client who is attending a wedding, prom, or any other special event. Consider the following points when providing a special occasion make-up.

- What type of lighting will the client most likely be in – is the special occasion during the day or in the evening?

- What clothes and accessories will she be wearing to the event, and what colours would complement her outfit.

- If it is an all-day event, she will require long-lasting products. A primer can be used to help ensure make-up stays on for longer.

Bridal make-up

Ensure the bride books two make-up appointments: a trial make-up and a bridal make-up for the wedding day. The make-up trial will help to ensure that the therapist is fully prepared for the wedding day, and that the bride knows she will be happy with the result. The following tips will help to create a perfect bridal make-up.

- Recommend using tanning products to give the face and body a sun-kissed glow.

- Brush shimmery powder over the shoulder and upper chest areas.

- Daytime bridal make-up should be minimal, with a natural-coloured blusher, neutral eyeshadows and rosy lips.

- Ivory and taupe (light brown) eyeshadows are recommended, and a neutral shimmer shadow can be added to the brow line.

Bridal make-up

Good practice

Remember to reshape the eyebrows at least a day before giving the make-up treatment, otherwise the eyebrow area may be reddened and bumpy and the open pores may become infected.

- Evening looks can be more dramatic, with sultry eyes and bold eyeshadows.

- Fill in brows with a taupe or brown shadow and set them with a clear mascara or wax.

- Always choose a waterproof mascara to prevent smudges. Black mascara is the best choice for every bride.

- Make sure you curl the eyelashes prior to mascara application, or apply artificial lashes.

- Use long-lasting products so the make-up stays on all day. A primer can be used to help ensure make-up stays on for longer.

- Use a lip stain to ensure the lip colour stays on all day.

Photographic make-up

You will need to discuss the requirements with the photographer before the photoshoot takes place. Bear in mind the following points when applying a photographic make-up.

- Bright lights will make the make-up less noticeable, so ensure you apply it strongly enough.

- Use matt colours, as the bright lights will highlight any shine.

- Apply artificial lashes to help accentuate the eyes.

- Under hot lights, the model might sweat and the make-up may slip off. Ensure you apply long-lasting products and have face powder and anti-shine products to hand. Also avoid oily make-up products.

For details of camouflage make-up, see **Unit B10: Enhance appearance using skin camouflage**.

Under hot lights make-up may slip off

UNIT OUTCOME 8

Know the contra-indications and contra-actions of make-up

Contra-actions

Occasionally a client may have an allergic reaction to a product being used. This will generally show itself as redness and swelling at the affected area. It may be itchy too. The product should be removed immediately. Calamine lotion or a cold compress can help to soothe the affected area.

Good practice

Always note any unwanted reactions to products on the client's record card/consultation form. This will ensure you do not use the same product again when they return for treatment.

UNIT OUTCOME 10

Know how to provide aftercare advice for clients following make-up services

Aftercare advice

You should record the details of the make-up treatment on the client's record card/consultation form, including: details of the treatment, the products used (particularly colours of cosmetics); client requests and preferences; products purchased; and any adverse reactions to products.

If the client returns to the salon to buy cosmetics, such as a certain shade of lipstick, the colour will be shown in the client's records.

Make sure you escort your client to the reception area so you can help them purchase any products they might wish to buy. Also ask them if they would like to make another appointment.

Provide the following aftercare advice and recommendations to your client.

- Remember to cleanse, tone and moisturise before applying make-up.

- Use a moisturiser with an SPF of at least 15. Explain the importance of using this product to the client and how it helps provide a good base for make-up.

- Recommend the use of a good eye make-up remover to avoid dragging of the skin when removing make-up, especially if waterproof mascara is worn.

UNIT OUTCOME 4

Know the organisational and legal requirements related to make-up application

See **Unit G20: Ensure responsibility for actions to reduce risks to health and safety**, for information on laws and regulations relating to salon treatments.

UNIT OUTCOME 7

Know anatomy and physiology related to make-up

To carry out an effective make-up treatment, you will need to have a good knowledge of the skin and its functions. See the **Anatomy and physiology** unit for information on the skin and its functions.

Providing a make-up lesson

It is very satisfying to impart your skills to a client, to help teach them how to apply make-up and show them which products and colours will best suit their features.

The consultation and contra-indications will be the same as for a make-up treatment. The equipment and products will also be the same, and the treatment room will be prepared in the same way.

You will need to discuss the make-up treatment with your client to find out her preference for colours and application. The client may prefer to be shown an evening make-up application rather than a day one, so suitable products need to be chosen. Make sure the client actively participates in the choice of make-up products and colours. This will help ensure she is satisfied with the final result.

Before you carry out the make-up lesson, you should make sure you are organised and that everything you need is close to hand.

Ideally, position your client in front of a large mirror, but if this isn't possible, ensure she has access to a good sized hand mirror.

When you are teaching make-up, it is important to explain everything clearly and in simple terms. Ensure you explain every stage carefully and show the client all the products that you intend to use during the make-up lesson.

Encourage your client to ask questions to help her to feel relaxed. Ensure you listen to her carefully and confidently answer any questions. Be patient with your client, she is probably learning a new skill and may find it difficult to correctly apply make-up.

A good way to evaluate how well you have instructed your client is to watch her applying the make-up to her own face. Many therapists will teach their client by applying make-up to one side of the face, then allowing the client to try out the colours and techniques on the other side. Ask her to describe what she is doing with every step, and ask her questions to check her understanding. The client could be asked to fill out an evaluation form asking questions about her level of understanding.

A make-up chart, which states the products and colours used, should be filled in and given to the client at the end of the lesson. Make sure that all the information she needs is written on a card for her to take home.

DON'T FORGET

The client may wish to use her own cosmetics for the make-up lesson.

Providing a make-up lesson

How are you doing?

1 Which of the following cosmetic ingredients are known to cause allergies?

  a Lanolin

  b Parabens

  c Perfume

  d All of the above

2 What is the purpose of a primer?

  a To provide a base for make-up and act as a barrier to stop it being absorbed into the skin

  b To enhance and thicken the natural lashes

  c To help produce an even skin tone and cover up blemishes

  d Helps to make the lips glossy and keep them moisturised for a long while

3 At what stage of the make-up treatment would you generally apply lipstick?

  a At the beginning of the treatment

  b After applying the eyeshadow

  c Before the application of a concealer

  d Towards the end of the treatment

4 Which colour corrective concealer would you use to conceal red-coloured broken capillaries?

  a Green

  b Lilac

  c Blue

  d Yellow

5 Which of the following is **not** a contour cosmetic?

  a Highlighter

  b Eyeshadow

  c Shader

  d Blusher

6 Which of the following describes a square face shape?

  a This face shape has a wide forehead and a narrow, pointed chin

  b This face shape has a narrow forehead and chin, and has the greatest width across the cheekbones

  c This face shape has a wide forehead and jawline

  d This face shape has greater length in proportion to its width

7 If a nose is too wide, where should you apply shader?

  a To the tip of the nose

  b To the sides of the nose

  c To the bridge of the nose

  d All of the above

8 What is a highlighter?

  a A product that draws attention to, and emphasises, features

  b A moisturiser that contains pigment

  c A make-up product that adds intense colour to the eyes

  d A cosmetic used to set foundation

9 Which of the following is **not** a type of mascara?

  a Liquid

  b Cream

  c Milk

  d Block

10 Which of the following is found in lipstick?

  a Wax

  b Oils

  c Pigment

  d All of the above

are you ready *for* assessment?

The evidence for this unit must be gathered in the workplace (salon) or realistic working environment (training centre).

Simulation (role play) is not allowed for any performance evidence within this unit.

You must practically demonstrate in your everyday work that you have met the required standard for this unit.

All outcomes, assessment criteria and range statements must be achieved.

Knowledge and understanding in this unit will be assessed by a mandatory (compulsory) written question paper. These questions are set and marked by VTCT.

Assessing your practical work

Your assessor will observe your performance of a practical task, such as carrying out a make-up treatment.

Your assessor will sign off an outcome when all criteria have been competently achieved.

On occasions, some assessment criteria may not naturally occur during a practical observation by your assessor. In such instances, you will be asked questions to demonstrate your knowledge in this area. Your assessor will document the criteria that have been achieved through oral questioning.

In this unit you must demonstrate competent performance of all practical outcomes on at least **three** occasions, each involving a different client, on a range of different skin tones.

Testing your knowledge and understanding

You will be guided by your tutor and assessor on the evidence that needs to be produced.

Your knowledge and understanding will be assessed using the assessment tools listed below.

- Mandatory written question paper
- Oral questioning
- Portfolio of evidence

B9 assessment criteria is the same as for B8 but with two exceptions:

- No mandatory written questions are required within this unit.
- In this unit you must demonstrate competent performance of all practical outcomes on at least **three** occasions, each involving instruction for a different look on a different client.

N2 & N3 Provide manicure services and provide pedicure services

On completion of this unit you will:

1. Be able to use safe and effective methods of working when providing manicure and pedicure services

2. Be able to consult, plan and prepare for the service with clients

3. Be able to carry out manicure and pedicure services

4. Understand organisational and legal requirements

5. Understand how to work safely and effectively when providing manicure and pedicure services

6. Understand how to perform client consultation, treatment planning and preparation

7. Know contra-indications and contra-actions that affect or restrict manicure and pedicure services

8. Know anatomy and physiology that relates to manicure and pedicure services

9. Understand manicure and pedicure techniques, products and service planning

10. Understand how to provide aftercare advice for clients

Introduction

A manicure improves the health and appearance of the hands and fingernails and will also help to prevent minor nail damage. Your client may have a particular problem, such as overgrown cuticles, and would like help to improve this condition; or they may have an event coming up, such as a wedding, and would like their hands and nails to look more attractive.

Painted fingernails

DON'T FORGET

A healthy nail is firm yet flexible, and can absorb minor shocks without splitting or chipping. The surface of the nail should be smooth with a slight shine and shouldn't peel or flake at the tip.

A pedicure is similar to a manicure, but involves treating the feet to improve the health and appearance of the toenails and skin.

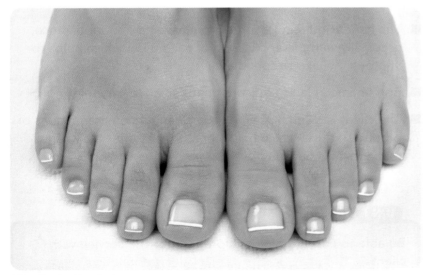

Attractive-looking feet

Benefits of a manicure or pedicure service

There are a wide range of benefits associated with manicure and pedicure treatment.

- A manicure or pedicure helps to make nails stronger, resulting in improved growth.

- Filing the nails helps to prevent them from splitting or breaking.

- Buffing the nails helps to improve their circulation, so they grow faster and stronger.

- Cuticles are softened, which reduces the likelihood of them growing onto the nail plate, or becoming dehydrated and splitting.

- The skin around the nails is softened, which helps to prevent the development of **hangnails**.

- Removing hard, dry and flaky skin from the feet makes them feel smoother and look more attractive.

- Having toenails nails cut and filed professionally will help prevent ingrowing toenails.

- Pedicures are helpful for people who can't reach their feet to cut their nails, file hard skin, etc.

- The hands and feet become more attractive in appearance, especially with the application of nail polish, which helps to improve the client's confidence.

- Both manicure and pedicure treatments are very relaxing.

- The client is given homecare advice and recommendations of products to use, which helps them to look after their hands, feet and nails outside the salon.

key terms

Hangnails: pieces of skin that split away from the cuticle, usually because the cuticles are dry. See a picture of a hangnail on page 250.

UNIT OUTCOME 2

Be able to consult, plan and prepare for the service with clients

UNIT OUTCOME 6

Understand how to perform client consultation, treatment planning and preparation

Consultation

During the consultation you should discuss the client's expectations of the treatment. They may need help with a particular problem, such as dry, overgrown cuticles, or weak, brittle nails; or, if the client has worn artificial nails for a long time, her nails may have become thin and ridged.

You can discuss a service or treatment plan with your client, which will allow you to put together an action plan to help with a particular issue. The client can be recommended to come for weekly treatments until the problem has been sorted out. You can also advise the client about additional treatments, such as hot oil and paraffin wax treatment.

However, a client may simply require a manicure or pedicure service to maintain the look and health of the nails and skin, or for relaxation and pampering purposes. In this case, recommend the client returns for treatment every four to six weeks. Some clients may only want a one-off treatment to make their hands or feet look more attractive for a particular event, such as a party.

As part of the consultation you will need to complete a record card/consultation form and ensure the client signs it.

For more information on the consultation process, see **Unit G20: Ensure responsibility for actions to reduce risks to health and safety.**

Good practice

If possible, advise your client to wear open-toed footwear, such as flip flops, when coming for pedicure treatment, as you don't want the nail polish to smudge when she puts on her shoes.

UNIT OUTCOME 7

Know contra-indications and contra-actions that affect or restrict manicure and pedicure services

Foot, hand and nail disorders

There are many diseases and disorders that can affect the nails, hands and feet, some of which may prevent or restrict treatment. Therefore, it is important that you observe the hands/feet and nails before giving treatment, to ensure there are no contra-indications.

The appearance and causes of some common disorders and diseases are listed below, along with advice as to what treatment would or would not be appropriate.

Arthritis

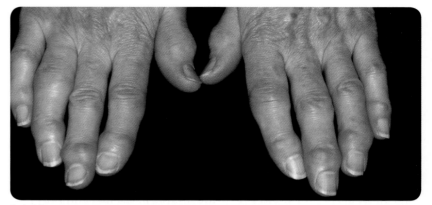

Arthritis

Description: a common condition that causes pain and inflammation of one or more joints. Pain and stiffness may also be present in muscles near the joint. It mainly affects older people.

Causes: the most common type is osteoarthritis, which is caused by ageing and wear and tear of the joints. The cartilage between the bones gradually wastes away, causing the bones to rub together and resulting in pain. Rheumatoid arthritis is more severe. It is an **autoimmune disorder** in which the membrane that lines the joint becomes thick and swollen. It usually affects the fingers and toes.

Advice: gentle treatment can be given as long as there is no discomfort to the client.

Athlete's foot (Tinea pedis)

Description: this common infection is caused by a type of fungus. The fungus likes warm, moist environments and feeds on keratin (a protein found in hair, nails and skin). Many people have the fungus present on their skin and are unaffected by it, but breaks in the skin allow the fungus to enter and may cause athlete's foot. This mostly affects the sole of the foot and the area between the toes. The skin becomes cracked and itchy with flaking pieces of dead, white skin, which may give off an unpleasant smell. The skin may also be swollen and blisters may form. It is more common in men and teenagers and, as the name suggests, in people who play a lot of sport.

key terms

Autoimmune disorder: an autoimmune disorder is a condition that occurs when the body's immune system mistakenly attacks and destroys healthy body tissue.

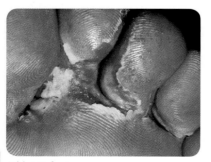

Athlete's foot

Causes: the infection is commonly spread in places such as communal showers and changing rooms. It can be spread through direct person-to-person contact or by skin particles left on towels, shoes, floors of shower cubicles, etc.

Advice: it is infectious, so the affected area should be avoided during treatment. The client should be encouraged to keep the feet cool, dry and clean. Anti-fungal powders can be used to treat the condition.

Beau's lines (transverse furrows)

Description: deep grooved lines and ridges that run from side to side on the nails. As the nail grows, the Beau's lines may disappear.

Causes: they are the result of any interruption in the protein formation of the nail plate, and are associated with injury to the nail, illness, poor diet and chemotherapy.

Advice: poor manicure techniques can cause ridges to form. Treatment may be given to the nails.

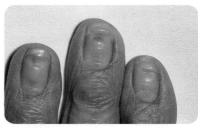
Beau's lines

Blue nails

Description: nails show a bluish colour and the hand and feet may feel cool. This is due to poor circulation of the blood to the fingers and toes.

Causes: this could be a sign of a heart condition, or a rare condition called Raynaud's disease, which affects the blood vessels, usually of the fingers and toes, and results in poor circulation to the hands and feet.

Advice: treatment can be given, and massage will be particularly beneficial to help boost the circulation.

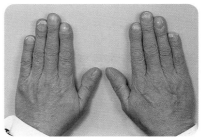
Blue nails

Bruised nail

Description: a bruise on the nail bed, which can vary in colour from maroon to black. If there is severe bruising the nail will fall off.

Causes: injury to the nail bed.

Advice: do not work on a bruised nail, although nail polish can be applied to help disguise it.

Bunion (hallux valgus)

Description: a hard swelling at the base of the big toe owing to displacement of the bone. The big toe points towards the other

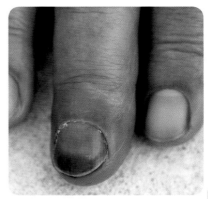
Bruised nail

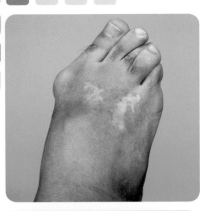

toes. The swelling will often rub against footwear, resulting in hard skin and discomfort.

Causes: bunions may be caused by poorly fitting shoes (so the condition is more common in women) and hereditary factors. It may also be the result of injury or weak ligaments. If it becomes worse over time, it can lead to other problems, such as arthritis within the big toe joint.

Advice: it may be painful, so handle the foot gently when giving treatment.

Calluses

Description: calluses are areas of hard skin that tend to form on the palm of the hand and the underside of the foot.

Causes: activities such as gardening can lead to calluses on the hands, as holding a spade while digging causes rubbing to the palms. Lots of walking or running can cause calluses to form on the feet.

Advice: if a client has calluses on the hands, they can be advised to use a moisturising product. Calluses on the feet can be treated by soaking the feet in warm, soapy water to soften the thickened skin, then drying them with a towel and using a foot file to help remove some of the dead skin. Homecare advice includes advising the client to moisturise the area and use a foot file regularly. Also advise them to have regular pedicure treatments. If the problem is severe the client could be referred to a chiropodist.

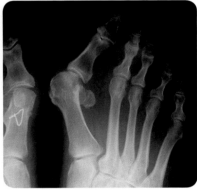

Bunion

> **DON'T FORGET**
>
> *A chiropodist treats minor foot conditions such as calluses.*

Corns

Description: these are areas of thick, hard and dry skin that build up in order to protect parts of the feet from friction or pressure. Hard corns are pea-sized and have a hard centre that can press into the skin causing pain and swelling. Hard corns commonly form over bony areas such as the little toe. Soft corns are whitish and feel rubbery; they often occur between the toes where the skin is kept moist. They are painful and can become infected by bacteria or fungi.

Causes: they are caused by badly fitting shoes and walking barefoot on hard and dry surfaces.

Advice: exfoliants and foot files help to get rid of dead skin build up. If a corn is infected or painful do not treat the affected area.

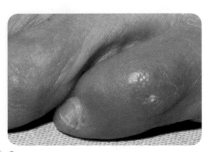

Corns

Diabetes

Description: a person with diabetes may have feet that are dry, pale and cool to the touch. There may be poor nerve and blood supply to the muscles and skin, which results in poor healing of the skin on the feet and an increased risk of infection. The sufferer may have poor sensation in the skin and the skin may also be fragile and thin.

Causes: diabetes is caused by insufficient production of the hormone insulin, or tissues that do not respond to insulin. This is the result of a build up of glucose (sugar) in the blood that leads to health problems.

Advice: ask the client to get their doctor's advice before carrying out treatment. A standard letter may be given to the client which they can give to their GP (see page 19 for an example).

Eggshell nails

Description: thin, white nails that are curved over the free edge.

Causes: eggshell nails are caused by poor diet, illness and medication.

Advice: care has to be taken when filing these nails, as they are fragile and will easily break. Apply a nail strengthener to help make them stronger.

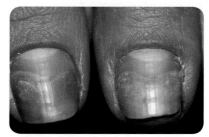

Eggshell nails

Gout

Description: a type of arthritis that typically affects the big toe, but can develop in any joint in the body. There may be pain, inflammation and swelling.

Causes: this condition is the result of an excessive amount of a substance called uric acid in the blood. This forms crystals in the joints, causing them to become painful and inflamed. This can be caused by too much protein in the diet, drinking alcohol or hereditary factors.

Advice: avoid the affected area when giving treatment.

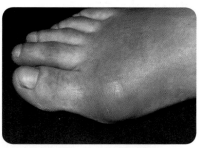

Gout

Hammer toes

Description: this is when there is a deformity of the toe joints resulting in bent toes. Corns will often develop on the joints of the toes. This condition may be painful.

Causes: this may be caused by arthritis, bunions, poorly fitting shoes or hereditary factors.

Advice: if there is no discomfort for the client, normal pedicure treatment can be given.

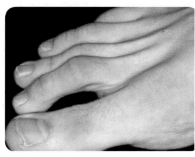

Hammer toes

Hangnail

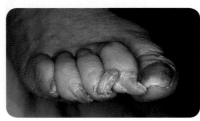

Leuconychia

Onychauxis

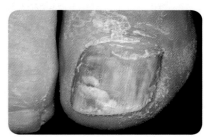

Onychia

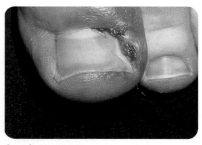

Onychocryptosis

Hangnail

Description: the cuticle around the nail splits, leaving a dry piece of skin. The area may become infected and painful.

Causes: dry cuticles and skin. Regular use of chemicals, such as household detergents, may cause the skin to become dry. Hangnails may also be the result of the client biting the skin around the nail.

Advice: cuticle nippers can be used to remove them; however, be careful not to pull the hangnail and rip the skin. Regular application of moisturiser and cuticle oil will help prevent them forming.

Leuconychia (loo-ko-nee-kee-ah) (white spots)

Description: a very common condition that shows as white spots on the nails; it will eventually grow out.

Causes: generally caused by injury to the nail, which causes air bubbles to form between the nail bed and the nail plate.

Advice: full treatment can be given.

Onychauxis (*on-ee-kawk-sis*) (thickened nail)

Description: nails are abnormally thick and overgrown.

Causes: this is a result of illness, injury, nail infection or hereditary factors.

Advice: if the client feels no discomfort, and the nails are not separating from the nail bed, treatment may be carried out, though it may need to be modified to suit the client's nails.

Onychia (*on-ee-ke-ah*) (infection of the nail)

Description: an infection will cause inflammation of the matrix and there may also be pus. The nail may separate and fall off.

Causes: this is the result of infection of bacteria through small wounds.

Advice: do not treat the affected nails.

Onychocryptosis (*on-nik-koh-crip-toe-sis*) (ingrowing toenail)

Description: inflammation caused by the corner of the nail growing into the skin. There is swelling and redness and it is often painful. It usually affects the big toe.

Causes: pressure from footwear and cutting nails down too far at the sides. There may also be hereditary factors, for example, the nails may be too large.

Advice: cutting and filing nails straight across can help prevent it occurring. If a client has an ingrowing toenail, they should be referred to a doctor. Treatment can go ahead if it is not painful and there is no risk of cross-infection.

Onycholysis (on-nik-koh-lee-sis) (nail separation)

Description: the nail, or more commonly part of the nail, separates from the nail bed.

Causes: it may be caused by illness, fungal infections, psoriasis or injury to the nail.

Advice: if the condition is mild, and there is no discomfort for the client, treatment may be carried out.

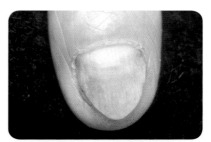
Onycholysis

Onychophagy (on-ee-co-fa-jee) (bitten nails)

Description: severely bitten nails, which may become deformed and bulbous at the fingertips.

Causes: nail biting.

Advice: regular manicures will help to improve the condition of the nails. Recommend bitter-tasting nail polishes, which give the nail biter a nasty taste when they bite their nails.

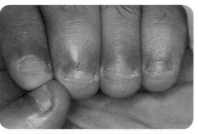
Onychophagy

Onychorrhexis (on-ee-co-rex-is) (split or brittle nails)

Description: nails that are split or brittle and have lengthwise ridges.

Causes: this may be caused by chemical use, injury, careless filing or poor diet.

Advice: use a nail strengthener and hand and nail creams, and also have regular manicures. Warm oil treatments will also help to moisturise and nourish the nails.

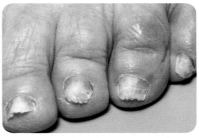
Onychorrhexis

Paronychia (par-on-ik-ee-ah)

Description: an infected area near to the nail which is quite hard to the touch. It shows itself as a swollen, red and painful lump around the nail wall. There may be pus, and the infection can spread. The nail may turn brown or black in colour.

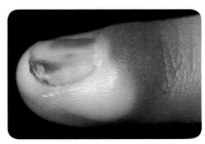
Paronychia

Causes: hands continually immersed in water and harsh chemicals, or an ingrown nail that pierces the surrounding skin, allowing bacteria or fungi to get into the opening. The latter may be caused by injury, bad manicure and poor cutting technique.

Advice: do not touch the affected area.

Pterygium (*ter-ridge-e-um*) (overgrown cuticle)

Description: the cuticle grows onto the nail plate and could possibly grow over the nail towards the free edge. It may lead to splitting of the cuticle and infection.

Causes: neglect of nails, very dry cuticles, and injury.

Advice: a manicure or pedicure will be very helpful for this condition. Also recommend using a cuticle oil/cream daily and having regular warm oil or paraffin wax treatments.

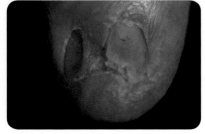

Pterygium

Ram's horn (club nail)

Description: overproduction of horny cells in the nail, which causes the nail plate to enlarge. This leads to curvature of the nail, similar in appearance to a ram's horn. This is more common in the elderly, and the big toe is mostly affected.

Causes: these include old age, injury, poorly fitting shoes and neglect. It may be associated with a heart and lung condition.

Advice: if severe, or painful for the client when touched, do not give treatment.

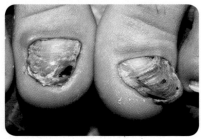

Ram's horn

Ridges

Description: ridges on the nail caused by uneven growth. The ridges may be horizontal or vertical depending on their cause.

Causes: factors such as stress, age, illness and injury can affect nail growth and the laying down of new nail, and can lead to the nails becoming ridged.

Advice: use a buffer and ridge filler polish to make the ridges less noticeable.

Ridges

Onychomycosis (*on-ee-co-my-co-sis*) (ringworm of the nail or Tinea unguium)

Description: at first, there are white or yellow patches of discolouration. Later, the nail becomes thickened, deformed and has a musty smell. It begins at the free edge and spreads downwards. The nail becomes brittle and rough, and may even separate from the nail bed.

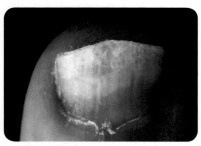

Ringworm of the nail

Causes: this is the result of fungal infection. Sweaty shoes and moist socks make ideal living conditions for the fungus. It may also be caused by injury or ingrowing toenails.

Advice: do not touch the infected area as it is contagious.

Warts and verrucas

Description: a wart is a raised, rough, whitish growth that usually occurs on the hands. Verrucas are a type of wart that appear on the soles of the feet and grow inwards, so that they look like flattened warts. Verrucas can be differentiated from corns and calluses as they contain areas of black speckling and fine bleeding points.

Causes: these are caused by a viral infection of the cells in the prickle cell layer of the skin. The cells rapidly divide in a localised area causing an irregular growth to appear above the surface of the skin. A wart/verruca is formed after hyperkeratinisation takes place and hardens the growth.

Advice: warts and verrucas are infectious, so should not be touched.

Other nail problems

Brown or black nails
Brown or black nails often results from occupational hazards: hairdressers, carpenters, photographers and factory workers who come into contact with harmful chemicals may be affected. Infections and illness may also be a cause. Do not treat brown or black nails. If the nails are not bruised, the client should seek medical advice, as they may have a fungal infection.

Dry nails that easily break
Dry nails, which break and flake easily, may be caused by insufficient nutrients in the diet, but can also be caused by contact with harsh chemicals. Recommend nail strengtheners/hardeners and moisturising products to the client, as well as regular manicures.

Slow-growing nails
Nails that grow slowly can be caused by hereditary factors, illness or poor diet. Regular manicures may be helpful.

Good practice
Advise your client that eating a nutritious, balanced diet will help to improve the condition of the nails.

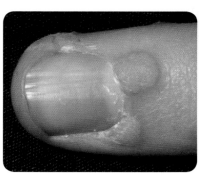
Warts

DON'T FORGET

Buffer kits can be purchased to help disguise light ridging and pitting of the nails. A certain type of buffer is used to smooth the surface of the nail, and another is used to give the nails a healthy shine.

HAVE A GO

Put together a game to help you learn the diseases and disorders of the nails, hands and feet.
- Create a table with five columns showing: the name of each disease/disorder, its appearance, its causes, if it is infectious and if it is a contra-indication.
- Cut the table into sections, so that you have separate boxes containing one piece of information each.
- Mix up the boxes and try to put them back together so that they correctly describe each disease/disorder.

To carry out professional manicure and pedicure services, you must have a good understanding of the structure of the nails and skin, and knowledge of the muscles and bones of the hands, arms, feet and lower leg. See the **Anatomy and physiology unit** for further information.

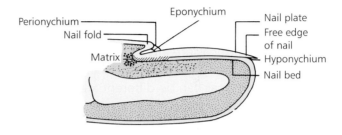

Structure of the nails

UNIT OUTCOME 8

Know anatomy and physiology that relates to manicure and pedicure services

UNIT OUTCOME 9

Understand manicure and pedicure techniques, products and service planning

Preparation for a manicure or pedicure service

Before giving a manicure or pedicure service, you should make sure everything is clean, tidy and close to hand. When setting up the treatment area make sure:

- the area is clean and tidy

- everything is safe, for example, there is no spillage of products on the floor or trailing leads

- you **disinfect** all surfaces and, if necessary, cover them in couch roll

- the trolley contains everything that is needed to carry out a treatment

- you sterilise tools such as scissors and clippers

- there is a clean bin near to where the treatment is being carried out

- there are enough clean towels.

If you are giving a manicure service, place a manicure cushion on the area where the treatment will take place, for the client to rest their hands upon. If a manicure cushion is not available, use a folded towel with a piece of couch roll or a disposable manicure mat over the top.

If you are giving a pedicure service, place a towel on the floor in preparation, for the client to put their feet on.

Manicure cushion

Good practice

A **Material Safety Data Sheet (MSDS)** for all the products you use while carrying out nail services should be kept in a file for reference.

Equipment, materials and products

The following items are usually required for manicure and pedicure services.

- Manicure trolley – ensure that it is clean and contains everything you need.

- Manicure bowl – this should contain warm water with some oil or antibacterial soap. Soaking the client's fingers in the water helps to soften the cuticles and cleanse the skin. Softened cuticles are easier to push back.

- Foot spa or bowl – contains warm water with antibacterial soap or essential oils, for soaking the client's feet.

- Emery boards (also known as nail files) – a wooden emery board is generally used to file and shape the nails. The darker, coarser side of the emery board is used to remove length from the nail. The finer, smoother side is used to file nails into shape and for **bevelling**. It should be used at a 45-degree angle, and in one direction only, working from the outside and moving into the middle of the nail.

- Foot file – used to remove dry, flaky and hard skin from the feet. A fast stroking action is used in one direction only. A sawing action may cause friction and so result in discomfort. Working in this way also helps you to keep control of how much skin you are removing, as this can be difficult to gauge if you are carrying out quick back and forth movements.

- Nail buffer or three-way buffer – stimulates the blood circulation to the nail, which helps to improve the health of the nails. Buffers also help to give the nails a slightly shiny appearance. They can be disposable or have a leather

key terms

Material Safety Data Sheet (MSDS): a form prepared by manufacturers and marketers of products that contain toxic chemicals. It outlines safe handling methods and control of hazardous substances used in the workplace.

Bevelling: to bevel the nails means to file with an upward stroke to the underside of the free edge. This removes any rough edges.

Emery boards

Foot file

Nail buffer and three-way buffer

Nail scissors

Cuticle knife

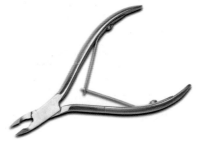

Cuticle nippers

Toenail clippers

Hoof stick

surface. They are used with an abrasive substance called buffing paste. The three-way buffer has sides that have slightly different textures. Firstly, the gritty side of the buffer is used to help remove roughness, ridges and stains; next the second roughest side is used to buff the nails. The first two sides are good for stimulating the blood circulation. Finally, the smooth side is used to polish the nails to make them shiny and glossy.

- Nail scissors – used to cut the nails. Nail scissors often have curved blades, which help to cut the nails without weakening them.

- Cuticle knife – a small metal tool that needs to be handled with care. It is used to free any cuticle that is stuck to the nail plate, and also to remove dead skin from around the cuticle and nail wall. It must be used flat, with light pressure, and care must be taken not to poke it into the cuticle. It should be kept wet, by dipping it into water containing some antiseptic, to prevent scratching of the nail plate.

- Cuticle nippers – if there is too much cuticle, or a hangnail, the cuticle nippers can be used to remove it. The cuticle nippers should be handled with care and must not pull or tear the skin.

- Toenail clippers – similar to cuticle nippers, but larger, and used to cut toenails. They may have either curved or straight jaws that come to a fairly fine point.

- Orange sticks – these are wooden sticks with a pointed end and a hoof end. The hoof end can be used for pushing back pre-softened cuticles. The pointed end can be tipped with cotton wool and used to clean around the nail and under the free edge. Both the pointed and hoof ends can be used to apply products such as cuticle and buffing cream to the skin and nails.

- Hoof stick – this is generally made of plastic, and has a pointed end and a rubber hoof end. The hoof end is used to push back the cuticle. The pointed end can be tipped with cotton wool and used to clean under the free edge of the nail.

- Cuticle remover – helps to soften and loosen the cuticle from the nail plate, which makes it easier to remove any excess cuticle. This product also helps to dissolve dead cuticle and skin around the nail. The potassium hydroxide found in cuticle remover is alkaline and may cause skin irritation, so remove it fairly quickly from the nails. Glycerol is added to help prevent the potassium hydroxide from being too drying to the nails and skin.

- Cuticle cream/oil – used to soften the cuticles so that they may be gently pushed back. Cuticle cream is made from a mixture of fats and waxes, including **beeswax**, lanolin and **white soft paraffin**, and is particularly useful for dry cuticles. Cuticle oil contains ingredients such as vegetable oil, mineral oil, vitamin E and jojoba (*ho-ho-bah*).

■ Buffing paste – used together with a buffer, it helps to smooth out ridges and removes stains from the nails. It consists of a gritty substance, such as talc, silica, kaolin or pumice, mixed with a combination of wax and mineral oil to form a paste. Only a little bit needs to be applied to each nail.

■ Exfoliator/rough skin remover – usually a creamy substance containing small granules that have an abrasive action, so help remove dry, flaky and rough skin. This helps to improve the skin's appearance and texture (feel of the skin).

■ Hand/foot cream/oil or lotion – used to massage and/or moisturise the skin and particularly useful for dry skin types. Hand and foot creams are made up of **emollients** and humectants. Hand and foot lotions have a thinner consistency owing to their higher oil content.

■ Nail polish – there is a vast range of different coloured nail polishes to choose from. Their main ingredient is nitrocellulose, which is a liquid mixed with tiny cotton fibres. Nitrocellulose is mixed with a plasticiser, such as castor oil, to prevent it drying too rapidly. Nail polish will also contain **resin** and colour.

■ Base coat – helps to prevent staining of the nails when using a coloured nail polish. It also provides a smooth base on which to apply nail polish. Ridge-filling base coat is useful to help make any ridges on the nail plate less noticeable, as it evens out the surface of the nail. Base coats contain more resin than nail polishes, to help improve adhesion to the nail plate.

■ Top coat – helps to protect the nail polish, so that it doesn't peel or chip as quickly. It also provides an attractive shine to the nails. The top coat contains increased nitrocellulose and plasticisers to enhance gloss and to resist chips.

■ Nail polish remover – used to remove nail polish and oil from the nails. It works by dissolving the nail polish. Removers contain ingredients such as **acetone**, ethyl acetate or butyl acetate and there are two main types: acetone and non-acetone removers. Oils, such as glycerol, are also added to help prevent the product from being too drying to the skin and nails. If a client has artificial nails, you should use non-acetone remover as acetone will damage them. Non-acetone remover is also preferable for clients with dry nails or skin, as acetone can be drying.

key terms

Beeswax: beeswax is a natural wax produced in the beehives of honey bees. The female worker bees have glands on their abdomens that produce the wax, and it is used to make their honeycombs. It makes a good humectant (helps to retain water so prevents drying of the cuticles) and emollient (helps to soften the cuticles and skin).

White soft paraffin: a white, odourless, solid substance that is derived from petroleum (also known as white petroleum jelly). It helps moisturise the skin by providing a layer of oil on the skin's surface that prevents water from evaporating from the skin.

Resin: a yellowish thick liquid or soft substance made from plants. Resin helps to ensure that the nitrocellulose found in nail polish adheres to the nail surface.

Acetone: a colourless, flammable liquid that can dissolve nail polish and nail extensions.

Nail polish

Base coat

Nail polish remover

- Nail white pencil – used under the free edge to give white nail tips when nail polish is not used.

- Nail strengthener/hardener – forms a protective coating that helps to strengthen the nails to prevent breakage. Chemicals called formaldehyde and dimethyl urea help make them effective hardeners.

- Nail polish dryer – helps to speed up the drying of nail polish. Types of nail polish dryer include a spray, oil, or light dryer.

- Nail polish thinner – used to thin polish if it has become thickened. Add a few drops to the polish and shake.

- Cotton wool pads/balls – can be used to tip orange sticks and to apply and remove products. They should be placed into clean bowls.

- Spatulas – used to remove products from pots and containers. Wooden spatulas can be thrown away after use.

Good practice

Always use a spatula to remove a product from a pot. If you use your fingers you will transfer bacteria to the contents. A lot of bacteria is found under the fingernails.

- Tissues – there are many uses for tissues, including protecting the clothing and separating toes.

- Towels – medium-sized towels are used for drying the client's hands and also for placing on the lap.

- Antiseptic wipes – used to clean client's hands before treatment.

- Bin – the bin should be placed near to the couch and should be lined with a plastic bin-liner

- Surgical spirit/sanitising solution – after use, items such as tweezers and scissors should be thoroughly cleaned with surgical spirit, then placed into a jar of sanitising solution such as barbicide.

- Client record card/consultation form – to record the client's personal details, treatment details and any products purchased.

The following table shows how manicure and pedicure tools and materials should be dealt with after use.

Disposable so can be thrown away	Can be cleaned	Can be disinfected	Should be sterilised
Cotton wool	Towels – wash at 60°C	Foot file	Cuticle knife
Tissues		Bowls	Cuticle nippers
Orange sticks		Buffer	Cuticle remover
Wooden spatula		Plastic spatula	Scissors
Couch roll		Plastic hoof stick	Nail clippers
Emery board		Trolley	
Disposable buffer			
Antiseptic wipes			

DON'T FORGET

Ensure metal tools are always made of stainless steel so they do not rust.

DON'T FORGET

All stainless steel tools can be sterilised in the autoclave.

Good practice ✓

Place metal tools into a disinfecting solution or ultraviolet (UV) cabinet in preparation for use.

Good practice ✓

It is not enough to clean and sterilise tools after use. They must also be stored hygienically to avoid them becoming recontaminated.

Good practice ✓

As emery boards and orange sticks are hard to sterilise, therapists may give them to the client at the end of the manicure as a small gift.

UNIT OUTCOME 1

Be able to use safe and effective methods of working when providing manicure and pedicure services

UNIT OUTCOME 3

Be able to carry out manicure and pedicure services

UNIT OUTCOME 5

Understand how to work safely and effectively when providing manicure and pedicure services

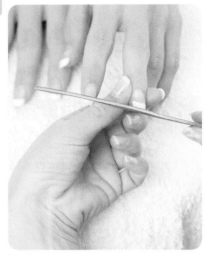

Manicure

Manicure service

A manicure service should take around 30–45 minutes, however this is dependent on the type of treatment being given. Some salons offer luxury manicures and specialised treatments, which means the service may take longer.

It is important to ensure the client is in a comfortable and relaxed position. Make sure they do not have to lean forward over the workstation as this will cause aching in the back and shoulder areas. The client's chair should have adequate back support.

The therapist should assess the condition of the hands and nails before treatment takes place in case any contra-indications are present.

Procedure for a manicure service

Most manicure treatments carried out in a salon will follow a procedure similar to the one below.

Step-by-step-guide

DON'T FORGET

If applying nail polish to the nails, make sure the client replaces jewellery beforehand to prevent smudging. This will also be a good time for your client to pay; otherwise, she may smear her newly painted nails when trying to get money from her purse!

1 Discuss the treatment plan with your client, and if she wishes to wear nail polish, ask her to choose which one she would like. If the client is wearing jewellery, remove it and put it in a safe place. Wipe over the hands with antiseptic, and then look at the nails and both sides of the hands to check for contra-indications.

2 Use a cotton wool pad with nail polish remover to get rid of any existing nail polish. Press the pad firmly onto the nail for a couple of seconds, then work from the nail base to the free edge to remove all of the polish. Use a tipped orange stick and nail polish remover to get rid of any nail polish remaining at the sides of the nails.

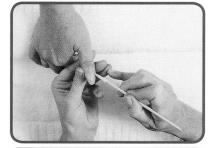

3 If required, cut the nails with nail scissors. Cut across the free edge of the nail, leaving the nail slightly longer than the desired length.

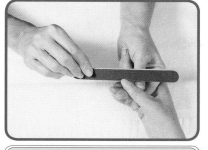

4 Work on one hand only for steps 4–6. Support each finger and use an emery board to file the nails into the desired shape (see page 264 for details of different nail shapes). Always file from the sides towards the middle, in one direction only – don't saw!

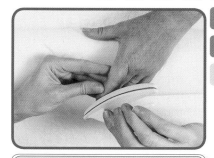

5 Apply a small amount of buffing paste to each nail, then use the buffer to stroke from the nail base to the free edge with light but rapid strokes. Apply about 10 strokes to each nail.

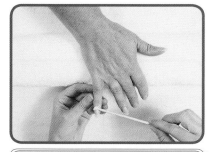

6 Use an orange stick to apply a small amount of cuticle cream/oil to the client's cuticle area. Use the thumb to massage the cream/oil into the cuticles. This will help soften the skin so excess cuticle will be more easily removed.

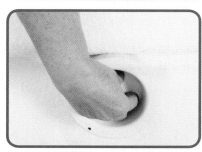

7 Soak the fingers in warm soapy water in the manicure bowl. Repeat steps 4–6 to the second hand. Dry the first hand and put the second hand into the manicure bowl to soak. Apply steps 8–11 to the first hand.

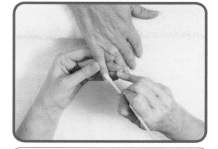

8 Apply cuticle remover to the cuticles with the pointed end of a tipped orange stick. Clean around the cuticle and under the free edge. With the hoof end (or a hoof stick) flat to the nail plate, use circular movements to gently push back the cuticles.

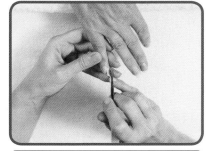

9 Use the cuticle knife to lift the cuticle from the nail plate, and to remove any dead skin from around the nail wall. The blade should be damp and kept flat to the nail surface to avoid scratching the nail plate. Work round the nail border with small circular movements, keeping the cutting edge facing towards the middle of the nail.

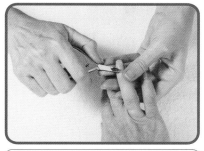

10 Use the cuticle nippers to remove excess cuticle. Place the pointed end of the nippers slightly under the lifted cuticle. Squeeze the blades together to ensure a clean cut is made before releasing the blades and moving further along the cuticle. Collect any bits of cuticle onto a tissue or cotton wool pad.

11 Use the fine side of the emery board to bevel the free edge of the nail to remove any roughness. Stroke the pad of your thumb across the free edge to check that it is smooth. Take the second hand out of the manicure bowl and dry it. Repeat steps 8–11 on the second hand.

DON'T FORGET

Following application of each coat, lightly touch the tip of the thumbnail to check whether the polish is dry. It is important to allow each coat to dry before applying another, otherwise it may smudge.

DON'T FORGET

While the nails are drying, advise the client about products that may be beneficial for the skin and nails, and that can be purchased from the salon for home use.

DON'T FORGET

If you use a back and forth movement to remove nail polish from the nail, you will end up smearing the polish over the fingers.

DON'T FORGET

It is better to use lint-free pads to remove nail polish as cotton wool may leave small fibres on the nails.

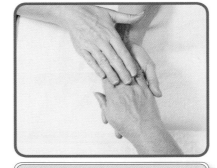

12 Apply either hand cream or lotion to the hands and forearms and carry out a hand and arm massage. See pages 272–273 for the massage routine.

13 Remove any oil from the nails with a cotton wool pad soaked with nail polish remover. If buffing is required as an alternative to nail polish, use an orange stick to apply a tiny amount of buffing paste to the middle of each nail and smooth it with a buffer towards the free edge.

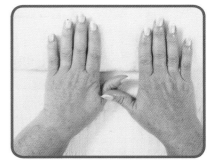

14 Apply a base coat – if the nails contain ridges choose a ridge filling basecoat. Some basecoats are also strengtheners.

15 Apply one coat of a coloured nail polish, leave it to dry, then apply a second coat. Finally, apply a top coat, but remember that pearlised polishes do not require it. See how to apply nail polish on pages 264–266. Record details of the client's treatment, including any product purchases, on the record card/consultation form and escort the client to reception.

Many salons will use a certain range of products, such as Jessica, to carry out a treatment and may also sell them. If a client likes a certain product, such as the colour of the nail polish you have applied, she is likely to want to purchase a bottle of the same coloured polish.

Good practice

Using a base and top coat will help to prevent the nail polish from chipping or peeling.

Quick-glance manicure routine

1 Remove nail polish from all nails.

2 File nails of the first hand from the sides to the centre.

3 Apply buffing paste and buff the nails.

4 Apply cuticle cream/oil and massage into the cuticles.

5 Soak the hand in a manicure bowl.

Repeat steps 2–5 on the second hand.

6 Dry the first hand.

7 Apply cuticle remover.

8 Clean around the cuticles and free edge of the nail, and gently push back the cuticles.

9 Use the cuticle knife.

10 Use the cuticle nippers.

11 Bevel the free edge of the nails.

Repeat steps 6–11 on the second hand.

12 Massage both hands and lower arms.

13 Remove oil from the nails.

14 Apply base coat, nail polish and top coat. If nail polish is not used, buffing may be carried out instead.

15 Allow the polishes to dry.

Ask Fran

Q: My client's nails are soft, weak and break easily. Which products can I recommend to improve the condition of her nails?

A: A weekly manicure can be recommended, until the condition improves.

Also, to help prevent her weak nails from chipping, advise her to gently file the nails with the finer surface of an emery board. Nails should be filed in one direction, working from the outside and moving into the middle of the nail. However, recommend she file only once a week, as excessive filing can cause the nails to become weaker.

Recommend using a nail hardener to help strengthen the nails and oil to prevent the layers within the nail plate from flaking. Massaging oil into the nails nourishes the nails and skin, and stimulates the blood circulation to help promote healthy nail growth.

Buffing the nails of a male client

Massaging oil into the nails

DON'T FORGET

Buffing is often required at the end of a manicure for a male client.

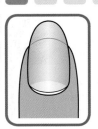

Oval nail

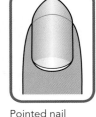

Pointed nail

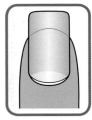

Square nail

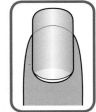

Squoval nail

Round nail

Fingernail shapes

Fingernails naturally come in a variety of shapes and sizes. A beauty therapist can help create a nail shape that suits the client's hands. Nail shapes include oval, pointed, square, squoval and round.

Oval nail

This is generally considered to be the most feminine and attractive nail shape. It is an ideal shape for short, thick fingers, as it adds length to the nails and helps to make the fingers look longer.

Pointed nail

A pointed nail can break easily as this shape weakens the nail. Ideally, the nails should not be filed into this shape.

Square nail

Short, square nails are often preferred by clients whose jobs would make long nails impractical, for example, typists and beauty therapists. It is also the shape often used for French manicures and for nail art designs.

Squoval nail

This is one of the most common shapes and, as the name suggests, it is a cross between a square and an oval shape. The nail is filed to a slightly rounded shape and then filed straight across the top of the free edge.

Round nail

This is a practical nail shape, as it is hard-wearing, strong and neat. This shape suits short nails and is used to create a natural, inconspicuous look. It is a common choice for male clients.

How to apply nail polish

Beginning at the centre of the nail, push the brush back towards the base of the cuticle and then apply three brush strokes down the length of the nail from the base of the cuticle to the free edge. If the nail is large you may need to apply four strokes of nail polish.

Follow the tips below to achieve the best results.

- When painting nails, try not to use more than four stokes of the brush.

- To make wide nails appear slimmer, leave a thin gap down each side of the nail.

- A French manicure can makes the nails appear longer.

- Dark nail polish makes the nails look smaller.

- Pearlised nail polish makes ridges in the nails more noticeable.

DON'T FORGET

Nail polish should not be applied to nails with severe ridging, because it is difficult to achieve a good finish.

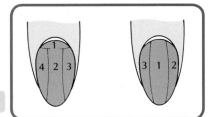

Three strokes of nail polish

- Always allow each coat to dry before applying the next, otherwise smearing will occur.
- Products such as nail polish drying spray will help speed up the drying process. A light dryer may also be used.

Good practice

If you flood the cuticle area with polish, use a tipped orange stick dipped in nail polish remover to get rid of it.

Pearlised nail polish

French manicure

A French manicure will give a clean, natural look to the nails. It involves applying a white polish to the free edge of the nail and a neutral coloured polish over the whole nail.

Step-by-step guide

1 Wipe the nails with nail polish remover to remove any existing nail polish or oil.

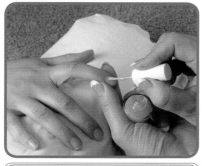

2 Apply a base coat and allow it to dry.

Ask Fran

Q: Why *do* dark nail polishes cause yellow stains on the nails?

A: This occurs when UV light reacts with the pigment in the nail polish. To prevent staining, it is important to apply a good base coat to act as a barrier between the polish and the nail. If staining has occurred, the tops of the nails can be lightly buffed to help remove it. There are also products available that lighten the nails and remove the yellow colouring.

DON'T FORGET

To correct any mistakes, use a cotton bud or tipped orange stick soaked in nail polish remover.

DON'T FORGET

Pearlised nail polishes are shimmery because they contain fish scales or chemicals such as bismuth oxychloride.

DON'T FORGET

To make short nails look longer, always leave a gap around the cuticle and along the sides of the nail.

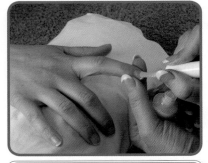

3 Apply white polish to the tip of the nail. Begin at one side of the free edge and sweep the brush across the top of the nail to the other side. Allow it to dry.

4 Apply neutral coloured (usually beige, pink or clear) polish to the whole of the nail using three or four strokes.

5 When the polish is dry, apply a top coat.

Q: Sometimes when I apply nail polish and allow it to dry, there are tiny bubbles in the polish. Why is this?

A: Bubbles can form if you apply too thick a layer of polish. It is better to apply two thin coats. Bubbles may also form naturally in the bottle of polish. Rolling the bottle between your palms will help to get rid of bubbles in the polish and stop new ones from forming.

Male manicure

A manicure service for a male client generally differs slightly from the manicure service for a female client.

- The nails are usually filed to a shorter length.
- The nails are usually filed to follow the shape of the fingertip.
- Non-perfumed oil/cream is used.
- Nail polish is not usually applied.
- The nails are usually buffed at the end of the treatment to give them a shine.

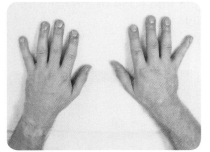

Male manicure

Pedicure service

Pedicure service

A standard pedicure service should take about 50 minutes.

Ensure the client is seated comfortably and, if required, place a towel over their lap for modesty reasons. You need to ensure you have everything close by and then place a towel across your own lap. A towel also needs to be placed on the floor between you and the client. This is for the client to put their feet on.

The therapist should assess the condition of the feet and nails before treatment takes place in case any contra-indications are present.

Good practice ✓

If a client is booked in for another service, such as a make-up service, on the same day as their pedicure, ensure you carry out the pedicure first; by the time the make-up service is finished the nail polish will be completely dry, so the client will be able to put on their shoes without smudging it.

Procedure for a pedicure service

Step-by-step guide

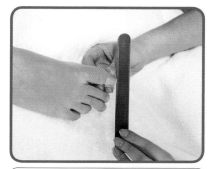

1 Discuss the treatment plan with the client and, if required, ask them to choose a nail polish colour. Check the feet and nails for contra-indications.

2 Ask the client to place their feet in a foot bath containing warm, soapy water. After soaking for 5–10 minutes, dry both feet with a clean towel. Throw away the water and refill the foot bath.

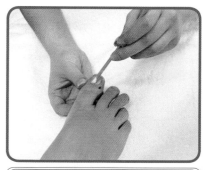

3 Remove any nail polish from the client's nails. Then use scissors or nail clippers to shorten the nails, if necessary.

4 Work on one foot only for steps 4–6. File the nails with an emery board (file straight across the nail).

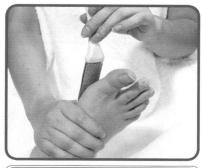

5 Use a foot file or exfoliating cream to remove dead skin cells and hard skin. Pay particular attention to the heel and ball of the foot.

6 Use a tipped orange stick to apply cuticle cream/oil to the cuticles, and use the thumbs to massage it in. Soak the foot in the foot bath. Then repeat steps 4–6 on the second foot. Dry the first foot with a towel.

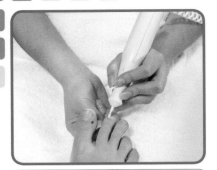

7 Apply steps 7–12 to the first foot. Apply cuticle remover to the cuticle area with a tipped orange stick. Clean around the cuticle and under the free edge of the nail.

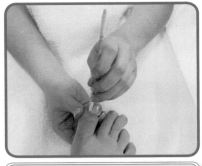

8 With the hoof end of the orange stick (or a hoof stick) flat to the nail plate, use circular movements to gently push back the cuticles.

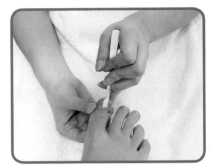

9 Use the cuticle knife to lift the cuticle from the nail plate, and to remove any dead skin from around the nail wall. The blade should be damp and kept flat to the nail surface to avoid scratching the nail plate. Work round the nail border with small circular movements, keeping the cutting edge facing towards the middle of the nail.

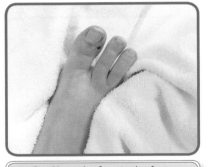

10 Clean the foot in the foot bath and then dry the foot.

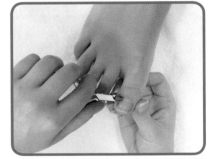

11 Use the cuticle nippers to remove excess cuticle. Place the pointed end of the nippers slightly under the lifted cuticle. Squeeze the blades together to ensure a clean cut is made before releasing the blades and moving further along the cuticle.

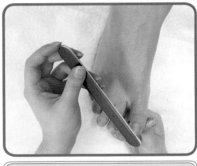

12 Bevel the nails to remove any rough edges. Dry the second foot and repeat steps 7–12.

13 Apply cream or oil to your hands and carry out lower leg and foot massage. See pages 273–274 for the massage procedure.

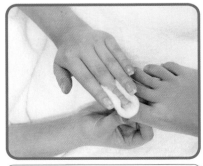

14 Remove any oil from the nails using cotton pads and nail polish remover.

15 Fold facial tissues and use them to separate the toes – this is more hygienic than using other types of toe separators.

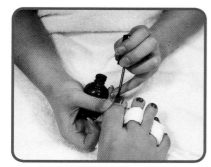

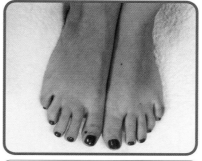

16 Apply a base coat, followed by two coats of nail polish and a top coat. Allow plenty of time for the nail polish to dry and then remove the toe separators.

17 Ensure the client is satisfied with the final result and discuss aftercare advice. If products are purchased, make a note of this on their record card/consultation form.

Good practice

Disposable toe separator footwear can be worn by the client, so they can freely walk around the salon as their toenails dry.

Quick-glance pedicure routine

1 Soak both feet in warm, soapy water, then dry.
2 Remove nail polish.
3 Shorten the nails if necessary.
4 File the nails of the first foot.
5 Remove hard skin.
6 Apply cuticle cream/oil and massage it in.
7 Soak the foot in the foot bath.

Repeat steps 4–7 on the second foot.

8 Dry the first foot.
9 Apply cuticle remover.
10 Push back the cuticles and clean around the free edge of the nail.
11 Use the cuticle knife.
12 Clean and dry the foot.
13 Use the cuticle nippers.
14 Bevel rough edges of the nail.

Repeat steps 8–14 on the second foot.

Ask Fran

Q: Why does streaking sometimes occur when using paler, whiter colours?

A: Streaking is more likely to occur when the nail polish contains a lot of white pigment. It may also happen if you are applying the nail polish too thickly, or if the product is past its best. Nail polish thinner will help to make it easier to apply and also extend its life.

15 Massage the feet and lower legs.

16 Remove oil from the nails.

17 Separate toes.

18 Apply base coat, nail polish and top coat.

19 Allow the polishes to dry.

Massage

There are many benefits of massage, including the following.

- It improves the condition of the skin.

- It increases the blood and lymphatic circulation. This helps to brings oxygen and nutrients to the part being massaged, and removes waste products that may be responsible for muscle stiffness, aches and pains.

- It relaxes tight muscles.

- It relieves stiff joints.

- It relaxes the mind and body.

- It helps to induce feelings of calmness.

- It creates a feeling of well-being.

The following massage techniques are used in hand and arm massage and foot and leg massage.

Effleurage

Effleurage involves using the hands to slowly stroke a body part. It can be applied superficially (with light pressure) or deeply (with slightly harder pressure). The hands may be used alternately or both together to perform this movement. The hands must completely relax and mould to the shape of the limb or part being treated.

Effleurage should be carried out in the same direction as blood travels in the veins (known as venous return). For example, it should be applied in an upward direction on the legs and arms, towards the heart. At the end of the movement the hands glide back over the body using almost no pressure at all.

It is mostly a restful movement, ideal to use at the beginning or the end of the massage.

DON'T FORGET

On small areas, such as the face, fingers and toes, the pads of the fingertips or thumbs may be used for effleurage instead of the whole hand.

Effleurage is used to:

- begin and end massage on a body part
- link one massage movement with another to help the massage flow smoothly
- help spread oil or cream over the area to be massaged
- promote relaxation
- calm the nerves
- improve lymphatic drainage, so it is useful for fluid retention (oedema)
- improve venous (blood in veins) drainage
- help eliminate toxins from an area after stimulating movements such as tapotement have been used.

Petrissage

Petrissage movements involve deeper pressure than effleurage movements, and are useful for working deep into the muscle tissue. These movements usually involve pressing the muscle against the bone or lifting the muscle away from the bone. Petrissage movements include kneading (the muscle is pressed on to the bone using firm movements) and thumb sliding.

Petrissage is used to:

- help relieve stiffness and pain in muscles by removing waste products from affected muscle
- stimulate poor blood circulation
- stimulate lymphatic drainage, therefore relieving fluid retention (oedema)
- relax tense muscles and break down knots
- improve the condition of the skin so that it looks healthier.

Tapotement

Tapotement movements include hacking and cupping, and are stimulating movements. Tapotement is used to:

- increase blood circulation to the area
- warm the area
- tone the muscles.

Procedure for hand and arm massage
Massage one hand and forearm at a time.

Step-by-step guide

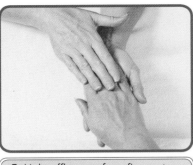

1 Light effleurage from fingers to elbow (a). Using one hand to support the client's hand and the other to carry out the massage, stroke over the whole outer forearm. Repeat this movement 6 times.

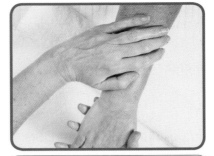

2 Light effleurage from fingers to elbow (b). As for step 1, but use slightly deeper pressure with the hand while stroking.

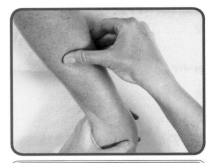

3 Thumb kneading to forearm. Use one hand to support the client's hand and the other hand to massage. Use the pad of the thumb to create circular movements over the outer forearm. Work over the whole area.

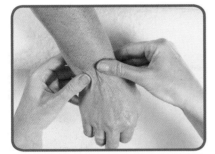

4 Thumb kneading to wrist. Place both thumbs on the upper wrist. Use the pads of the thumbs to create small, circular movements around the joints of the wrists.

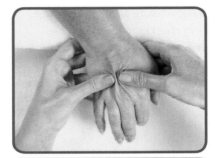

5 Thumb kneading to back of hand. Hold the client's hand firmly with both hands. Use the thumbs to create small circular movements to the back of the hands working between the tendons (these feel and look rather like bones on the back of the hands, and run from the knuckles to the wrist).

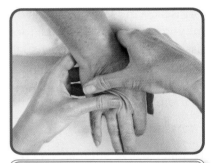

6 Cross-thumb sliding to back of hand. Use your thumbs to carry out a zigzag movement to the back of the hand.

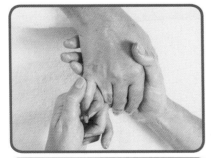

7 Thumb kneading to joints of fingers. Hold the client's hand firmly and use the pad of the thumb of the other hand to make small, circular movements to all the joints of the fingers.

8 Thumb kneading to joints of thumb. Hold the client's hand firmly and use the pad of the thumb of the other hand to make small, circular movements to the joints of the thumb.

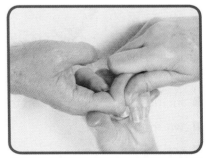

9 Pushing against a resistance. Clasp the client's fingers one at a time and ask them to pull against yours to create a resistance. Repeat 6 times to each finger and thumb.

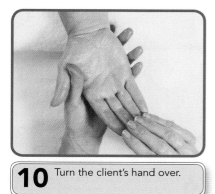

10 Turn the client's hand over.

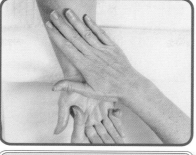

11 Light effleurage from fingers to elbow (inner forearm). Use one hand to support the client's hand and the other hand to massage. Effleurage over the entire inner forearm and use light pressure to stroke back down the arm. Repeat this movement 6 times.

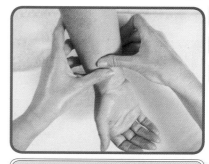

12 Thumb kneading from elbow to palm. Use one hand to support the client's hand and the other hand to massage. Use the pad of the thumb to create circular movements over the palm and whole inner forearm area.

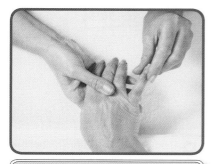

13 Finger rotation. Hold each finger with your index finger and thumb, then simply rotate each finger and then the thumb. Repeat 6 times with each finger and thumb.

14 Wrist rotation. Support the client's wrist with your hand and then use the other to grasp the client's fingers with your fingers. Rotate the hand at the wrist 6 times in each direction.

15 Light effleurage from fingers to elbow. Use one hand to support the client's hand and the other hand to massage. Effleurage over the whole outer forearm and use light pressure to stroke back down the arm. Repeat this movement 6 times. Now massage the other lower arm and hand.

Procedure for foot and lower leg massage
Massage one foot and lower leg at a time.

Step-by-step guide

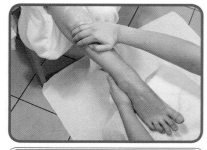

1 Light effleurage from the toes to the knee. Using alternate hands, stroke up the front of the lower leg, then slide down the back of the lower leg. Repeat 6 times with each hand.

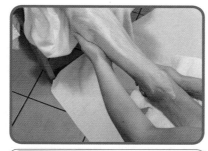

2 Palmar knead to calf. Use the palm of the hand to create circular movements to the back of the lower leg.

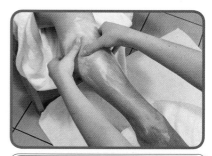

3 Thumb knead to tibialis anterior muscle. This runs down the side of the tibia bone. Use the pad of the thumb to create circular movements. Do not massage directly onto the bone.

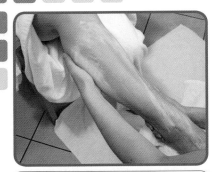

4 Cupping to calf. Ensure the foot is supported, and with the hands in a cupped position, alternately strike them against the leg. Work over the back of the lower leg.

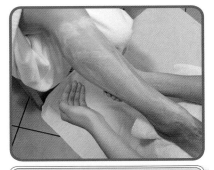

5 Hacking to top of the foot. Gently hit the top of the foot with light strokes using the sides of the hands.

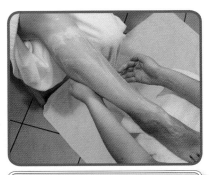

6 Light effleurage to foot. Use both hands to stroke the whole of the foot. Repeat 6 times.

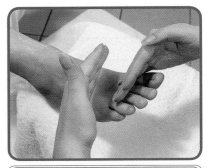

7 Kneading to Achilles tendon. Support the foot with one hand and use the index finger and thumb of the other hand to carry out the massage. Create circular movements with the finger and thumb working in an upwards direction on the back of the lower leg.

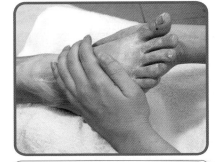

8 Thumb kneading to bottom of foot. While supporting the foot, use the pads of the thumbs to carry out circular movements covering the whole bottom of the foot and also the toes.

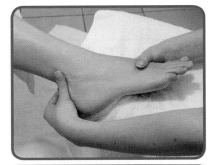

9 Thumb slides to bottom of foot. While supporting the foot, use the thumbs to slide across the foot, working from the base of the toes to the heel of the foot.

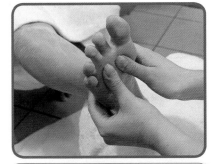

10 Palmar knead to bottom of foot. Support the foot with one hand and use the palm of the other hand to knead the whole bottom of the foot. Work from the base of the toes to the heel of the foot.

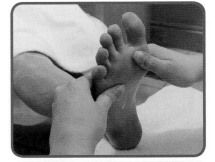

11 Thumb knead to medial side of foot. Support the foot with one hand and use the pad of the thumb on the other hand to create circular movements. Work over the whole inner side of the foot.

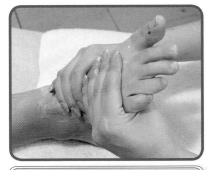

12 Effleurage to foot and lower leg. Support the foot with one hand, and use the other hand to stroke up the front of the lower leg and then stroke down the back of the lower leg. Repeat 6 times.

Additional services for feet, hands and nails

Warm oil treatment for nails

This treatment may be carried out in the salon or given as homecare advice. The warm oil helps to soften the cuticles and is particularly beneficial for dry skin and flaky nails. Use oils such as sweet almond oil or olive oil.

Procedure for warm oil treatment

1 Place a large bowl of hot water on a flat surface. Put oil into a small bowl and allow it to stand in the hot water. This will help to warm the oil.

2 Soak the client's nails in the warm oil for five minutes.

3 Remove the fingers from the bowl and massage the oil into the nails and hands.

4 To further nourish the skin and nails, wrap the oil covered fingers in tin foil and leave for 5–10 minutes.

5 Remove the foil and massage the oil into the skin and nails. Remove any excess oil with a tissue or a towel.

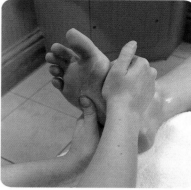
Warm oil treatment

Paraffin wax treatment for hands and feet

This treatment softens and moisturises the skin, so it is particularly useful for hydrating dry skin. Paraffin wax is heated in a special container to a temperature of around 50–55 °C and is applied to moisturised hands or feet. The wax has excellent heat-sealing properties and the warmth helps the moisturiser to penetrate into the skin. This treatment also increases blood circulation and reduces joint stiffness, so it is beneficial for clients with arthritis. It is also a pleasant and relaxing experience.

DON'T FORGET

Paraffin wax treatment may be given to clients with artificial nails.

Good practice

Never try to heat the wax using anything other than the proper equipment.

Procedure for paraffin wax treatment
The paraffin wax should be heated about half an hour before giving treatment.

1 Ensure the client does not have any contra-indications.

2 If treating the hands, ask the client to roll up long sleeves. If treating the feet, ask the client to roll up their trouser legs.

3 Rest the client's hands/feet on tin foil that has a towel placed underneath it.

4 Apply moisturising lotion to the client's hands/feet and massage into the skin.

5 Test the temperature of the paraffin wax on your skin.

6 Transfer the paraffin wax into a bowl lined with tin foil.

7 Use a brush to apply the paraffin wax to the client's skin.

8 Apply an even coating of wax to both sides of the hands/feet. Work quickly otherwise it will set.

9 Wrap the hands/feet in the tin foil, then wrap the towel around them too. This will help to keep in heat so the moisturiser can penetrate more easily.

10 The wax can be left on the skin for 10–15 minutes.

11 To remove the wax, massage the hands/feet to loosen the wax, starting at the wrist/ankle, then peel it away and dispose of it.

1. Apply paraffin wax to a moisturised hand; ensure the whole hand is covered and sufficient wax is applied.

2. Wrap the hand in foil to help keep in heat.

3. Wrap a towel around the foil to also help retain heat.

Thermal mitts and boots

Thermal mitts and boots are electrically heated to provide warmth to the hands or feet. The level of heat may be adjusted to suit the client. The heat, combined with a moisturising cream or lotion, helps to:

- moisturise and hydrate the skin

- make the skin feel smooth and so improve its texture

- increase the blood circulation, so nutrients are brought to the skin

- soothe aching joints and reduce joint stiffness.

Procedure for using thermal mitts or boots

1 Apply moisturiser to the hands/feet.

2 Wrap the hands/feet in cling film.

3 Ask the client to put their hands into the thermal mitts or their feet into the thermal boots.

4 The hands/feet can remain in the thermal mitts/boots for 10–15 minutes.

5 A massage may be given after the treatment or, as this treatment also helps to soften the cuticles, it can be followed by cuticle work.

Thermal mitts

UNIT OUTCOME 7

Know contra-indications and contra-actions that affect or restrict manicure and pedicure services

Contra-actions

The skin may react to products being used. If a reaction such as redness or itching occurs, remove the product from the client's skin immediately. If necessary, a soothing lotion can be applied to the area to help calm down any redness. Remember to enter these details on the client's record card/consultation form.

Thermal boots

UNIT OUTCOME 10

Understand how to provide aftercare advice for clients.

Aftercare advice

Aftercare advice is an important part of giving a professional service, and will help the client keep their hands, feet and nails in good condition. Aftercare advice includes the following.

■ Follow a healthy, well-balanced diet to help keep the nails healthy and strong.

■ Wear gloves in the winter to protect the hands from exposure to cold weather, which may cause chapping.

■ Wear gloves when gardening and when washing-up or cleaning, to protect the hands from detergents and other household chemicals.

> **key terms**
>
> **SPF (sun protection factor):** this is a rating given to sun creams, which tells you how much protection they provide from the burning (UVB) rays of the sun. For example, if a person normally burns in the sun after 15 minutes of exposure, a lotion with an SPF of 4 allows them to stay out four times longer (i.e. one hour) in the sun without burning.

Ask Fran

Q: My client suffers with extremely dry skin and cuticles. What should I recommend?

A: If the cuticles are dry, they are more likely to split, and so may allow bacteria to enter and cause infection; also, dry cuticles are more likely to adhere to the nail plate, which can spoil the look of the nails.

Your client would benefit from having regular manicure treatments to help soften and hydrate the cuticles and the skin around them. Regular use of an exfoliating product during the treatment will help to remove dead skin cells and make the skin feel smoother. Thermal mitt or paraffin wax treatments can also be recommended, as these are moisturising to the skin and nails.

At home, recommend that your client uses a good hand cream and cuticle oil to moisturise the hands and nails; for a really effective nourishing treatment, suggest they put gloves (either cotton or rubber) on top of the oil and moisturising cream. This will trap in warmth, which will aid the penetration of the products into the skin and nails.

- Regularly apply hand cream to keep the hands and nails moisturised and to help prevent brittle and split nails.

- Wear hand creams that contain an **SPF (sun protection factor)**, which will help to slow down the ageing of the skin and help prevent the formation of liver spots.

- Use an emery board frequently, to keep the nails smooth and free of splits.

- Wear a base coat and nail strengthener to help protect the nails, especially if they are weak.

- Do not use nails as tools, for instance when opening a ring-pull on a can.

- If the nails and the skin around them are dry, use acetone-free nail polish remover, as acetone is drying.

- Dry the hands thoroughly after washing (or the skin may become dry).

- Ensure that the feet are thoroughly dry after washing to help prevent fungal infections.

- When cutting the toenails, always cut straight across the nail to help prevent ingrowing toenails.

- Recommend products the client can purchase from the salon that will be beneficial for the skin and nails of the hands and feet.

- Advise the client what action to take if there is a contra-action to any of the products used.

UNIT OUTCOME 4

Understand organisational and legal requirements

For information about legal requirements see **Unit G20: Ensure responsibility for actions to reduce risks to health and safety**.

How are you doing?

1 Which of the following does **not** make up part of the nail?
  a Matrix
  b Paronychia
  c Free edge
  d Lunula

2 A hangnail is:
  a a contra-indication to treatment
  b found on the free edge of the nail
  c a small, torn piece of skin near to the nail
  d caused by bacteria

3 Which of the following is the medical term for white spots on the nail plate?
  a Fungus
  b Psoriasis
  c Paronychia
  d Leuconychia

4 A wart is caused by:
  a a bacterial infection
  b a viral infection
  c a fungal infection
  d a parasite

5 A fungal infection of the foot that commonly spreads in places such as communal showers and changing rooms is called:
  a athlete's foot
  b arthritis
  c a bunion
  d psoriasis

6 Onychophagy is the term for:
  a brittle nails
  b overgrown cuticles
  c an infected toenail
  d bitten nails

7 The free edge of the nail is:
  a the area of the nail plate near to the matrix
  b part of the nail bed
  c the part of the nail that extends over the fingertip
  d the skin around the nail

8 The ideal nail shape is considered to be:
  a oval
  b triangle
  c diamond
  d rectangle

9 When using an emery board to shape the nails you must ensure that you:
  a carry out a back and forth (sawing action)
  b work from the side to the middle in one direction only
  c only use the roughest side of the emery board
  d file the nails as quickly as possible

10 Which of the following is **not** used during a nail treatment?
  a Cuticle cream
  b Orange stick
  c Buffing paste
  d Headband

11 The buffing method involves:
  a buffing in one direction from the nail base to the free edge
  b banging the buffer directly onto the nail plate
  c vigorous strokes from side to side across the nail plate
  d working in fast, circular motions across the nail plate

12 Which of these products is alkaline and can cause irritation to the skin if left on for too long?
  a Cuticle remover
  b Buffing paste
  c Cuticle oil
  d Ridge-filling base coat

13 Which of the following is **not** generally an additional service for feet, hands and nails?
  a Warm oil treatment
  b Steaming
  c Paraffin wax treatment
  d Thermal mitts

14 The nails should be free from grease when:
  a applying cuticle remover
  b applying nail polish
  c applying massage oil
  d placing the fingers into the manicure bowl

15 Which of the following is **not** aftercare advice for a manicure treatment?
  a Apply nail strengthener to weak nails
  b Regularly apply hand cream
  c Use coloured nail polish every day
  d Wear gloves when washing-up or gardening

are you ready *for* **assessment**?

The evidence for this unit must be gathered in the workplace (salon) or realistic working environment (training centre).

Simulation (role play) is not allowed for any performance evidence within this unit.

You must practically demonstrate in your everyday work that you have met the required standard for this unit.

All outcomes, assessment criteria and range statements must be achieved.

Knowledge and understanding in this unit will be assessed by a mandatory written question paper. These questions are set and marked by VTCT.

Assessing your practical work

Your assessor will observe your performance of a practical task, such as a manicure.

Your assessor will sign off an outcome when all criteria have been competently achieved.

On occasions, some assessment criteria may not naturally occur during a practical observation. In such instances you will be asked questions to demonstrate your knowledge in this area. Your assessor will document the criteria that have been achieved through oral questioning.

In this unit you must demonstrate competent performance of all practical outcomes on at least **three** separate occasions (each occasion must involve a different hand and nail treatment from the range).

Assessing your knowledge and understanding

You will be guided by your tutor and assessor on the evidence that needs to be produced.

Your knowledge and understanding will be assessed using the assessment tools listed below.

- Mandatory written question paper
- Oral questioning
- Portfolio of evidence

Carry out waxing services

On completion of this unit you will:

1. Be able to use safe and effective methods of working when waxing

2. Be able to consult, plan and prepare for waxing treatments with clients

3. Be able to remove unwanted hair

4. Understand organisational and legal requirements

5. Understand how to work safely and effectively when providing waxing treatments

6. Understand how to consult, plan and prepare for the treatment

7. Know anatomy and physiology that relates to waxing treatment

8. Understand contra-indications that affect or restrict waxing treatments

9. Understand equipment, materials, products, techniques and treatment planning for waxing

10. Be able to provide aftercare advice for clients

Introduction

There are many different hair removal methods, most of which are temporary. This unit mainly focuses on waxing services but also discusses other methods. Both temporary and permanent methods are usually offered within a salon.

Waxing is a very popular treatment, especially during the summer months, and owing to regrowth of hair, the client will return regularly for this treatment. There are different types of waxing, including hot, warm and cold waxing.

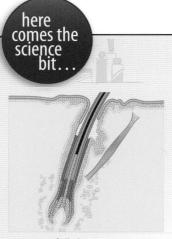

here comes the science bit…

Hair in its follicle

Waxing is a very popular salon treatment, especially throughout the spring and summer months. It is a method that involves pulling the hairs out from the roots, resulting in a smooth clear skin that lasts for around four weeks.

DON'T FORGET

Cold wax products can be bought from most chemists and large supermarkets, and are available as pre-waxed strips. However, beauty therapists would not use these in a salon.

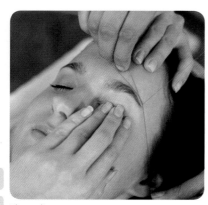

Threading

Temporary methods of hair removal

Most methods of hair removal are temporary. The hairs regrow, so regular treatments are required.

Depilatory waxing

Depilatory waxing is an effective temporary method of removing unwanted hair. Cold, warm or hot wax can be used. The wax is applied to the skin, and when it is removed it takes the hair with it. Regrowth takes about four weeks, depending on the area waxed.

Sugaring

Sugaring is similar to waxing, but uses a paste containing sugar, lemon and water. The hairs stick to the sugar paste, so when it is removed the hairs are removed too.

Plucking

Plucking or tweezing the hair from its follicle is the simplest and cheapest method of hair removal. It involves using tweezers to pull out hairs from the root. This method can be time consuming, so should be used only on small areas such as the eyebrows. Regrowth of hairs takes about four weeks.

Tweezing

Threading

Threading is an ancient form of hair removal, most commonly used for eyebrow shaping and removing facial hair. A cotton thread is wrapped around the fingers and twisted over hair to pull out it out from the roots. It is a faster and less painful method than plucking because many hairs are removed at once.

Cutting

Cutting hairs with scissors only removes hair from the skin's surface and not from the root. This is a fast and painless method, but will not produce a completely smooth result, and the hair grows back quickly.

> **Good practice**
>
> Advise a client to cut the hairs of a hairy mole. Waxing or tweezing may cause the hairs to become thicker and stimulate growth of more hairs.

Shaving

A razor blade is used to remove hairs at the surface of the skin. This is a quick and generally painless method, but regrowth of hair will occur quickly.

Both cutting and shaving result in hairs growing back with a blunt edge, which makes them feel spiky.

Depilatory (hair removal) cream

The alkaline chemical (calcium thioglycolate) in the depilatory cream, reacts with the protein (keratin) in the hair, so the hair dissolves and can then be wiped or washed away. It is a quick and painless way of removing hair. However, most creams have an unpleasant odour and the hair usually grows back within a few days.

Depilatory cream

Abrasive mitt

An abrasive mitt fits onto the hand and has a rough surface, rather like sandpaper, which is rubbed in circular motions against the skin. This action causes the hair to be broken off at the surface of the skin. A pumice stone can also be used for this purpose. It is a fairly painless method, but can be time consuming, and hair will regrow quickly.

Permanent methods of hair removal

Some methods can remove hairs permanently. This usually requires several treatments, but will eventually result in no further regrowth of hair.

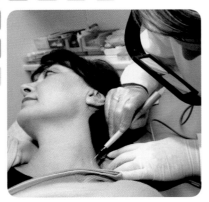

Electrolysis

Electrolysis

Electrolysis involves passing an electrical current into the hair root through a fine needle. The needle is placed into a hair follicle and the current destroys the dermal papilla (the area that provides nutrients for hair growth) so preventing further regrowth. Electrolysis is expensive and time consuming compared to other hair removal methods, however, it is an effective permanent method. The client may feel some discomfort while the treatment is being carried out.

Laser hair removal

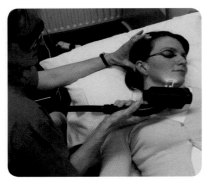

Laser hair removal

This method uses laser light to prevent hair growth. The laser produces a light that targets the melanin (the pigment that gives the hair its colour) in the hair follicle. The melanin absorbs the laser energy, which is turned into heat. The heat destroys the dermal papilla and the matrix of the hair follicle (where cells divide to make the hair). Therefore new hair growth is slowed or stopped. Once an area has been treated with the laser it can take up to 14 days for the destroyed hair to fall out. The laser only affects hairs that are in the growth phase (anagen stage) of the hair cycle. This is why around four treatments are usually required to see a noticeable hair growth reduction.

Intense pulsed light (IPL)

This works in a similar way to laser hair removal. However, whereas laser light produces only one colour of light, intense pulsed light (IPL) systems produce many different colours. The light produces heat that affects the lower third of the follicle and destroys the hair cells, thereby preventing further hair growth.

UNIT OUTCOME 2

Be able to consult, plan and prepare for waxing treatments with clients

UNIT OUTCOME 6

Understand how to consult, plan and prepare for the treatment

Consultation

Make sure you explain the treatment to the client. If it is the client's first time for waxing treatment, warn them there may be some discomfort. The feeling is similar to having a plaster ripped off the skin.

Ask the client about their expectations of the treatment and if they have any contra-indications to treatment.

Always ensure the client signs the record card/consultation form, as this may be a requirement of your salon's insurance company.

> **Good practice**
>
> Clients under 16 years old should be accompanied by a parent or guardian who will be expected to sign a consent form.

For more information on the consultation process, see **Unit G20: Ensure responsibility for actions to reduce risks to health and safety**.

Service times

Ensure your client is clear about how long the treatment will take. The following table shows you how long each waxing treatment should take.

Treatment	Time
Full leg wax	45 minutes
Half leg wax	30 minutes
Bikini line wax	15 minutes
Full arm wax	20 minutes
Underarm wax	15 minutes
Eyebrow wax	15 minutes
Upper lip wax	10 minutes
Chin wax	10 minutes

Skin sensitivity test

If a client has sensitive skin, they should ideally have a skin sensitivity test before having waxing treatment. This test should be carried out at least 24 hours before the treatment is given.

1   Test the wax on your wrist to ensure it is not too hot, and then remove it.

2 Apply some wax to the client's inner forearm, then remove it with a small piece of strip.

3 If the client notices any changes in the patch test area within the next 24 hours, such as redness, itchiness and swelling, they should not go ahead with treatment. You could offer the client an alternative treatment such as sugaring.

UNIT OUTCOME 8

Understand contra-indications that affect or restrict waxing treatments

key terms

Doctor's referral note: a doctor can advise if their patient can go ahead with a treatment, despite having a condition such as diabetes.

Contra-indications

If the client has any of the following contra-indications, you should either avoid the affected area, or advise the client to get a **doctor's referral note**.

- Skin disorders and infections
- Recent haemorrhage
- Recent operations
- Recent fractures or sprains
- Diabetes
- Bruising – the area around a bruise can be waxed
- Swellings – the area around them can be waxed
- Warts or moles – the area around them can be waxed
- Varicose veins – the area around them can be waxed
- Areas of scar tissue – the area around them can be waxed
- Areas with lack of sensation – the area around them can be waxed
- Cuts or abrasions – the area around them can be waxed

Without causing alarm to the client, suggest they seek medical advice regarding a contra-indication, or return for treatment when the contra-indication is no longer present.

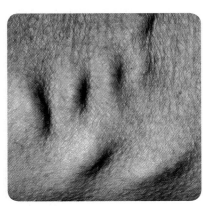
Varicose veins

Good practice

People with diabetes may have thin and fragile skin that heals poorly, so waxing treatment may not be suitable for them. They need to seek a doctor's advice.

key terms

Skin tag: these are soft lumps attached to the skin by a stalk, which tend to occur in areas such as the armpits, face and neck. They are quite common and are harmless.

UNIT OUTCOME 9

Understand equipment, materials, products, techniques and treatment planning for waxing

Equipment, materials and products

The following equipment, materials and products are required for a waxing treatment.

- Couch with plastic cover – the plastic cover helps to protect the couch

- Trolley – should be disinfected and lined with couch roll

- Pot of wax-heated in a wax heater or roller wax system

- Wax removal strips – paper and material (can be cut to suit the area being waxed)

- Antiseptic or pre-wax lotion – to cleanse the area before waxing treatment and remove any oils that could prevent the wax from sticking to the hairs

- After wax lotion – to help get rid of any stickiness after waxing and to soothe the skin

- Talcum powder – to absorb any moisture on the skin

- Petroleum jelly – for protecting the skin during eyebrow waxing, or for covering moles etc.

- Scissors – to trim long hair and cut strips

- Tweezers – to remove any hairs that remain after waxing

- Disposable spatulas – to apply wax

- Orange sticks – to apply wax to small areas

DON'T FORGET

Wax contains a wax base (usually beeswax or paraffin), resin to help the wax stick to the hair and skin, and an oil or fat to make the removal of hair easier.

DON'T FORGET

Hot wax heaters used to be supplied with a filter so you could recycle and reuse the wax. This was stopped because it was found that skin cells, sweat, sebum and even blood, could not be filtered!

Warm wax heater

Cream wax

- Mirror – for discussing facial waxing with the client

- Towels – to protect the client's clothing

- Apron – to protect the therapist's uniform

- Disposable gloves – may be required for hygiene reasons

- Headband – to keep hair off the face during facial waxing treatments

- Cotton wool pads – for cleansing the skin

- Disinfecting solution, such as barbicide, in a jar – to store items such as tweezers and scissors

- Tissues – used to protect clothing while carrying out the waxing treatment, and to cover small areas of wax spillage on the couch

- Client record card/consultation form – used to record client information, such as their contact details and treatment given

- Aftercare leaflets – these give aftercare advice that should be carried out following treatment

Good practice

All metal tools, such as tweezers and scissors, should be sterilised in an autoclave before use.

Good practice

Ensure the couch has a plastic cover to protect it from wax spillage.

DON'T FORGET

Cream waxes are useful for sensitive skin types as they contain moisturisers and azulene, which has anti-inflammatory properties. They are good for all skin types but are specifically formulated to calm and soothe the skin.

Gel waxes are also available which, because of their consistency, can be spread very thinly onto the skin.

UNIT OUTCOME 1

Be able to use safe and effective methods of working when waxing

UNIT OUTCOME 3

Be able to remove unwanted hair

UNIT OUTCOME 5

Understand how to work safely and effectively when providing waxing treatments

Hot wax treatment

Because of its high temperature, hot wax is useful for removing strong hair growth, such as that found on the underarm and bikini line areas. The wax is applied to the skin with a spatula and allowed to cool a little. The wax tightens around the hairs, so when it is pulled away the hairs are lifted off too.

The wax consists of beeswax and resins and should be heated to 55 °C. When the wax is at the correct temperature it should be soft in consistency and pleasantly warm rather than hot. The wax can become very hot, so care needs to be taken to maintain a safe working temperature throughout the treatment.

Hot wax

Good practice

Don't heat hot wax to too high a temperature, as once it is cooled to working temperature it may become brittle and hard to use.

DON'T FORGET

If the wax becomes too brittle, apply some new wax on top of it to help soften it and make it easier to remove.

Procedure for a hot wax treatment

Step-by-step guide

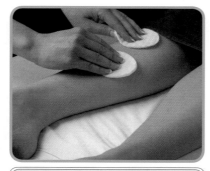

1 Ensure the client's clothing is protected with towels.

2 Wipe over the area being treated with an antiseptic or pre-wax lotion. This will clean the skin and remove any oil and so on that would prevent the wax from sticking to the hair.

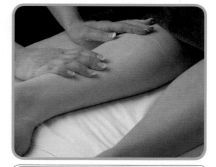

3 Apply a fine dusting of powder against the direction of the hair growth. This raises the hair and absorbs any moisture on the skin, thereby helping the wax stick to the hair.

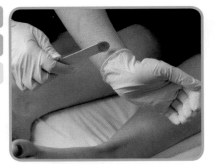

4 Put on disposable gloves and test the temperature of the wax on the inside of your wrist, and then on either the client's wrist or ankle. Use the fingertips to peel off the hot wax from the wrist.

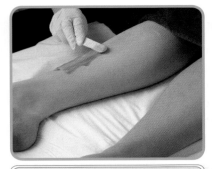

5 Use a wooden spatula to apply the wax to the skin – twist it frequently to avoid drips. The wax should be applied in strips approximately 5 cm wide by 10 cm long, and about 3 mm thick. First apply a layer of wax against the direction of the hair growth.

6 Then apply a layer in the direction of the hair growth, and finally another layer against the growth. Make sure the outer edges of the strip are slightly thicker so they can be gripped easily and don't break.

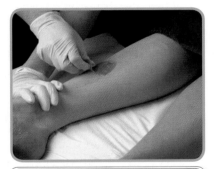

7 Leave the strip to cool for about 30 seconds while firmly pressing it down with your fingers. As it cools it will tighten around the hairs. When it feels soft but dry to the touch, flick the edge of the wax up with your fingers, grasp it firmly, and pull against the direction of the hair growth. Use the other hand to stretch the skin, which will help to make the removal of the wax less uncomfortable.

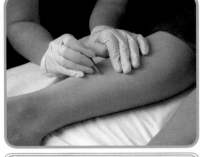

8 Remove any remaining hairs with tweezers and apply after wax lotion.

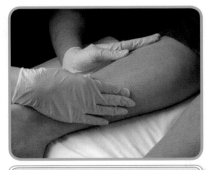

9 Apply after-wax lotion. Give aftercare advice, fill out the client's record card/consultation form, and book the client for their next appointment – usually about four weeks later.

Good practice

Try to make sure that the edge of the hot wax that is to be gripped and pulled off is positioned onto a hair-free area. This will cause less discomfort to the client when the wax removed.

Warm wax treatment

Warm waxing is a popular treatment for removing hair growth, such as that found on the legs, underarm, bikini line and facial areas. The wax is commonly applied to the skin with a wooden spatula, however, many therapists use a roller wax system, which involves using a special device to roll the wax onto the skin. In both methods, the wax is removed using paper or fabric strips,

DON'T FORGET

Hot wax can be used on any area of the body, but if a smaller area is being treated a smaller strip will need to be applied.

and as it is removed it pulls the hairs out from the skin. The wax should be heated to around 43°C. Regrowth of hairs takes around four weeks.

Good practice

Always check the wax heater is set at the correct temperature, and test the wax on yourself before applying it, to a client. If the wax is too hot it can burn.

Procedure for a warm wax treatment using a spatula

Step-by-step guide

DON'T FORGET

1. Apply a layer of hot wax against the direction of hair growth.
2. Apply a layer of hot wax in the direction of hair growth.
3. Apply a layer of hot wax against the direction of hair growth

1 Clean the skin with an antiseptic or pre-wax lotion, to ensure it is clean and oil free. Blot dry with tissues, and if the skin is damp owing to perspiration, add a little talcum powder to the area.

2 Remove some wax from the wax pot with a wooden spatula and wipe the excess onto the sides of the pot. Test some wax on your wrist to make sure it is at the correct working temperature. Use the fingertips to peel off the hot wax from the wrist.

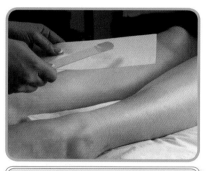

3 As the spatula is taken towards the client, ensure the wax strip is held underneath it to catch any drops of wax. Test the temperature of the wax on a small area of the client's skin.

4 Hold the spatula at a 90-degree angle on the skin, and thinly spread the wax in the direction of the hair growth.

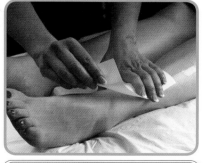

5 Fold back the end of the wax strip – you will hold on to this when you pull off the strip.

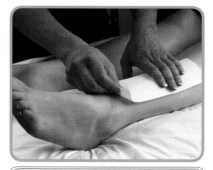

6 Place the strip onto the wax, press firmly, and rub over it a few times. Ensure the folded part is placed at the correct end.

7 Support the skin with one hand, and use the other to grasp the folded end of the strip, then quickly pull it off against the direction of the hair growth. Ensure the strip is pulled in a horizontal direction and not upwards, as that would be uncomfortable for the client and might result in breakage of hair.

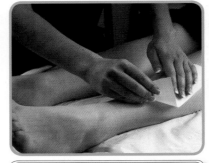

8 Apply more wax near to the previous area treated and repeat. Reuse the strip until the wax build up is too thick and it becomes ineffective at removing more wax. A new strip can then be used.

9 Use tweezers to remove any remaining hairs and apply after wax lotion.

DON'T FORGET

Incorrect removal of wax strips can tear or bruise skin.

Good practice ✓

Do not pull the waxing strip off in an upwards direction, as this may result in breakage of hair and could also cause the skin to bruise.

Good practice ✓

It is generally not considered good practice to re-dip the spatula at all during the waxing treatment, in case cross-infection occurs. Instead, the wax should be transferred from the 'dipping' spatula to another spatula, which is then used to apply the wax. However, the method used will depend on the training centre or workplace.

DON'T FORGET

It is cheaper to refill the wax cartridges rather than keep buying new ones.

DON'T FORGET

You can also buy sugaring roller systems.

Roller wax treatment

Roller waxing systems are commonly used in salons. The wax is contained within a tube or other container, often called a cartridge, which is heated in a special wax heater. There are various sized cartridges – some are designed for use on the body, and so are bigger, and others are for smaller areas such as the face. A special roller head is attached to the cartridge and then the wax is rolled onto the skin. This is a very hygienic system, because the roller head spreads fresh wax onto the skin with every application. When all the wax in one cartridge has been used, the roller head can simply be removed and placed onto another full cartridge.

The method for a roller wax treatment is the same as for a warm wax treatment using a spatula, except that the warm wax is rolled onto the skin. Between each application of wax the cartridge should be place back into the heater, or into a thermo sleeve, to keep the wax warm.

Roller wax system

Good practice

If the roller wax container is a little too warm for your hands, wrap a wax strip around it to hold onto. The strip will absorb some of the heat.

To ensure an effective waxing treatment

- Ensure the skin is clean and oil free before you apply the wax.

- Make sure the wax is applied thinly to the skin.

- Apply wax in the direction of the hair growth, but pull the strip off against the direction of the hair growth.

- Make sure the strip is parallel to the skin as it is pulled off, and remove it with a quick flick.

- When pulling the wax off, hold the skin taut and ensure it is well supported.

- Do not go over a sensitive area of the body, such as the face, underarms or bikini line, more than twice with wax, as it could result in skin breakage and bruising.

- If necessary, reposition your client to make it easier for you to apply and remove wax in certain areas. Putting your body into awkward positions will put you at risk of suffering from aches and pains.

DON'T FORGET

Warm wax needs to kept at a temperature of about 40–43 °C so it can be spread thinly onto the skin.

DON'T FORGET

If a client has been having waxing treatments for a long time, hair growth may become sparse or even stop altogether.

HAVE A GO

Practise applying small strips of wax to your leg or arm as thinly as possible. Cut out small pieces from wax strips to remove the wax.

DON'T FORGET

In hot conditions, such as during the summer months, the wax may become sticky and so more difficult to remove with a wax strip. In cold conditions, such as during the winter months, cold legs can make the wax set more quickly, which means it tends to spread more thickly and is more difficult to remove. However, with experience, you will soon learn how to overcome these problems.

DON'T FORGET

As knees are bony, they can be a tricky area to wax. Remember to bend the knee when waxing over it.

DON'T FORGET

If the legs are cold, thick lumps of wax may form, which are difficult to remove. If this happens, take a new strip, press it onto the lump, and remove it slowly in the direction of the hair growth.

DON'T FORGET

Ensure your client is warm, because being cold causes the hair follicles to tighten around the hairs. This means the hairs will be more difficult to remove, and the treatment will be more uncomfortable for the client.

Procedure for a half leg wax treatment

A half leg wax involves waxing both legs from the knee to the foot. It can take 15–30 minutes, depending on the amount and thickness of hair growth. If the client has had their legs waxed many times before, the hairs will generally be easier to remove than if the client has previously shaved their legs.

Good practice

Have a facial tissue handy in case some wax dribbles onto the couch cover. Bits of tissue can be placed on top of any blobs of wax, so the client doesn't get sticky.

Step-by-step guide

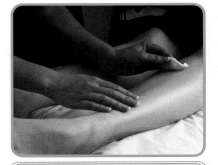

1 Position the client in a raised, sitting position. Use an antiseptic or pre-wax lotion to clean the lower legs.

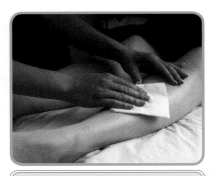

2 Use tissue to blot the legs to remove any moisture, and apply some talcum powder if necessary.

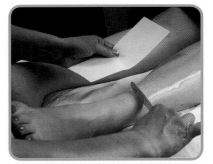

3 Working on the front and sides of one lower leg, use the spatula to spread wax from the bottom of the knee towards the ankle (in the direction of the hair growth). The leg may need to be repositioned at times to make it easier to wax the sides.

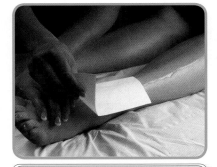

4 Use a paper strip to remove the wax, starting at the ankle, and pulling up towards the knee.

5 When the front and sides of the lower leg have been waxed, bend the knee, position the spatula at the top part of the knee, and spread the wax in a downwards direction over it.

6 Place the strip at the bottom part of the knee and pull it in an upwards direction. Then place the strip on the upper part of the knee and remove the wax.

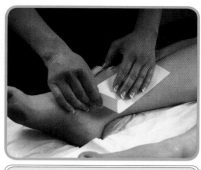

7 Repeat on the other lower leg.

Ask Fran

Q: I've noticed that if the treatment room is hot, blobs of wax can become stuck to the client's skin and are difficult to remove. I'm afraid that if I keep trying to remove them, the skin may become damaged. What do you suggest?

A: This is a fairly common occurrence during the summer months. My advice is to get a new wax strip, press down onto the blob, and remove the strip in the direction of the hair growth. This usually solves the problem.

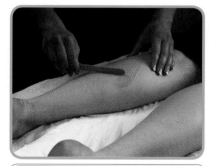

8 Lower the backrest of the couch and ask the client to turn over. Notice that the pattern of hair growth on the back of the lower leg is usually from the outside of the leg towards the inside; therefore the wax needs to be applied across the leg rather than down it.

9 Use a paper strip to remove the wax. (Note: most clients like to have their toes waxed too. When applying wax to them, be aware that the hair may grow in different directions. Small strips can be used to remove the wax.)

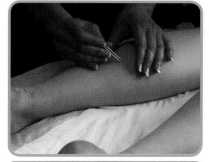

10 After both lower legs have been fully waxed, use tweezers to remove any remaining hairs.

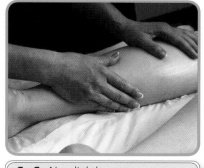

11 Now lightly massage some afterwax lotion into the legs.

DON'T FORGET

If a client has used self-tanning lotion on her legs, they will probably look blotchy after being waxed. This is because dead skin cells containing the tan will be removed along with hair.

Procedure for a full leg wax treatment

A full leg wax includes the upper legs as well as the lower legs. The techniques used are the same as for the lower legs. Ensure you support the skin well, as bruising is more likely to occur on the upper legs. Also, notice the direction of hair growth on the back of the upper legs – it often follows a similar pattern to the hair on the back of the lower legs.

Procedure for a bikini line wax treatment

Step-by-step guide

DON'T FORGET

If you are using a lot of strips, perhaps more than six to carry out a full leg wax, it may be because you are applying the wax too thickly. Practise applying it as thinly as possible.

DON'T FORGET

You can buy plastic tubes containing wax that are heated and thrown away after use. The wax is applied to the skin directly from the tube. This is less messy and more hygienic than using the spatula method, but it is also more expensive.

1 Lie the client in a flat position. (If she is pregnant, or suffers from blood pressure problems, raise the couch head slightly.) Position facial tissues over the client's underwear and ask the client to tuck them into each side; this will help to stop wax from getting onto the underwear. Ask the client to help position the underwear so you know how much hair to remove.

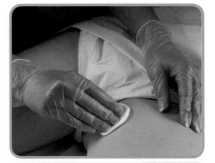

2 Put on disposable gloves, and use an antiseptic or pre-wax lotion to cleanse the bikini line area. Blot the area dry using tissues and apply talcum powder if necessary.

3 Ask the client to bend the leg and allow it to flop to one side, so that the knee is turned outwards. This will create a flat surface, making the bikini line hairs easier to remove. A pillow can be placed under the leg if the client finds this more comfortable.

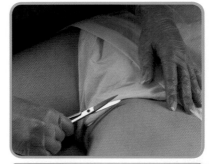

4 If the hairs are quite long, use scissors to cut them shorter – this will make it easier to remove the hairs and will be less painful for the client.

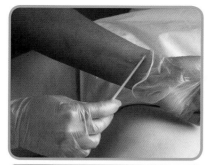

5 Test a little wax on your inner wrist to make sure the temperature is comfortable, and then test it on the client's skin. Use a small piece of wax strip to remove the patch of wax.

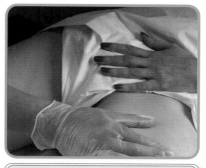

6 Ask the client to stretch the skin of the area being treated with her hands, as this makes it easier to wax. Also use your free hand to support the skin.

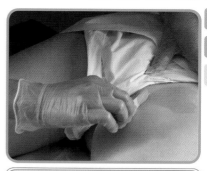

7 Apply the wax to one side of the bikini line and then remove it with a strip. Do not work over the same area more than twice as the skin can be quite sensitive. When the whole area has been treated, move to the other side of the couch and treat the other side. Tweeze out any remaining hairs.

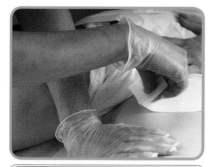

8 Remove the wax with a strip. Do not work over the same area more than twice as skin can be quite sensitive. When the whole area has been treated, move to the other side of the couch and treat the other side.

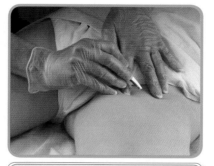

9 Tweeze out any remaining hairs.

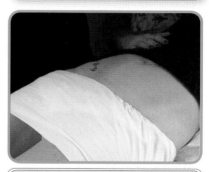

10 To remove hairs from the abdomen area, firstly tuck a tissue into the top of the client's underwear and then slightly pull it down. Discuss with the client how much hair she would like removed from this area. Notice that the hairs usually grow from the outside edge of the bikini area inward, and then upwards to the navel.

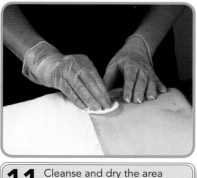

11 Cleanse and dry the area and, if required, trim the hairs.

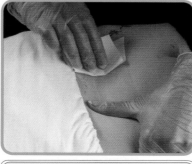

12 Wax this area using small strips, then tweeze any remaining hairs.

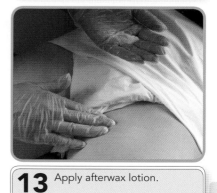

13 Apply afterwax lotion.

DON'T FORGET

A Brazilian wax involves removing all hair from the pubic area except for a thin line – known as the landing strip.

A Hollywood wax involves removing all of the hair from the pubic area.

Unsurprisingly, many clients find these treatments very painful!

DON'T FORGET

You may notice a tendon – a hard and protruding bump – as you apply wax to the upper, inner thigh area. It is advisable to firstly wax above it and then below it. Do not wax over it as bruising may result.

Good practice

If a client suffers with back pain, they may find it more comfortable to have a pillow placed under their lower back when lying on the couch.

Good practice

You may be expected to wear disposable gloves when carrying out a waxing treatment, especially for the bikini and underarm areas, as there may be some slight bleeding. Wearing gloves will help to prevent any cross-infection.

Good practice

If your client is going on holiday, ask her to wear her swimming costume or bikini bottoms, so you know exactly how much hair needs to be removed.

Good practice

Sometimes there will be tiny dots of blood after giving waxing treatments, especially to the bikini and underarm areas, as the hairs here tend to be thick and have deep roots.

Anything contaminated with blood must be sealed into a bag and disposed of in accordance with the local environmental health regulations. Remember to wear gloves when you put it into the bag.

VTCT advises that all waxing waste is treated as contaminated waste and is disposed of in a yellow bag. The yellow bags are available from local authorities, local hospitals and private waste management companies (the same people who collect the sharps boxes).

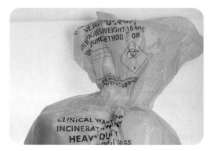

Yellow bags

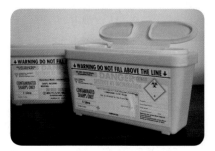

Sharps box

Procedure for an underarm wax treatment

Step-by-step guide

1 Lie the client in a flat position. (If she is pregnant, or suffers from blood pressure problems, raise the couch head slightly).

2 Place a towel over the client's chest, and tuck facial tissues into the sides of her bra to prevent wax getting onto it. Ask the client to lift one arm over her head and rest it on the couch head.

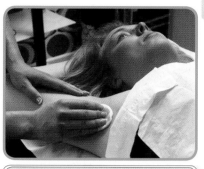

3 Use an antiseptic or pre-wax lotion to cleanse the underarm area and then blot with a tissue.

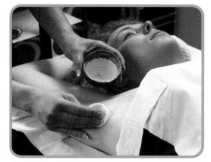

4 If the underarm area is slightly damp, perhaps owing to perspiration, use a cotton wool pad to spread a light dusting of talcum powder onto it. Notice the hair growth patterns, which can run in many different directions under the arm – even forming shapes like crop circles!

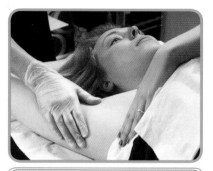

5 Put on disposable gloves. The client can help to stretch the skin by pulling down underneath her underarm area with her other hand.

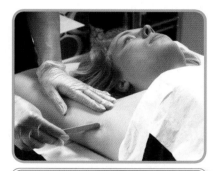

6 Test the temperature of the wax on yourself and then on the client. Use a small piece of wax strip to remove the patch of wax.

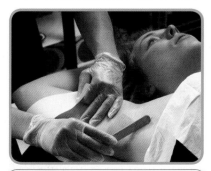

7 Apply the wax to the underarm and then remove it using a small strip. Do not work over the same area more than twice as the skin can be quite sensitive.

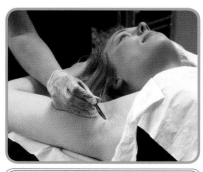

8 Tweeze out any remaining hairs and apply after wax lotion.

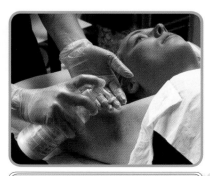

9 Move to the other side of the couch and treat the other underarm.

DON'T FORGET

Some therapists prefer to use material strips for underarm and bikini line waxing, as this type of strip fits snugly into the curved shape of these areas.

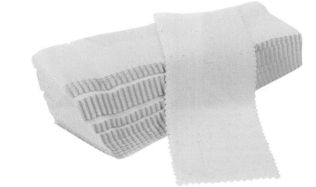

Material wax strips

DON'T FORGET

Advise the client not to bleach facial hair before coming for a waxing treatment. Bleached hair tends to break off when waxed.

Procedure for an arm wax treatment

- The client can either sit in an upright position on the couch, or sit on a chair with their arm resting on the couch.

- Make sure you protect their clothing using tissues and towels.

- Notice the direction of the hair growth. It often grows across the arm rather than down it.

- Cut strips in half, as this will make it easier to wax across the arm.

- Carry out the waxing treatment as you would for other areas of the body.

- Make sure the arm is bent when working over the elbow.

Facial waxing treatments

Procedure for an eyebrow wax treatment

Step-by-step guide

1 Ensure the client is in a semi-reclined position and that their clothes are protected. The hair may need to be secured back from the face with a headband. With the help of a mirror, discuss the client's expectations of the treatment.

2 Cleanse the area with an antiseptic or pre-wax lotion and then blot dry with a tissue.

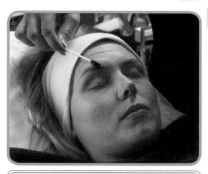

3 Brush the eyebrows and measure them with an orange stick.

4 Apply petroleum jelly to the eyebrows hairs that you do not want to be removed. This creates a barrier to stop the wax sticking to the hairs.

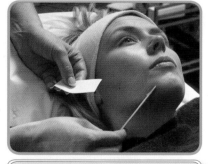

5 Test the temperature of the wax on your inner wrist and then on the client's jawline. Use a small piece of wax strip to remove patch of wax from the wrists.

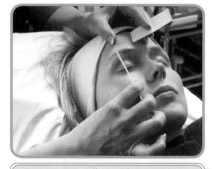

6 Using a small spatula or orange stick, apply a small amount of wax to the eyebrow in the direction of the hair growth.

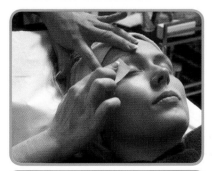

7 Apply a small piece of strip, then pull the strip off towards the direction of the bridge of the nose. Remember to support the skin with your free hand. Wax the other eyebrow.

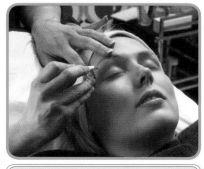

8 Use tweezers to remove any remaining hairs.

9 Apply afterwax lotion to the treated area.

Good practice

When carrying out an eyebrow wax, you may want to put some damp cotton wool pads onto the eyes to protect them from any dripping wax.

See **Unit B5: Enhance the appearance of eyebrows and eyelashes**, for more information about shaping eyebrows.

Procedure for an upper lip and chin wax treatment

Step-by-step guide

1 Lift the couch head so that the client is in a semi-reclined position. Place towels over the chest and, if required, secure the hair back from the face with a headband.

2 Cleanse the upper lip area with an antiseptic or pre-wax lotion, then dry it with a tissue.

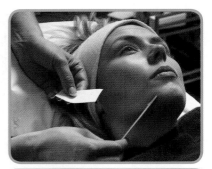

3 Test the temperature of the wax on your inner wrist, then on the client's jawline. Use a small piece of wax strip to remove patch of wax from the wrist.

4 Apply wax to the upper lip from the outer corners of the mouth to the area under the nose.

5 If it is comfortable for your client, ask her to stretch the skin around her mouth by pulling the face shown above. Or you could ask her to smile, which will have the same effect.

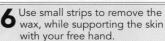

6 Use small strips to remove the wax, while supporting the skin with your free hand.

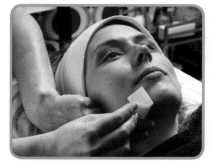

7 If treating the chin too, be aware that the hairs can be thick and strong in this area. Also, they can be tricky to remove because of their growth pattern, which is usually down over the chin.

8 Tweeze any remaining hairs and apply afterwax lotion.

Good practice

If the chin hairs are long, cut them with scissors before carrying out the waxing treatment.

Sugaring and strip sugar

Sugaring is an ancient method of hair removal that involves using a paste containing sugar, lemon and water. As it uses natural ingredients, it is ideal for people with sensitive skin. The hairs stick to the sugar paste, so when it is removed the hairs are removed too.

The sugar paste can be applied to the skin using the hand or, in a method called strip sugar, it is applied with a spatula and removed with material strips.

Benefits of using sugar paste

- It is made from natural products, so is good for use on allergy-prone and sensitive skin types.

- Sugar dissolves in water (water soluble) so it can easily be cleaned from surfaces.

- Sugaring with the hands requires little equipment.

- The sugar paste sticks to the hair and not to the skin, which means it can be reapplied to the same area, if required.

- Clients often say it is less painful than warm waxing treatments.

- It is good for desquamating the skin (getting rid of dead skin cells) so it makes the skin feel smooth.

Ask Fran

Q: How did I cause a small bruise to form while waxing my client's legs?

A: We all make mistakes, but bruising shouldn't happen. It is caused by faulty technique – perhaps you didn't support the skin well enough or you pulled the strip off too slowly. Also, the client could possibly have an illness that has made the skin fragile or more prone to bruising.

Equipment, materials and products

The equipment, materials and products required are similar to those required for warm waxing, but sugar paste is used instead. Sugar paste is available in a hard or soft paste consistency. Hard paste is better to use in a warmer environment, such as during the summer months.

Sugar paste

Good practice

Be very careful if heating the sugar paste in a microwave, as it can easily become too hot and burn the skin.

Procedure for a sugaring treatment

Step-by-step guide

1 Heat the sugar paste in a heater. Cleanse the area being treated with an antiseptic or pre-wax lotion and blot dry.

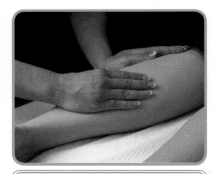

2 Dust some talc over the area being treated.

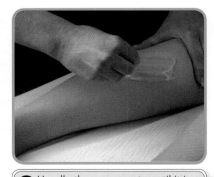

3 Handle the sugar paste until it is the right consistency, and then apply in the direction of the hair growth.

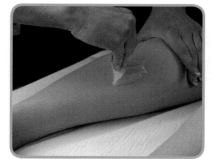

4 Remove it by flicking quickly against the direction of the hair growth.

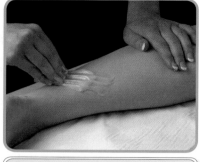

5 If several hairs remain, apply the paste to the area again.

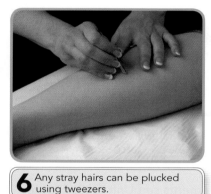

6 Any stray hairs can be plucked using tweezers.

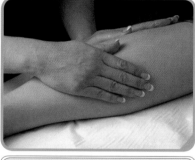

7 Apply an afterwax lotion to the treated areas. Give aftercare advice and fill out your client's record card/consultation form.

Procedure for a strip sugar treatment

1 Heat the sugar paste until it is runny.

2 Cleanse and then blot the skin with tissues.

3 Apply the sugar paste with a spatula in the direction of the hair growth.

4 Use a strip to remove the sugar paste against the direction of the hair growth.

5 Tweeze any remaining hairs.

6 Apply after wax lotion.

7 Give aftercare advice and fill out the client's record card/ consultation form.

> **DON'T FORGET**
>
> *Sugaring is a skill that requires a lot of practice to master.*

Good practice

Used sugar paste contains dead skin cells, hairs and maybe even blood, which poses a risk of cross-infection. Make sure it is quickly and hygienically thrown away.

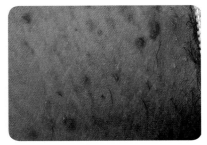

Ingrowing hairs

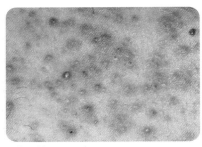

Folliculiltis

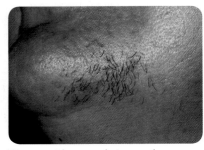

Woman with excess hair growth

key terms

Seborrhoea: a condition where the skin produces too much sebum and so becomes very oily.

Contra-actions

Some skin redness (erythema) is normal after waxing treatment, but if there is excessive redness a cool compress and soothing antiseptic lotion should be applied.

Waxing may cause the hair follicles to become distorted, leading to ingrowing hairs. Advise the client to exfoliate the area with an exfoliating product such as a loofah. This will help to remove dead skin cells and make it easier for the hairs to grow up to the surface of the skin. Ingrowing hairs may also be a result of dry skin forming over the follicle, so the skin should be regularly moisturised to help control the dryness. Wearing tight clothing or boots can also cause ingrowing hairs.

A sterile needle can be used to expose the opening of the follicle so the hair can be released. An antiseptic can then be applied. This should only be carried out in the salon.

UNIT OUTCOME 4

Understand organisational and legal requirements

For information about legal requirements see **Unit G20: Ensure responsibility for actions to reduce risks to health and safety.**

UNIT OUTCOME 7

Know anatomy and physiology that relates to waxing treatment

For more, see the **Anatomy and physiology** unit.

here comes the science bit…

Superfluous hair means excessive hair growth.

This can be caused by heredity factors or ethnic background – women from certain ethnic groups naturally have more terminal hair on their bodies than others.

Excessive hair growth can also occur because of hormonal changes, illness, medication, or even long-term stress.

Women may develop hair in places where usually only men grow hair, for instance facial hair around the lip and chin areas. This is known as hirsutism. Hirsutism is also linked to acne or **seborrhoea**.

Aftercare advice

Be able to provide aftercare advice for clients

- If you suffer from ingrowing hairs, exfoliate and moisturise the area regularly.

- Do not sunbathe or use a sunbed for 24 hours after treatment, otherwise irritation could occur, resulting in itching and pain.

- Wear loose clothing so that it does not rub against the treated area. Tight clothing can cause irritation and ingrowing hairs.

- Do not use a steam room or sauna for 24 hours, as the heat could affect the open follicles.

- Avoid having a hot bath or shower for 24 hours. However, warm water and unperfumed soap can be used to clean the body.

- Do not swim in a swimming pool for 24 hours, as the water could cause irritation of the skin.

- Do not touch or scratch the treated area, as bacteria can be transferred into the follicles and lead to infection.

- Do not apply any products, such as perfumes, self-tanning lotions or make-up, to the treated area for 24 hours, as they may irritate the skin and cause blocked pores.

- Clients should be advised to return for treatment in around four weeks time, depending on the area treated and the hair growth and thickness. Facial waxing is usually done every three to four weeks and body waxing every four to six weeks.

- Hairs should ideally be about 0.25 cm long or more for waxing treatment. If the hairs are too short the wax will not be able to grip them.

DON'T FORGET

Occasionally after hair removal treatment some little whiteheads may appear. This happens because the sebaceous glands have been stimulated and too much sebum is being produced. The client should be advised not to touch them and be reassured that they will disappear within a few days.

Good practice

After waxing, give the client a written aftercare leaflet for reference. Many insurance companies will require that you do this.

How are you doing?

1 Which of the following is a permanent method of hair removal?

- **a** Laser hair removal
- **b** Warm wax treatment
- **c** Threading
- **d** Sugaring treatment

2 What is responsible for giving hair its colour?

- **a** Hair root
- **b** Melanin
- **c** Capillaries
- **d** Dermal papilla

3 Which of the following would **not** commonly be used during a waxing treatment?

- **a** Massage oil
- **b** Tweezers
- **c** Spatulas
- **d** Disposable gloves

4 Which of the following is a normal reaction to waxing treatment?

- **a** Bruising
- **b** Burns
- **c** Removal of skin
- **d** Erythema

5 If the client has long hairs, for example on the bikini and leg areas, what action would you take before carrying out waxing treatment?

- **a** Apply talcum powder
- **b** Cut the hairs to a shorter length
- **c** Tweeze the hairs out
- **d** Apply wax in a different direction

6 If the area to be waxed is damp due to perspiration, what action can you take?

- **a** Apply pre-wax lotion
- **b** Tweeze out the hairs
- **c** Apply talcum powder
- **d** Apply petroleum jelly

7 What is the best way to remove warm wax from the skin?

- **a** Remove the strip with a quick flick, ensuring it is parallel to the skin as it is pulled off
- **b** Remove the strip with a quick flick in an upward direction
- **c** Remove the strip with a quick flick ensuring the strip is held loosely
- **d** Remove the strip with a quick flick in the direction of the hair growth

8 Which of the following is aftercare advice given after a waxing treatment?

- **a** Apply perfumed products to the treated area
- **b** Return for further waxing treatment in 12 weeks
- **c** Ensure the area is not scratched following treatment as bacteria may pass into the hair follicles and cause an infection
- **d** Have a hot bath or shower directly after the waxing treatment

9 Which of the following best describes the action of hot wax?

- **a** The hot wax sticks to the hairs, so when it is pulled away the hairs are stuck to the wax
- **b** The hot wax tightens around the hairs, so when it is pulled away the hairs are lifted off too
- **c** The hot wax dissolves the hairs, so when it is pulled away the hairs disappear
- **d** The hot wax reaches a high temperature and melts the hairs from the surface of the skin

10 Which of the following would you commonly find in sugar paste?

- **a** Sugar
- **b** Lemon
- **c** Water
- **d** All of the above

are **you ready** *for* **assessment**?

The evidence for this unit must be gathered in the workplace (salon) or realistic working environment (training centre).

Simulation (role play) is not allowed for any performance evidence within this unit.

You must practically demonstrate in your everyday work that you have met the required standard for this unit.

All outcomes, assessment criteria and range statements must be achieved.

Knowledge and understanding in this unit will be assessed by a mandatory (compulsory) written question paper. These questions are set and marked by VTCT.

Assessing your practical work

Your assessor will observe your performance of a practical task, i.e. a waxing treatment.

Your assessor will sign-off an outcome when all criteria have been competently achieved.

On occasions, some assessment criteria may not naturally occur during a practical observation. In such instances you will be asked questions to demonstrate your knowledge in this area. Your assessor will document the criteria that have been achieved through oral questioning.

In this unit, you must demonstrate competent performance of all practical outcomes (waxing treatments) on at least **four** occasions, each involving a different client.

Testing your knowledge and understanding

You will be guided by your tutor and assessor on the evidence that needs to be produced.

Your knowledge and understanding will be assessed using the assessment tools listed below.

- Mandatory written question paper
- Oral questioning
- Portfolio of evidence

B7 Carry out ear piercing

On completion of this unit you will:

1. Be able to use safe and effective methods of working when piercing ear lobes

2. Be able to consult, plan and prepare for ear lobe piercing with clients

3. Understand the ear-piercing procedure

4. Understand organisational and legal requirements

5. Understand how to work safely and effectively when piercing ear lobes

6. Understand how to consult, plan and prepare for ear-lobe piercing

7. Know anatomy and physiology that relates to ear-piercing treatments

8. Understand contra-indications that affect or restrict ear piercing

9. Understand equipment, materials, products, techniques and treatment planning for ear piercing

10. Understand the aftercare advice to provide for clients

Introduction

Ear piercing involves piercing the ear lobe area using an ear-piercing gun. The gun holds a sterilised stud and clasp to pierce the ear. The treatment only takes about 15 minutes, which makes it a profitable one.

UNIT OUTCOME 2

Be able to consult, plan and prepare for ear lobe piercing with clients

A pierced ear

Understand how to consult, plan and prepare for ear lobe piercing

Consultation

Clients who come for an ear-piercing treatment may be nervous, so it is important to make them feel as relaxed as possible. Ensure the client understands what the treatment entails, so they know what to expect. As you are carrying out the treatment, explain every step to the client to help them feel at ease.

Make sure you ask the client about any possible contra-indications to treatment, and that you fill out a record card/consultation form and get them to sign it.

For more information on the consultation process, see **Unit G20: Ensure responsibility for actions to reduce risks to health and safety**.

Good practice

Anyone under the age of 16 years old must be accompanied by a parent/guardian who should sign a consent form. The consent form should be kept for three years so it can be inspected if necessary.

Understand contra-indications that affect or restrict ear piercing

Contra-indications

Contra-indications for ear piercing include: the client having a condition that means they might be prone to infection or slow to heal; a current infection; a physical injury; or some kind of obstruction.

A client should seek medical advice before having their ears pierced if they have any of the following.

- Circulation disorders
- High or low blood pressure
- History of thrombosis/embolism

DON'T FORGET

Clients with keloid scarring should be advised not to have their ears pierced. If they insist, always pierce 4mm away from any keloids/scar tissue.

If there is an open hole, pierce 1cm away from it.

- Epilepsy (a client with epilepsy must be accompanied by someone if they are having their ears pierced)

- Pregnancy

- Any disorder that requires they take **anticoagulant drugs**

- Diabetes

- Inflammation of the ear

- Skin disorders affecting the ears

- Bruises or recent haemorrhage of the ears

- Scar tissue or keloids on the ears

- Warts or moles on the ears (you may pierce through freckles)

- Cuts, abrasions or recent operations to the ears

An extremely nervous client may also be a contra-indication. If a client is nervous, warn them that if they flinch or 'jump' when the trigger is pulled, it could lead to incorrect placement of the earring or even injury.

Good practice

All materials and equipment used while carrying out an ear-piercing treatment should be appropriately cleaned, disinfected and/or sterilised.

UNIT OUTCOME 5

Understand equipment, materials, products, techniques and treatment planning for ear piercing

key terms

Anticoagulant drugs: these drugs help to prevent or slow down the clotting of blood, e.g. a medicine called Warfarin.

Clasp: the clasp is attached to the post of the earring to prevent the earring from falling out.

Post: the part of the earring that is pierced through the ear.

Equipment, materials and products

The following equipment, materials and products will be required to carry out an ear-piercing treatment.

- Trolley – should be disinfected and lined with couch roll

- Ear-piercing gun – this fires the stud through the lobe of the ear and also fixes the **clasp** to the **post**

- Sterile ear studs and clasps (which come in an intact, sterile package) – there are a variety of styles for clients to choose from. The ear studs are made from hypoallergenic material, which means they do not cause allergies or irritate the ear lobes

- Alcohol-based sterile cleaning wipes (such as **medi-swabs**) – used to clean the ear lobes

- Non-toxic, sterile, skin-marker pen (usually a violet colour) – used to mark a dot onto each ear, this will let the therapist know exactly where to pierce the ear

- Disposable gloves – a new pair of gloves is used for each client, to help prevent cross-infection occurring

- Headband – to secure the client's hair back from the face

- Mirror – for the client to check the position of marker dots, and see the final results

- Cotton wool and tissues in a bowl – used to apply lotions

- Tissues – to protect the client's clothing

- Sharps box – to dispose of studs

- Waste bin with a lid (should contain a yellow-coloured waste liner) – for clinical waste

- Disinfectant (70 per cent alcohol) such as surgical spirit – used to clean the gun after use

- Ultraviolet (UV) light cabinet – a clean place to store the ear-piercing gun while not in use

- Consent form – used if the client is under 16 years old

- **Aftercare lotion** – used by the client for homecare

key terms

Medi-swabs: small, individually wrapped alcohol wipes used to clean the skin. They can be used to clean the ear lobes before carrying out the ear-piercing treatment.

Aftercare lotion: a solution that is usually provided by the salon to help the client care for their pierced ears. It has antibacterial properties to help keep the area clean.

DON'T FORGET

Ear-piercing instruments must be cleaned between each use by thoroughly wiping them down with a disinfectant, such as surgical spirit.

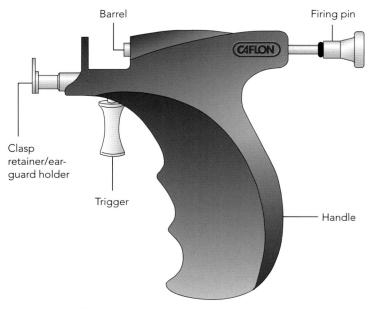

Ear-piercing equipment

Barrel

Firing pin

CAFLON

Clasp retainer/ear-guard holder

Trigger

Handle

■ Aftercare leaflet – following the instructions on the leaflet will aid healing and help prevent infection

■ Record card/consultation form – contains the client's personal details, any contra-indications, and the details of the treatment and the products used

Good practice

Waste materials, such as used cotton wool, that have come into contact with bodily fluids, are called clinical waste and should be bagged separately from the normal waste.

UNIT OUTCOME 1

Be able to use safe and effective methods of working when piercing ear lobes

UNIT OUTCOME 3

Understand the ear-piercing procedure

UNIT OUTCOME 5

Understand how to work safely and effectively when piercing ear lobes

Preparation for an ear-piercing treatment

You must carry out the following steps to ensure a hygienic and successful ear-piercing treatment.

■ Wash your hands.

■ Check the client is sitting comfortably.

■ If required, secure the client's hair back away from the face.

■ Observe the ears to make sure there are no contra-indications.

■ Place a facial tissue on each of the client's shoulders.

■ Put on disposable gloves.

■ Clean the lobules (lobes) of the ears with a suitable alcohol wipe, such as a medi-swab, or surgical spirit applied on cotton wool. This will remove any bacteria from the area. Remember to clean both sides of each ear.

DON'T FORGET

If the client isn't happy with the position of the dots, you can wipe them off, allow the ears to dry, and start again.

DON'T FORGET

Faces are not symmetrical, so the client may have slightly different-shaped ears.

- Allow a few seconds for the ears to dry.

- Using a hand mirror, discuss the preferred position of the dots with the client.

- With the client's agreement, mark a dot on each ear lobe. Check that the dots are in the correct position and look balanced.

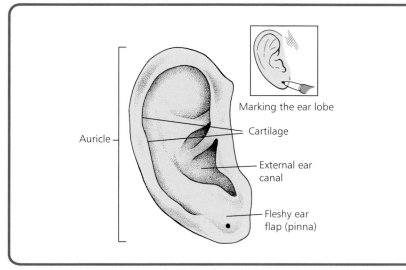

Marking the ear lobe

Auricle

Cartilage

External ear canal

Fleshy ear flap (pinna)

Positioning dots on the ears

Procedure for an ear-piercing treatment

- Peel off the back of the stud pack.

- Pull back the plunger on the back of the gun until you hear a 'click' noise which means it is in the correct position.

- Pick up the plastic cartridge from the stud pack (do not touch the studs or clasps).

- Position the back clasp into the slot and push the cartridge down as far as it will go.

- Another part of the cartridge holds the stud, which can be placed into the stud barrel of the gun. A plastic protective ring will be automatically positioned around the barrel of the gun and stud.

- The stud holder can be pulled away in an upwards direction, which leaves the stud in the barrel.

- Hold the gun horizontally to the ear lobe – take a few seconds to check you have the right angle.

Ask Fran

Q: What should I do if my client has thick ear lobes?

A: If the client has thick lobes, the clasp can be pulled back slightly after the ear has been pierced, to make more room. Ear lobes thicker than 6 mm may require studs with longer posts.

DON'T FORGET

If you are piercing a second hole, ensure the earrings are at least 9 mm apart.

DON'T FORGET

If you drop the cartridge or earring onto the floor you will need to open a new pack containing sterile studs.

DON'T FORGET

It is very important to get the right angle when piercing the ear, as an incorrect angle can cause the earring to point upwards or downwards.

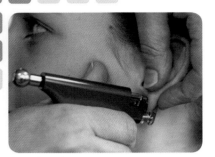

Gun placed onto ear

- Squeeze the trigger – this will allow you to check that the tip of the earring is correctly positioned so it will pierce through the dot on the ear lobe.

- To pierce the ear, you need to squeeze the trigger again. A successful piercing will show the clasp securely attached to the tip of the stud.

- Now throw the plastic ring into the waste bin.

- Pull back the plunger of the gun and add the next stud and clasp.

- Now pierce the other ear.

- Use a hand mirror to show the client the final result.

The ear-piercing gun is designed so that it doesn't actually touch the skin of the ears. It is the clasp retainer/ear guard that touches the skin and is thrown away after use.

Pierced ears

The post of the stud that is used for ear piercing has a slightly larger diameter than a regular earring post. This allows for the shrinkage that commonly occurs during the healing process, which usually takes four to six weeks. This ensures that a regular earring will fit easily into the resulting hole.

Occasionally the gun may fail to attach the clasp to the post. If this happens, take the clasp out from the plastic casing, while wearing gloves, and put it onto the post of the earring. This can usually be done quite quickly and easily.

HAVE A GO

Mark dots on thick pieces of cardboard and practise using the ear-piercing gun to pierce through the dots.

Good practice

Only recognised ear-piercing systems should be used to pierce the ears.

First-aid kit

Good practice

There must be a first-aid kit in the salon that complies with the Health and Safety (First Aid) Regulations (1981), and it is recommended that at least one person on site holds a basic first-aid qualification.

UNIT OUTCOME 4

Understand organisational and legal requirements

Legislation relating to ear piercing

The Local Government (Miscellaneous Provisions) Act (1982) (part VIII), requires that the premises and the people carrying out ear-piercing treatment should be registered with their local authority. Officers will inspect the premises and, if everything is satisfactory, a registration certificate will be issued which should be displayed in the salon. A charge will be made for this. In addition, the local authority may have by-laws that come under this legislation and relate to ear piercing.

Do not pierce the ears of anyone under the age of 16 without the presence of a parent or legal guardian. If you do, you could be at risk of being charged with grievous bodily harm to a child, despite the fact that the child requested the treatment. Also, do not accept consent by telephone or letter. You should witness the parent or guardian signing the consent form.

If a parent chooses to have a small child's ears pierced, they should be advised that, because of ear growth, the earrings may not look balanced in the future. Also, owing to the child's age, aftercare may be difficult for the child to follow. Therefore, parents must take responsibility for ensuring that the child's piercings are properly maintained and seek medical advice if a problem occurs.

Child with pierced ears

UNIT OUTCOME 7

Know anatomy and physiology that relates to ear-piercing treatments

here comes the science bit…

The ear
The outer ear includes the part that we can see, called the **pinna** (Latin for feather), and the ear canal. The pinna includes the **helix** and the **lobule** (lobe).

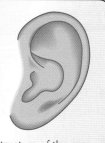

Structure of the ear

key terms

Pinna: the part of the ear we can see. It collects sound waves travelling in the air and directs them into the ear canal.

Helix: the rim of the ear, which contains cartilage. If pierced, it does not heal quickly, and hard, lumpy scar tissue can often result.

Lobule: (lobe) the fleshy part of the ear. It contains fatty tissue but does not contain cartilage.

Ear pierced many times

If a client would like to have any other part of the ear pierced, besides the lobe, or a part of their body pierced, they should seek the advice of a body piercer. Your insurance may not cover you for piercing any part of the body other than the ear lobe.

UNIT OUTCOME 10

Understand the aftercare advice to provide for clients

Aftercare advice

The following aftercare advice must be given to the client, preferably in written form. If it is not carried out properly, the client could get an infection, and the earrings would need to be removed.

■ Wash hands thoroughly before touching the studs or ear, to avoid getting bacteria into the piercing.

Aftercare lotion

■ Cleanse both the front and back of the ears twice a day with antiseptic or aftercare lotion. Afterwards, rotate the studs a quarter turn to the left and then a quarter turn to the right, three times. This will ensure that the hole stays open. Do not turn the stud round completely, because this may result in hair getting wrapped around the post at the back of the lobe, and bacteria from the hair may get into the pierced ear.

■ The clasp should always be positioned at the tip of the post, not pushed into the back of the ear.

■ Do not fiddle with the studs, as you may get bacteria into the piercing.

■ Make sure that soap and shampoo do not collect behind either the stud or clasp. After shampooing, the ear should be rinsed with clear water, and then cleansed with antiseptic or aftercare solution.

- Cover the ears when spraying perfume or hairspray.
- Leave the studs in the ears for six weeks. After six weeks, the studs can be removed and other post-type earrings may be worn. These should be gold or silver, and should be worn for another six months.

Contra-actions

Directly after treatment, it is normal for the pierced ears to look red, feel warm and for there to be some slight discomfort. However, this soon settles, usually within 48 hours, provided proper aftercare is carried out.

Infection and irritation

If the client thinks a pierced ear has become infected, they should return to the salon as soon as possible. The client may need to be reminded of aftercare advice. The ears can be checked to make sure the clasps are in the correct position – if they are too tight it may lead to inflammation. If the infection looks serious – such as excessive redness, weeping, itching and soreness – they should be referred to their doctor and should consider removing the earrings.

Keloids

Some clients may develop keloid scarring when they injure the skin. A keloid is a type of scar that grows lumpy and large, and can spread outside the original area of skin damage. Keloids are shiny and hairless, raised above the skin, and feel hard and rubbery to the touch. They usually develop on the shoulders, head and neck. This can happen to anybody, but it is more common in people with black skin. Keloid scars can last for years, and sometimes don't appear until months after an injury to the skin. People who have previously had keloid scarring should avoid having ear-piercing treatment.

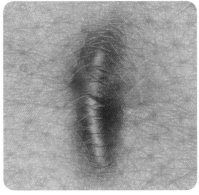

Keloid scarring

If the client returns to the salon suffering with a contra-action, this should be noted on the record card/consultation form. It is important to do this for insurance purposes and in case of any future action taken against you by the client.

How are you doing?

1 Which of the following is the part of the ear you should pierce?

   a Helix

   b Lobule

   c Ear canal

   d Cartilage

2 You will need a parent or guardian's consent to pierce the ears if your client is:

   a over 16 years old

   b under 18 years old

   c under 16 years old

   d any age

3 The Local Government (Miscellaneous Provisions) Act (1982) ensures that:

   a ear piercing may only be carried out by a person in a premises registered by the local authority

   b a premises has the correct equipment and materials to carry out treatment

   c there is adequate light and ventilation for carrying out ear-piercing treatment

   d proper aftercare advice is given

4 Which of the following reactions after ear piercing is **not** considered normal?

   a Slight redness

   b Warmth

   c Minor discomfort

   d Bleeding

5 Which of the following makes up part of the earring?

   a Post

   b Barrel

   c Keloid

   d Trigger

6 Which of the following would be used during ear-piercing treatment?

   a Mirror

   b Non-toxic marker pen

   c Disposable gloves

   d All of the above

7 Which of the following is **not** aftercare advice given after ear piercing?

   a Cover the ears when spraying perfume or hairspray

   b Push the clasp along the post towards the ear

   c Rinse any soap or shampoo that collects around the earrings

   d Always wash the hands before touching the earrings

8 After ear-piercing treatment, studs should be kept in the ears for:

   a two weeks

   b three weeks

   c six weeks

   d eight weeks

are you ready *for* assessment?

The evidence for this unit must be gathered in the workplace (salon) or realistic working environment (training centre).

Simulation (role play) is not allowed for any performance evidence within this unit.

You must practically demonstrate in your everyday work that you have met the required standard for this unit.

All outcomes, assessment criteria and range statements must be achieved.

Knowledge and understanding in this unit will be assessed by a mandatory (compulsory) written question paper. These questions are set and marked by VTCT.

Assessing your practical work

Your assessor will observe your performance of a practical task, i.e. an ear-piercing treatment.

Your assessor will sign off an outcome when all criteria have been competently achieved.

On occasions, some assessment criteria may not naturally occur during a practical observation. In such instances you will be asked questions to demonstrate your knowledge in this area. Your assessor will document the criteria that have been achieved through oral questioning.

In this unit you must demonstrate competent performance of all practical outcomes (ear-piercing treatment) on at least **two** occasions. Your assessor will want to see preparation activities for **two** different clients.

Testing your knowledge and understanding

You will be guided by your tutor and assessor on the evidence that needs to be produced.

Your knowledge and understanding will be assessed using the assessment tools listed below.

- Mandatory written question paper
- Oral questioning
- Portfolio of evidence

S1 Assist with spa operations

Introduction

There are many different types of spa, from day spas to luxury holiday resort spas. Spa treatments are the services that are provided by spas. Some common spa treatments are discussed in this unit.

Heat treatments

The following heat treatments may be offered in spas.

- Saunas
- Infrared treatments
- Steam baths and rooms
- Spa pools
- Foam baths
- Hydrotherapy baths

A spa

Effects of heat treatments on the body

- Increases the blood circulation, which brings nutrients and oxygen to the body's cells

- Increases the lymphatic circulation, which helps speed up the removal of waste products and toxins

- Raises the body temperature

- Causes erythema (reddening) of the skin and also warmth

- Relaxes tense muscles and, if used after exercise, can reduce the build-up of lactic acid in the muscles that can lead to stiffness

- Lowers blood pressure owing to the widening of the blood vessels (vasodilation)

- Stimulates the sweat glands, which helps the removal of waste products and toxins

- Stimulates the sebaceous glands, which helps the to improve the condition of the skin

- Increases heart and pulse rates

- Soothes nerve endings and helps the client feel relaxed

- Promotes feelings of well-being and cleanliness

Relaxing image

Saunas

A sauna is a dry heat treatment, which means it has low humidity (around 10–20 per cent) or, in other words, there is little moisture in the air.

Types of sauna include the Finnish or Tyrolean sauna, the laconium sauna and the infrared sauna.

Finnish or Tyrolean sauna

Saunas have been used in Finland for over 1000 years, and pine log saunas are often positioned next to a lake so that users can jump into freezing water during the sauna. Modern saunas are based on Finnish-style log cabins, which are commonly made from pine trees. There is insulating material in between the wooden panels to help keep the warmth inside.

Sauna cabins are heated by electric stoves to between 70 and 100 °C. The stoves contain rocks or coals to give off heat, and water is poured onto the rocks to raise the humidity level to around 10 per cent. Because the humidity level is low, and the heat produced is dry heat, clients can tolerate higher

A sauna

temperatures, as the sweat can evaporate from the skin and cool the body down.

A Tyrolean sauna is a wood-lined cabin that is very similar to a Finnish sauna. It was established in the Tyrol region of Austria. Users will often follow this heat treatment with an ice shower.

Laconium sauna

This type of sauna has a higher humidity (15–20 per cent) than the Finnish sauna. The temperature is evenly distributed and is cooler than the Finnish sauna. The average temperature is about 55 °C, and the heat is created by under-floor heating.

This gentler treatment suits those with sensitive skin and those who cannot bear excessive heat. This type of sauna is cleansing to the body, and pleasant aromatic essences are used to induce relaxation. There are often lighting and sound effects to enhance the experience.

Infrared sauna

Clients who find the heat of a traditional sauna too excessive may prefer infrared saunas. The infrared rays penetrate into the body at a depth of 45 mm, and the heat produced will help to relax muscles, relieve pain and rid the body of waste products and toxins.

Effects of a sauna

- Increases the blood and lymphatic circulations
- Produces erythema on the skin
- Raises body temperature
- Slightly increases metabolic rate
- Stimulates sweat glands
- Slightly stimulates sebaceous glands
- Reduces blood pressure
- Induces relaxation and feelings of well-being

DON'T FORGET

The sauna is intended to be a dry heat treatment, but it should not be so dry that it is uncomfortable to the nose and throat. That is why water is poured onto the coals.

DON'T FORGET

Recommend that your client spends around 20 minutes in the Finnish sauna, with a relaxation period afterwards, about twice a week.

DON'T FORGET

Recommend that your client remains in the laconium sauna for around 20 minutes, with a relaxation period afterwards, two or three times a week.

Good practice

Ensure the client removes any jewellery before entering a sauna. Jewellery made from metal will heat up quickly and cause a burning sensation.

Steam baths and rooms

Water is heated to 100 °C to create water vapour (steam). Steam is a moist heat, with up to 90 per cent humidity.

Steam bath (Turkish bath)

Steam baths originate from ancient Turkey and are a popular way of preheating the body before treatment in a spa. A steam bath is commonly made out of fibreglass, but sometimes metal, and allows one person to sit comfortably with their head sticking out through an opening at the top. The seat is adjustable for the height of each client. The steam bath temperature varies between 50 °C and 55 °C. An electrical element, which is controlled by a thermostat, heats water in a tank, which is found under the seat, and when the water boils it produces steam, which circulates inside the cabinet.

Steam room

In spas, a steam room is usually large, and has a boiler in which water is heated to produce steam. The steam is channelled through pipes into the room so the room fills with steam. The recommended temperature is 40 °C.

Caldarium

The caldarium is a Roman-style, aromatic steam room, which uses essences such as jasmine and rose to help promote relaxation. The air temperature is commonly 42–45 °C. A **Kneipp hose** may be used to cool the body down.

Hamam

A hamam is a Turkish-style sauna. It is a communal bathhouse which is often decorated with blue and yellow tiles. Several clients will relax together in a room (known as the warm room) where there is a constant flow of hot, dry air that induces sweating. Some clients may move to an even hotter room (known as the hot room) and then will splash themselves with cold water before moving to the cooling room to relax. There may also be a cold plunge pool for the clients to plunge into to help bring down the body temperature.

> **DON'T FORGET**
>
> The service time for a steam room is around 10–15 minutes.
> The service time for a steam bath is around 15–20 minutes.

> **key terms**
>
> **Kneipp (ka-nipe) hose:** used for Kneipp therapy, which involves alternately using hot and cold treatments to help stimulate the blood and lymphatic circulations.

Steam room

Caldarium

Hamam

Effects of a steam bath/room

- Increases the blood and lymphatic circulations

- Produces erythema on the skin

- Raises body temperature

- Slightly increases metabolic rate

- Stimulates sweat glands

- Slightly stimulates sebaceous glands

- Reduces blood pressure

- Induces relaxation and feelings of well-being

Hydrotherapy

Hydrotherapy, or water therapy, is the use of water for therapeutic effect and to promote physical well-being.

Spa pool

A spa pool, also known as a jacuzzi, hot tub or whirlpool, contains warm water in which clients sit. Warm air is forced through small holes in the sides of the pool, producing bubbles that help to massage the body. Essential oils can be added to the pool to help relax the user. This treatment is particularly beneficial for people with joint and muscular pain.

Effects of a spa pool

- Induces sweating and so releases toxins

- Increases the blood and lymphatic circulations

- Relaxes tense muscles

- Increases the body temperature

Good practice

Inform the client not to wear jewellery or plasters in the pool, as these can easily come off in the water and clog the filters.

Baths

These are a form of hydrotherapy and include foam and hydrotherapy baths.

Ask Fran

Q: What is the difference between dry heat and wet heat?

A: Dry heat (such as that found in a pine sauna) is heat with little humidity (moisture in the air); wet heat (such as that found in a steam bath) has a high humidity (a lot of moisture in the air).

---

key terms

Hydrotherapy: water treatment.

DON'T FORGET

The service time for a spa pool is around 10–15 minutes.

DON'T FORGET

It would be impractical for the spa pool to be drained regularly, so the water is recycled instead. It is kept safe and hygienic by a filter system that collects matter such as hair, plasters, fluff and so on. The filters should be cleaned regularly.

Foam bath

Foam baths found in spas are similar to a normal bath in appearance, but contain a lot of holes from which air is jetted out into the bath water. A small amount of water is required, 10–15 cm, and it is heated to around 40 °C. A concentrated foam product is added to the water and the jets of air cause bubbles to form. When the bath is full of bubbles, the client can lie in it and relax. The foam traps heat and so acts as an insulator, allowing heat to build, so there is a rise in body temperature which induces sweating. Essential oils may also be added to the bath. This is an ideal service to have before a massage treatment.

Foam bath

Effects of a foam bath

- Induces sweating and so releases toxins

- Increases the blood and lymphatic circulations

- Relaxes tense muscles

- Increases the body temperature

Hydrotherapy bath

This bath is similar in appearance to a household bath and is filled with warm water. Substances such as essential oils may be added for relaxation. Air is forced out of holes in the bath which forms bubbles. A hose can be used under the water to direct air over the body and can be used to work on specific muscle groups.

Effects of a hydrotherapy bath

- Induces sweating and so releases toxins

- Increases the blood and lymphatic circulations

- Relaxes tense muscles

- Increases the body temperature

Flotation

Flotation helps to induce calmness and relaxation.

Dry flotation tank

This is called dry because the client has no contact with water. The client lies on a raised bench which is lowered into a water tank or bath. The warm water is covered with a heavy waterproof sheet. The client will benefit from the warmth given off by the water.

DON'T FORGET

The service time for a foam bath is around 15–20 minutes.

DON'T FORGET

The service time for a hydrotherapy bath is around 15–20 minutes.

DON'T FORGET

The service time for a dry flotation tank is around 40 minutes.

DON'T FORGET

The service time for a wet flotation tank is 20–60 minutes.

DON'T FORGET

The pH of the water in the wet flotation tank should be 7.2–7.4.

DON'T FORGET

The service time for body wrapping is around 60 minutes.

Wet flotation tank

A shallow pool or tank is filled with about 30 cm of water. It contains a high level of salt, enabling the client to float.

Body wrapping

A body wrap involves first covering the body in substances such as mud, seaweed and algae, then wrapping materials such as wet bandages, plastic or foil around the whole body, or specific body parts, depending on the treatment. The client may be asked to wear a plastic suit over the top of the bandages, or be covered with a thermal blanket to help keep in warmth.

The effects of the treatment are inch loss and detoxification. The skin will feel smoother, firmer and tighter. A client will be measured with a measuring tape, both before and after treatment, and should lose inches from their body.

Other treatments

Fango therapy

Fango therapy is a treatment using various types of mud, which are rich in minerals and nutrients. Mud helps to remove impurities from the skin and also aids exfoliation. 'Fango' is from the Italian word meaning 'mud'.

Thalssotherapy

Thalassotherapy is any treatment that uses seawater and marine by-products, which are full of minerals and nutrients.

Herbal wrap

This popular spa treatment involves using strips of cloth soaked in a heated herbal solution to wrap around the body. It is used to aid relaxation and also to help detoxify the body.

Salt glow

A salt glow involves massaging small amounts of oil and salt into dampened skin. It helps to exfoliate the skin and stimulate the blood and lymphatic circulations.

Be able to clean and set up spa work areas

Be able to check, maintain and shut down spa work areas

Cleaning and maintaining spa treatment areas

Microorganisms

Because of its high heat and moisture content, a spa is an ideal environment for growth of bacteria, fungi and other harmful (pathogenic) microorganisms (germs). Therefore it is important to ensure that the spa and its equipment and materials are kept as clean as possible. Maintaining high standards of hygiene and using disposable items, where possible, will help to reduce the risk of infection.

Microorganisms

Saunas

■ Follow the manufacturer's instructions regarding cleaning the inside of the sauna cabin. Many spas will use only fresh clean water to clean the sauna area.

■ When not in use, ensure there isn't any water left in the bucket, as this will result in the formation of mould growth.

■ If the sauna is not being used, ensure the door is left open to enable fresh air to circulate inside.

■ Carry out a risk assessment – check for any broken bits of wood on the benches or anything else that could be potentially hazardous.

Steam baths/rooms

■ Use a disinfectant to clean the steam unit after each client, paying particular attention to the seating area and floor.

■ At the end of the day, leave the door open to allow air to circulate.

■ Carry out a risk assessment to ensure everything is in working order and not broken or unsafe.

DON'T FORGET

Steam baths are usually made from fibreglass, which makes them a difficult environment for microorganisms to grow on and means they can be easily cleaned.

Spa pool

- Check the equipment is working properly and ensure the water is being continually filtered to keep it clean.

- Chemically treat the water as recommended by the manufacturer.

- Test the temperature, pH and bromine levels of the water (see 'Water safety and testing' on pages 331–332).

- Regularly dry the area around the spa pool; a wet floor could result in somebody slipping over.

- Regularly clean the exposed parts of the spa pool to remove any oil, fluff, etc.

- Carry out a risk assessment to ensure everything is in working order and that there is nothing that could harm a client.

Baths

- Hydrotherapy baths and foam baths must be emptied and cleaned after use.

- Use recommended products to thoroughly clean the baths.

- Clear the area around the bath and wash the floor.

- Carry out a risk assessment and ensure everything is safe and in good working order.

Dry flotation tank

- Regularly clean the waterproof sheet with products recommended by the manufacturer

- Regularly clean and dry the floor.

Wet flotation tank

- Ensure the pH of the water is 7.2–7.4 (this should be checked every day).

- Ensure the bromine level is not higher than 2 milligrams per litre (mg/L) (this can be checked once a week).

- Use the correct amount of recommended products to clean the water.

- Remove any bits floating in the water, such as fluff or hair.

- Ensure the water is filtered after every treatment.

- Add the correct amount of **Epsom salts**, as recommended by the manufacturers.

key terms

Epsom salts: (also known as magnesium sulphate) are named after the mineral springs of Epsom, an English spa town. It is a salt that helps to detoxify and soften the skin, and relaxes muscles and soothes joints.

Body wrapping equipment

- Wash the bandages after each use as recommended by the manufacturer.
- Thoroughly wash and clean all equipment used during the treatment.
- Carry out a risk assessment, making sure all equipment is in good working order.

Good practice

Towels should be washed at 60 °C to help ensure they are thoroughly clean and to prevent cross-infection.

Water safety and testing

Bacteria, fungi and viruses can all grow in spa water, and some of them are harmful (pathogenic) and can cause infection and illness. As spa pools are not emptied daily, they rely on a filter system and chemicals to keep them clean and safe.

Bromine tablets, which contain chemicals that kill microorganisms, are used to help keep pool water safe. Levels of bromine in the pool must be regularly measured and should be 2–4 milligrams per litre (mg/L). If the readings are not within this range, it may lead to the growth of microorganisms and algae.

Good practice

If you notice a strong odour, resembling bleach, this is probably a sign there is too much bromine in the water.

Good practice

A swimming pool temperature should be maintained at around 37–40 °C.

The pH level of the water also needs to be checked regularly, as if it is too low the water can cause discomfort to the skin and eyes. The pH of the water should be 7.2–7.6.

The temperature must also be checked to ensure it is comfortable for the client. The temperature of the pool should be 37–40 °C.

In addition, there needs to be a balanced level of calcium salt in the water, or there will be corrosion of pool fixtures and equipment, leading to costly repairs.

DON'T FORGET

Legionnaires' disease is a type of pneumonia caused by legionella bacteria. These bacteria can live in water and grow quickly in warm temperatures. Although it cannot be spread from person to person, tiny water droplets can pass the disease.

Symptoms of Legionnaires' disease include high temperature, feverishness, headaches and muscle pains, and can lead to death. Fatal cases of Legionnaires' disease have been associated with spa pool services.

Appropriate water treatment and cleaning routines can help to prevent the spread of this type of bacteria.

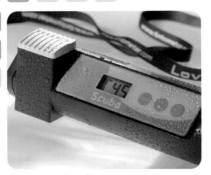

A water-testing device

DON'T FORGET

Chlorine is similar to bromine, and is a disinfectant commonly used in swimming pools. Too much chlorine in the water will result in the eyes becoming sore.

The following tests are carried out every two hours.

■ Temperature – the temperature of the spa pool is measured with a thermometer.

■ Bromine levels – a sample of water is taken from the spa pool, and DPD tablets are added to it. These change the colour of the water depending on the bromine levels. The colour of the sample can be compared against a coloured chart.

■ pH levels – a sample of water is taken from the spa pool, and a phenol red tablet is added to the sample. This changes the colour of the water depending on its pH levels. The colour of the sample can be compared against a coloured chart.

Alkalinity and calcium-hardness tests need to be carried out every week.

Good practice

Report to your manager if the water test results are abnormal.

Good practice

Spa chemicals can be hazardous, so ensure they are stored safely, preferably in a locked cupboard.

here comes the science bit…

Keeping water balanced

If the water in a spa becomes too alkaline, it can cause limescale to build up on the equipment and affect its functioning. However, if the water is too acidic it will cause erosion of equipment (such as spa pumps and heaters), which will also affect its functioning.

The total alkalinity (TA) of the water must be tested, followed by a pH check. A correct TA will also help to ensure that the pH level is correct. Products can be used to increase or reduce total alkalinity and pH levels, if required.

Calcium hardness of water is also measured. If the level is insufficient, it can lead to equipment corrosion and result in water foaming problems. If there is too much calcium in the water, this can result in the formation of limescale on surfaces and the water will become cloudy. Water softeners can be used to decrease the amount of calcium in the water, which helps to increase the lifespan of the equipment. A product called Hardness Increase helps to raise the level of calcium in the water, if necessary.

Luxury swimming pool

Langelier Saturation Index

The Langelier Saturation Index is a means of evaluating water quality to determine if the water is corrosive or limescale forming. It is used to work out:

- temperature of pools – a spa pool should ideally be 37–40 °C

- pH of water – should be 7.2–7.6

- calcium hardness in the water – should be 75–150 milligrams per litre (mg/L)

- alkalinity – should be 100–150 milligrams per litre (mg/L).

These are all considered to be safe levels, and samples of water are measured against the index.

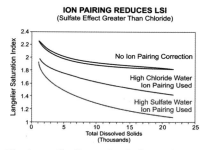

The Langelier Saturation Index

Preparation for a sauna treatment

Equipment, materials and products

- Sauna

- Wooden bucket containing water – to pour over the coals or stones using a ladle

- Electric stove – to heat the coals or stones

- Temperature gauge – to monitor the temperature of the sauna heat

- Hygrometer – to measure relative humidity, which should be between 50 and 70 per cent

- Essential oils – to provide pleasant and relaxing smells inside the sauna

- Disposable footwear – this type of footwear can be thrown away after use and helps to provide comfort for the client while walking around the spa. It also helps to prevent the spread of germs

- Shower with soap and shampoo – the client may want to have a shower after the treatment

- Couch roll to go on the floor – this will help to keep the floor clean and free of germs

- Towels – clients need towels to wrap around themselves while having the sauna treatment and can use them to wipe away sweat. They will also require towels to dry themselves after having a shower

- Drinking water – the client may be thirsty following the sauna treatment

Preparing the sauna

- Follow the manufacturer's instructions for turning on the sauna.
- Set the temperature – a Finnish/Tyrolean sauna should be 70–100 °C and a laconium sauna should be 55 °C.
- Ensure the air vents are working correctly.
- Ensure floor mats are clean and safely positioned.
- If there is a bucket, fill it with water and check there is also a ladle.

DON'T FORGET

Allow the sauna about an hour to heat up; however, this is dependent on how big it is.

DON'T FORGET

A sauna treatment service is usually around 30 minutes.

- Clients can be given towels to sit on.
- Check the temperature and the relative humidity before the client enters the sauna.

Preparation for a steam treatment
Equipment, materials and products

- Steam bath or room
- Distilled water – to fill the tank (ordinary water would cause limescale to form and would damage the equipment)
- Essential oils – to provide pleasant and relaxing smells inside the sauna

Essential oils

- Shower with soap and shampoo – the client may want to have a shower after the treatment, to wash off the sweat

- Couch roll to go on the floor – this will help to keep the floor clean and free of germs

- Towels – clients need towels to wrap around themselves while having the steam treatment and can use them to wipe away sweat. They will also require towels to dry themselves after having a shower

- Disposable footwear – this type of footwear can be thrown away after use and helps to provide comfort for the client while walking around the spa. It also helps to prevent the spread of germs

- Drinking water – the client may be thirsty following the steam treatment.

Good practice

Suggest to clients that they wear swimwear while having a steam treatment. Disposable pants can be given to clients if they forget their swimwear.

Preparing the steam bath

- Ensure towels are positioned on the seat of the steam bath and also on the floor for the client to place their feet on.

- Pour water into the tank, ensuring there is at least 5 cm of water above the heating element.

- Place a towel over the top of the steam bath (covering the hole) to help keep warmth inside.

- Switch on the steam bath – it will take about 15 minutes to heat up.

- Follow the manufacturer's instructions regarding setting the temperature.

Preparation for a spa pool treatment

Equipment, materials and products

- Spa pool

- Plant room containing the power supply for the spa pool

- Water testing equipment

Spa pool

- Shower with soap and shampoo – the client may want to have a shower after the treatment

- Towels – clients need towels to dry themselves after having a shower

- Disposable footwear – this type of footwear can be thrown away after use and helps to provide comfort for the client while walking around the spa. It also helps to prevent the spread of germs

- Drinking water – the client may be thirsty following the treatment.

Preparing the spa pool

- Refer to the manufacturer's instructions regarding switching on the spa pool.

- Ensure the water level is sufficient.

- Ensure the temperature is correct.

- Ensure the pH and bromine levels are correct.

- Ensure the water is clean.

- Ensure everything is presented well and the client has towels and anything else they need.

Preparation for a foam bath treatment

Equipment, materials and products

- Foam bath

- Foaming product

- Shower with soap and shampoo – the client may want to have a shower after the treatment

- Towels – clients need towels to dry themselves after having a shower

- Disposable footwear – this type of footwear can be thrown away after use and helps to provide comfort for the client while walking around the spa. It also helps to prevent the spread of germs

- Drinking water – the client may be thirsty following the treatment.

Preparing the foam bath

- Fill the bath with around 10–15 cm of hot water.

- Check the temperature is roughly 38–43 °C.

- Add the foaming product to the water as recommended by the manufacturer.

- Switch on the air jets – turn them off when the foam reaches near the top of the bath.

Preparation for a hydrotherapy bath treatment

Equipment, materials and products

- Hydrotherapy bath

- Essential oils – to provide pleasant and relaxing smells in the hydrotherapy bath

- Shower with soap and shampoo – the client may want to have a shower after the treatment

- Couch roll to go on the floor – this will help to keep the floor clean and free of germs

- Towels – clients require towels to dry themselves after having having the hydrotherapy bath and also following a shower

- Disposable footwear – this type of footwear can be thrown away after use and helps to provide comfort for the client while walking around the spa. It also helps to prevent the spread of germs

- Drinking water – the client may be thirsty following the hydrotherapy bath.

Hydrotherapy bath

Preparing the hydrotherapy bath

- Ensure the jets are properly cleaned and that there are no blockages.

- Fill the bath with warm water so that all the holes are covered.

- Add any products, such as essential oils, to the water while the bath is being filled.

- Ensure the temperature of the water is around 36–40 °C.

- The bath jets can be activated after the client has got into it.

DON'T FORGET

The water temperature of a hydrotherapy bath should be 36–40 °C.

Preparation for a dry flotation treatment

Equipment, materials and products

- Flotation bed
- Couch roll – to cover the waterproof sheet for hygiene purposes
- Towels – clients require towels to dry themselves after having the treatment and also following a shower
- Shower with soap and shampoo – the client may want to have a shower after the treatment
- Couch roll to go on the floor – this will help to keep the floor clean and free of germs
- Disposable footwear – this type of footwear can be thrown away after use and helps to provide comfort for the client while walking around the spa. It also helps to prevent the spread of germs
- Drinking water – the client may be thirsty following the treatment.

Preparing the dry flotation tank

- Refer to the manufacturer's instructions regarding the correct temperature of the water.
- Ensure everything is thoroughly clean.
- Ensure the board is at the top of the tank.
- Cover the waterproof sheet with couch roll.
- Protect the floor from products being used during the treatment.

Preparation for a wet flotation treatment

Equipment, materials and products

- Flotation tank
- Epsom salts – to enable the client to float
- Cleaning chemicals – to ensure cleanliness of the water
- Ear plugs – to prevent water entering the ears

- Towels – clients require towels to dry themselves after having the treatment and also following a shower

- Shower with soap and shampoo – the client may want to have a shower after the treatment

- Couch roll to go on the floor – this will help to keep the floor clean and free of germs

- Disposable footwear – this type of footwear can be thrown away after use and helps to provide comfort for the client while walking around the spa. It also helps to prevent the spread of germs.

Preparing the wet flotation tank

- Check the level of the water.

- Check the temperature of the water is around 35 °C.

- Check the water is clean and that there is nothing floating in it, such as hair.

- Check everything is in working order.

- Carry out any other tests recommended by the manufacturer.

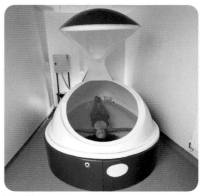
Wet flotation

Preparation for a body-wrapping treatment

Equipment, materials and products

- Tank filled with water and bandages (depending on the system being used)

- Products such as seaweed and essential oils – to infuse into the bandages

- Brushes – to apply products

- Towels – clients require towels to dry themselves after having the treatment and also following a shower

- Couch roll to go on the floor – this will help to keep the floor clean and free of germs

- Bowls – for the client to stores items such as jewellery

- Disposable footwear – this type of footwear can be thrown away after use and helps to provide comfort for the client while walking around the spa. It also helps to prevent the spread of germs

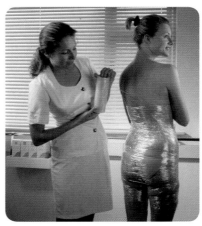
Body wrapping

- Disposable underwear – this can be thrown away after use and helps to prevent the client's underwear from becoming stained during the body wrapping treatment

- Tape measure – to measure parts of the client's body

- Plastic suit – to be positioned over the bandages, or thermal blankets – to keep in warmth.

Preparing the body-wrapping treatment area

- Switch on the water tank (depending on the system being used).

- Ensure everything is clean and close to hand

- As the client may be in their underwear, make sure the room is warm.

- Ensure you have sufficient amounts of bandages and towels.

UNIT OUTCOME 1

Be able to use safe and effective methods of working when assisting with spa operations

UNIT OUTCOME 5

Understand how to work safely and effectively when assisting with spa operations

UNIT OUTCOME 6

Understand client care for spa treatments

Consultation

A consultation helps the therapist find out if the client has any contra-indications, such as those that could spread infection. Items such as disposable footwear will help to prevent the transfer of infections such as athlete's foot.

Make sure the client signs the client record card/consultation form.

For more information on the consultation process, see **Unit G20: Ensure responsibility for actions to reduce risks to health and safety**.

Contra-indications to heat treatments

A heat treatment cannot be given to a client if they have any of the following.

- Pregnancy
- Breathing difficulties, including colds and asthma (this depends on which treatment the client is having)
- Recent scar tissue
- Severe bruising, recent haemorrhage or undiagnosed swelling
- Hepatitis
- Any bacterial, fungal or viral infections
- Are highly nervous, especially if they suffer with **claustrophobia**
- Have recently had a heavy meal
- Are under the influence of drugs or alcohol

The client should seek medical advice from their doctor before having a heat treatment if they have any of the following conditions.

- High or low blood pressure
- Heart or circulatory conditions
- Severe skin condition
- Diabetes
- Kidney/liver/pancreatic problems
- Epilepsy
- Diseases of the nervous system, such as **Parkinson's disease**
- Recent operations (depending on the type of operation carried out)
- History of thrombosis

key terms

Claustrophobia: the fear of having no escape and being closed in. It is often associated with an anxiety disorder.

Pregnant woman

key terms

Parkinson's disease: usually affects older people and is caused by the loss of nerve cells in the brain. The symptoms include tremors and slowness of movement.

key terms

Adverse reaction: an unwanted reaction to treatment, such as an allergic reaction.

Caring for the client during the treatment

Sauna

- Inform the client that it is cooler to sit on the lower benches rather than the higher ones (because heat rises).
- Advise the client to take regular cool showers to help the body cool down.
- Check on the client throughout the treatment.
- Offer a glass of water at the end of the treatment.
- Advise the client to relax after the treatment to allow the body to return to its normal state.

Steam bath

- Check the temperature of the steam bath before the client enters it.
- Adjust the seat to suit the client's height.
- After closing the door of the steam bath ensure the client feels relaxed and doesn't need anything.
- Put a large towel around the client's neck to prevent loss of steam through the opening of the steam bath.
- After the treatment, advise the client to take a shower and ensure clean towels are available to use.
- After the shower, the client should be encouraged to relax and drink some water.

Spa pool

- Ensure the client knows where to find a shower after the treatment.
- Regularly check on the client during the treatment.
- Ensure the client is provided with water and towels.
- Advise the client to rest and relax after the treatment.

Bath treatments

- If required, help the client into the bath.
- Ensure the client is safely and comfortably positioned inside the bath.

- Offer the client fresh water to drink.

- Advise the client to take a shower after the treatment.

- Advise the client to rest and relax after taking a shower.

Dry flotation

- Advise the client to take a shower before having the treatment.

- If the client is having other treatments at the same time, such as body wrapping, ensure they know what to expect and how long the whole treatment will take.

- Offer the client fresh water to drink.

- Ensure the client rests and relaxes after the treatment.

Wet flotation

- Advise the client to take a shower before entering the flotation tank; this will prevent make-up from entering the water.

- Fully explain the treatment to the client and inform them how long it lasts. This will help the client to feel relaxed about the treatment.

- Ensure the client is correctly positioned in the water to get the most out of the treatment.

- Offer the client ear plugs and ensure they are able to insert them properly.

- Offer the client neck support.

- Regularly check on the client in case there is a problem.

Body wrapping

- Fully explain to the client what you are doing throughout the body-wrapping treatment.

- Encourage the client to ask questions.

- Offer fresh water to drink and perhaps a magazine to read (depending on the type of body-wrapping treatment being carried out).

- Advise the client to take a shower after treatment.

Contra-actions to heat treatments

If any of the following occur during a heat treatment, do not continue with the treatment.

- Dizziness or fainting
- Excessive redness of the skin
- Allergic reaction to products, such as a skin rash
- Nosebleeds
- Nausea
- Cramp
- Headache

Good practice

If the client feels overheated in the sauna, escort them to a cooler area, sit them down and offer a drink of water.

UNIT OUTCOME 4

Understand organisational and legal requirements

Aftercare advice

- Ensure the client is comfortable and feels well after the treatment.
- Ask the client if they require a bathrobe, another towel or a glass of water.
- Advise the client to relax for a time after the treatment.

See **Unit G20: Ensure responsibility for actions to reduce risks to health and safety** for information regarding organisation and legal requirements.

How are you doing?

1 Hydrotherapy is a term that means:

  a mud treatment

  b steam treatment

  c water treatment

  d seaweed treatment

2 Which of the following is **not** a heat treatment commonly offered in spas?

  a Sauna service

  b Steam bath

  c Foam bath

  d Mud bath

3 Which of the following is **not** an effect of heat treatments on the body?

  a Increase in blood circulation

  b Creates areas of redness on the skin

  c Relaxation of tense muscles

  d Stimulates the nerves

4 A sauna is which type of treatment?

  a Dry heat

  b Wet heat

  c Cold heat

  d Damp heat

5 Humidity means:

  a the amount of moisture in the air

  b the amount of heat circulating in the air

  c the amount of people allowed into a sauna at one time

  d the presence of microorganisms in a sauna cabin

6 Which of the following is **not** another name for a spa pool?

  a Hot tub

  b Jacuzzi

  c Hamam

  d Whirlpool

7 Wet flotation involves which of the following?

  a A client lies on a bench and has jets of water sprayed onto their back

  b Lying in shallow water which contains a high level of salt

  c Adding a foaming product to a bath

  d All of the above

8 The Langelier Saturation Index is used to work out which of the following?

  a pH of water

  b Calcium hardness of water

  c Alkalinity of water

  d All of the above

9 What is the function of bromine tablets?

  a To test relative humidity levels

  b To create bubbles for the foam bath

  c They contain chemicals to kill microorganisms

  d To use during a body wrap treatment

10 A phenol red table is used to measure:

  a calcium hardness of water

  b pH of water

  c alkaline levels of water

  d bacterial levels in water

are you ready *for* assessment?

The evidence for this unit must be gathered in the workplace.

Simulation (role play) is not allowed for any performance evidence within this unit.

You must practically demonstrate in your everyday work that you have met the required standard for this unit.

All outcomes, assessment criteria and range statements must be achieved.

Knowledge and understanding in this unit will be assessed by a mandatory, written question paper. These questions are set and marked by VTCT.

Assessing your practical work

Your assessor will observe your performance of a practical task, such as cleaning a sauna.

Your assessor will sign off an outcome when all criteria have been competently achieved.

On occasions, some assessment criteria may not naturally occur during a practical observation. In such instances you will be asked questions to demonstrate your knowledge in this area. Your assessor will document the criteria that have been achieved through oral questioning.

In this unit you must demonstrate competent performance of all practical outcomes on at least **four** separate occasions, which must include wet areas and changing rooms.

Testing your knowledge and understanding

You will be guided by your tutor and assessor on the evidence that needs to be produced.

Your knowledge and understanding will be assessed using the assessment tools listed below.

- Mandatory written question paper
- Oral questioning
- Portfolio of evidence

Glossary

Acetone: a colourless, flammable liquid which can dissolve nail polish and nail extensions.

Achilles tendon: a tendon that connects the heel of the foot to the muscles of the lower leg (calf muscles).

Acid mantle: a slightly acidic oil layer on the skin's surface, made from sebum and sweat, which protects against harmful bacteria, viruses and other contaminants that might penetrate the skin.

Acne rosacea: a common disorder that causes redness on the nose, cheeks and forehead and, if not treated, red solid bumps and pus-filled pimples can develop. The nose may become bulbous and swollen-looking. Broken capillaries are also associated with this condition.

Adverse reaction: an unwanted reaction to treatment, such as an allergic reaction.

Aftercare lotion: a solution that is usually provided by the salon to help the client care for their pierced ears. It has antibacterial properties to help keep the area clean.

Alpha hydroxy acid and beta hydroxy acid: products that contain acids, such as alpha hydroxy acids (AHAs) and beta hydroxy acids (BHAs), are used to slough off dead skin cells from the skin's surface. They come in various forms, including creams, gels and lotions, and can be used for all skin types.

Antibodies: these are chemicals made by the body in response to bacteria and any other harmful matter. They have the function of destroying the harmful matter so that it is no longer a threat to the body.

Anticoagulant drugs: these drugs help to prevent or slow down the clotting of blood, e.g. a medicine called Warfarin.

Antioxidant: a substance that helps to fight free radicals. Free radicals cause damage to cells, including skin cells.

Antiseptic: a substance that can be applied to the skin to destroy and prevent the growth of harmful microorganisms. Alcohol is a common antiseptic.

Autoimmune disorder: an autoimmune disorder is a condition that occurs when the body's immune system mistakenly attacks and destroys healthy body tissue.

Automatic tweezers: these types of tweezers have a spring-loaded action, so they can work very quickly to remove hairs. They are useful for removing a lot of hair at one time.

Beeswax: beeswax is a natural wax produced in the beehives of honey bees. The female worker bees have glands on their abdomens that produce the wax, and it is used to make their honeycombs. It makes a good humectant (helps to retain water so prevents drying of the cuticles) and emollient (helps to soften the cuticles and skin).

Bevelling: to bevel the nails means to file with an upward stroke to the underside of the free edge. This removes any rough edges.

Birthmarks: birthmarks may be flat or raised and can have different shades of colouring, commonly brown to red. The two main types of birthmarks are: red, vascular birthmarks, such as port-wine stains and strawberry naevus; and pigmented birthmarks, such as moles and dark brown pigmented areas.

Body language: how people interpret the movements and gestures of a person's body. For example, a slouched receptionist with folded arms may be interpreted as being unfriendly, bored and disinterested in dealing with the client. Positive body language with good eye contact sends the correct signals.

Bone mass: refers to the amount of minerals (mostly calcium and phosphorous) a specific volume of bone contains. A person with low bone mass is at risk from fractures and osteoporosis.

Carbohydrate: a major class of foods that includes sugars and starches. Carbohydrates provide energy for the body.

Carbon dioxide: a gas that is found in the atmosphere, and is breathed out by humans during respiration.

Caucasian: refers to a racial group that has white skin, especially a person of European origin.

Chip and PIN: a security system for ensuring that the holder of a debit or credit card is the owner. Cards have a silicon chip where the four-digit personal identification number (PIN) of that card is stored. When the card is used, the owner enters the PIN into a keypad and this number is compared with the one stored on the chip.

Chloasma: known as the 'mask of pregnancy' when present in pregnant women. Also associated with the contraceptive pill and hormone replacement therapy (HRT) medication. It causes darkened patches on the skin, and is commonly found on the upper cheek, nose, upper lips and forehead.

Clasp: the clasp is attached to the post of the earring to prevent the earring from falling out.

Claustrophobia: the fear of having no escape and being closed in. It is often associated with an anxiety disorder.

Client base: the individuals who regularly visit a beauty therapist for treatments.

Clinical waste: refers to waste products that cannot be considered general waste. It may contain needles, blood or other bodily fluids, and so may be hazardous.

Colleague: a person you work with.

Consent form: a form, usually pre-prepared, that shows the date, name, date of birth, address and contact numbers for the client, the details of the treatment being carried out, and the signature of the parent/guardian. Sometimes, instead of there being a separate consent form, the consultation form will include a paragraph asking the parent/guardian to sign the form if the client is under 16 years of age.

Consumer rights: what the consumer can expect when they buy the product. Consumer rights include protection from hazardous goods, and false and misleading claims in advertising and labelling practices. Consumer rights are protected by consumer law.

Contouring: using shaders, highlighters and blushers to help disguise the less attractive features of the face, and accentuate the more attractive features.

Contract of employment: an agreement between an employer and employee that details the rights, responsibilities and duties agreed between them.

Contra-action: a reaction that happens during or after treatment. This may be an unwanted reaction, such as irritation caused by a product, or a desirable reaction, such as erythema (reddening of the skin) following a facial.

Contra-indication: any medical reason, or other factor, that would either prevent or restrict treatment.

Cross-infection: passing on infection, either by direct person-to-person contact, or by indirect contact such as by using contaminated make-up tools.

Desquamation: shedding of dead skin cells.

Diabetes: a condition caused by insufficient production of the hormone insulin, or tissues that do not respond to insulin. In people with diabetes, the skin may be paper thin and, because of poor circulation, healing may also be poor. There may also be loss of skin sensation.

Disinfect: the process of destroying or helping to prevent the growth of harmful microorganisms (pathogens) with the aid of heat, radiation or chemicals.

Disinfection: a process that reduces the number of harmful microorganisims to a level where they can no longer cause disease.

Distilled water: water that has been cleaned to remove substances such as mineral deposits.

Doctor's referral note: a doctor can advise if their patient can go ahead with a treatment, despite having a condition such as diabetes.

Elastin: a protein that allows many tissues in the body, such as the skin, to resume their shape after being stretched.

Electrocution: electric shock, perhaps caused by electrical wires or faulty equipment – may lead to death.

Emollients: these fill in the spaces between the cells in the skin, helping replace lipids (fats) and helping to smooth and moisturise dry skin. They also help to prevent water loss from the skin.

EPoS system: this system handles the calculations involved in sales of services and products, including change given and total amounts. It issues receipts, and keeps track of stock levels and customer information.

Epsom salts: (also known as magnesium sulphate) are named after the mineral springs of Epsom, an English spa town. It is a salt which helps to detoxify and soften the skin, and relaxes muscles and soothes joints.

Erythema: erythema is redness of the skin caused by increased blood circulation.

Flare lashes: flare lashes are small bundles of single lashes connected at the end in a little knot. 'Flare' describes the way in which the eyelash is shaped.

Glycerol: a colourless, odourless liquid that comes from fats and oils.

Haemorrhage: an excessive loss of blood.

Hair follicle: a tube-like opening from which a hair grows.

Hangnails: pieces of skin that split away from the cuticle, usually because the cuticles are dry. See a picture of a hangnail on page 250.

Hazard: a situation that may be dangerous.

Helix: the rim of the ear, which contains cartilage. If pierced, it does not heal quickly, and hard, lumpy scar tissue can often result.

Hepatitis: occurs when there is inflammation of the liver, often caused by a virus. There are different kinds of hepatitis.

Hirsutism: excessive hair growth in women in areas where usually only men grow hair, such as the chin. Some women with hirsutism have a condition in which the ovaries do not work properly, called polycystic ovary syndrome (PCOS).

Humectants: substances which help to increase the water content of the skin. Useful for moisturising dry skin and softening thickened or scaly skin.

Humidity: the amount of moisture (water) in the air.

Hydrotherapy: water treatment.

Hypoallergenic: unlikely to cause an allergic reaction.

Iris: the circular, coloured part of the eye.

Keratin: a hard, waterproof protein that is found in hair and nails.

Kneipp (ka-nipe) hose: used for Kneipp therapy, which involves alternately using hot and cold treatments to help stimulate the blood and lymphatic circulations.

Lanolin: a thick oil that comes from the wool of animals, such as sheep, where it helps to make the wool waterproof. When used in cosmetics, it makes an effective moisturiser, but some people are allergic to it.

Lateral side: the part of the body that is furthest from the middle of the body and is on the outer side; it is also used to describe the side of a body part, e.g. when describing the foot, 'lateral' refers to the outside of the foot.

Legally binding: enforceable in a court of law.

Lobule: (lobe) the fleshy part of the ear. It contains fatty tissue but does not contain cartilage.

Lymph: a watery, colourless fluid that plays an important role in protecting the body from infection.

Lymphatic circulation: a clear fluid called lymph travels around the body in tube-like vessels. The lymphatic system makes up part of the immune system and so helps protect us from disease.

Lymphocytes: white blood cells that produce antibodies.

Manual tweezers: these types of tweezers have two ends, which vary in shape (although the slanted ends are preferable) and that should meet together at the bottom to make them effective at pulling out hairs. They are ideal for removing stray hairs and creating the final shape.

Material Safety Data Sheet (MSDS): a form prepared by manufacturers and marketers of products that contain toxic chemicals. It outlines safe handling methods and control of hazardous substances used in the workplace.

Matt: doesn't reflect light, so isn't shiny.

Medial side: the medial side of the foot is the inside part of the foot and the lateral side is the outside part of the foot.

Medi-swabs: small, individually wrapped alcohol wipes used to clean the skin. They can be used to clean the ear lobes before carrying out the ear piercing treatment.

Melanin: a pigment responsible for skin and hair colour. Vitiligo is a skin condition in which there is a lack of melanin.

Melanocytes: melanin- or pigment-producing cells that are found in the basal layer of the epidermis.

Merchandising strategy: a method of promoting particular products by, for instance, placing them in a prominent position.

Microorganisms: tiny living organisms including bacteria, viruses and fungi.

Mitosis: the division of a cell into two identical daughter cells. It is the process by which the body grows and replaces cells.

Monocytes: white blood cells that destroy harmful matter, e.g. bacteria, by engulfing and digesting them. These cells gather around wounds and kill invading bacteria to prevent them from entering the body.

Motor nerves: nerves that cause movement when stimulated.

Non-comedogenic: does not cause blocked pores or blackheads.

Non-pathogenic: not capable of causing disease.

Nucleus: the part of the cell that contains DNA and is responsible for growth and reproduction of the cell.

Oestrogen: a hormone that is produced by the ovaries in women, and is responsible for female sexual characteristics such as pubic hair and breast development.

Oxidation: the chemical reaction caused by the combination of a substance with oxygen.

Parkinson's disease: usually affects older people and is caused by the loss of nerve cells in the brain. The symptoms include tremors and slowness of movement.

Pathogenic: a pathogen is able to cause a disease, such as a pathogenic bacteria.

pH: the measure of the acidity or alkalinity of a solution. The pH of the skin is 5.5, which is slightly acidic.

Pinna: the part of the ear we can see. It collects sound waves travelling in the air and directs them into the ear canal.

Post: the part of the earring that is pierced through the ear.

Pustules and papules: a pustule is a spot containing pus and a papule (pimple) is an inflamed, raised, irritated spot.

Record card: also known as a **consultation form**. It includes the client's name, address, date of birth, contact details and health questionnaire. The client should sign and date the record card before any treatment takes place.

Resin: a yellowish thick liquid or soft substance made from plants. Resin helps to ensure that the nitrocellulose found in nail polish adheres to the nail surface.

Risk assessment: to observe any potential hazard that could result in injury, illness or a dangerous situation.

Sales commission: percentage of money earned from every product sold.

Sales figures: the amount of money generated from the sale of products and treatments carried out in the salon.

Sanitisation: a method that helps to kill germs and make an environment more hygienic.

Seborrhoea: a condition where the skin produces too much sebum and so becomes very oily.

Sensory nerves: nerves that pass messages to the brain and make us aware of feelings of heat, cold, touch and pain.

Service time: commercially acceptable time to carry out a treatment.

Sharps box: a special container, usually coloured yellow, which is used to dispose of sharp items such as needles.

Skin tag: these are soft lumps attached to the skin by a stalk, which tend to occur in areas such as the armpits, face and neck. They are quite common and are harmless.

SPF (sun protection factor): this is a rating given to sun creams, which tells you how much protection they provide from the burning (UVB) rays of the sun. For example, if a person normally burns in the sun after 15 minutes of exposure, a lotion with an SPF of 4 allows them to stay out four times longer (i.e. one hour) in the sun without burning.

Sterilisation: a process that kills microorganisms to prevent cross-infection.

Stock levels: the amount of products a business has in stock for carrying out treatments and for retail purposes.

Strip lashes: strip lashes are a strip containing many lashes. These generally cover the whole width of the eye.

Tendon: a tough band of inelastic tissue that attaches muscle to bone.

Terminal hair: a type of thick hair that grows on the head, eyebrows, underarm and pubic regions.

Testosterone: a hormone produced by the testicles from the start of puberty that is responsible for male characteristics, such as muscle growth, deepened voice and hair growth under the arms. Smaller quantities of testosterone are produced in females and are believed to help maintain muscle and bone strength.

Thoracic cavity: the chest area.

Thrombosis: the formation of a blood clot inside a blood vessel, which obstructs the flow of blood through the circulatory system.

Thyroid: gland found in the neck that produces hormones including thyroxine.

Treatment/service plan: the therapist puts together a plan of action that includes choice of products, client preferences and so on, to ensure the best possible treatment is given and that it meets with the client's expectations.

Ultraviolet (UV) cabinet: a cabinet with an ultraviolent lamp producing rays that prevent the growth of bacteria. It provides a hygienic environment for storage of equipment. Equipment such as manicure tools, tweezers and brushes can be stored in the cabinet.

Urea: a waste chemical produced from the break down of protein. Urea is taken by the kidneys from the blood and removed from the body by urine.

Vitiligo: vitiligo causes the skin, and sometimes the hair, to turn white in patches. This is due to melanoctyes (pigment cells) being either damaged or destroyed. It is thought that the body's own immune system attacks the pigment cells.

White soft paraffin: a white, odourless, solid substance which is derived from petroleum (also known as white petroleum jelly). It helps moisturise the skin by providing a layer of oil on the skin's surface which prevents water from evaporating from the skin.

Index

Note: Key terms (glossary terms) are in **bold** type.

A

abrasive mitts (hair removal) 283
acetone 257
Achilles tendon 87
acid mantle, skin 76
acne rosacea 29
acne vulgaris 29
adverse reactions 342
aftercare advice
　ear piercing 318–19
　facial treatment 162–3
　make-up 237
　manicure services 277–8
　pedicure services 277–8
　spa treatments 344
　waxing services 307
aftercare lotion, ear piercing 313
ageing, skin effects 135–6
alcohol, skin effects 133
alopecia 82
alpha hydroxy acids (AHAs) 145
antibodies 95
anticoagulant drugs 312
antioxidants 131
antiseptics 23, 256
anxiety attacks 120
appeals, grievance procedures 56
appointments 40–3
appraisals, work 51–3
arms
　see also limbs, upper
　arm wax treatment 300
　underarm wax treatment 299–300
arteries 106–10
arthritis 246
artificial eyelashes 168, 172–3, 176–7, 187–90, 192
assessment
　anatomy and physiology 121
　ear piercing 320–1
　effectiveness 58–9
　eyebrows/eyelashes 193–4
　facial treatment 164–5
　health and safety 31–3
　make-up 239–41
　manicure services 279–80
　pedicure services 279–80

promoting products and services 69–70
reception duties 48–9
spa treatments 345–6
waxing services 308–9
astringents, facial treatment 143
athlete's foot (tinea pedis) 246–7
autoclaves 23
autoimmune disorders 106, 246
automatic tweezers 174

B

bacterial infections 24–5
basal cell carcinoma 30
Beau's lines (transverse furrows) 247
beeswax 257
beta hydroxy acids (BHAs) 145
bevelling, nails 255
birthmarks 207
black nails 253
blood
　cardiovascular system 104–6
　cells 105
　clotting 106
　haemoglobin 106
　plasma 105
　platelets 105
　red blood cells 105
　white blood cells 105
blood pressure 109
blood vessels 106–10
　arteries 106–10
　body 109
　capillaries 106–10
　head, face and neck 108
　veins 106–10
blue nails 247
blushers, make-up 212–14
body language, communicating with clients 37
body wrapping, spa treatment 328, 331, 339–40, 343
boils 25
bone mass 87
bones 84–95
　anatomical terms 87–8
　conditions 86–7
　feet 92–4
　hands 91–2
　joints 94–5

limbs, lower 92–4
limbs, upper 91–2
osteoporosis 86–7
skull and face 88–9
spine 89–90
upper body 90–1
botox, skin effects 133
bridal make-up 235
bronzers, make-up 214
brown nails 253
bruised nails 247
brushes, make-up 202–4
bunions (hallux valgus) 247–8

C

caffeine, skin effects 133
caldariums 325
calluses 248
cancer, skin 30
capillaries 106–10
carbohydrates 132
carbon dioxide 75
carbuncles 25
cardiovascular system 104–12
　blood 104–6
　blood vessels 106–9
　circulatory system 109–12
　conditions 111–12
　heart 104
cash, customer payment 43–4
cashing-up, reception duties 46
Caucasian skin 136, 137
cells 71–3
　blood 105
central nervous system (CNS) 118–19
Chemicals (Hazard Information and Packaging for Supply) Regulations (2002) 12
cheques, customer payment 44–5
chip and PIN, customer payment 45
chloasma 27, 130
circulatory system 109–12
　see also cardiovascular system
clasps, ear piercing 312
claustrophobia 341
cleaning, equipment 22
cleaning and maintenance, spa treatments 329–33
cleansing the skin, facial treatment 138–43

client base 61
clinical waste 14
closing the sale 64–5
code of ethics 16
codes of conduct 56–7
codes of practice 16–21
cold sores 26
colleagues 53–4
comedones 29
    facial treatment 162
communicating with clients,
        reception duties 37–40
complaints 39
concealers, make-up 206–8
conjunctivitis 25
consent forms 18
consultation forms 17–18
consultations 17–19
Consumer Protection Act (1987) 15
consumer rights 68
continuing professional development
        (CPD) 62
contouring 198, 205
contouring cosmetics, make-up
        212–14
contra-actions 17–18
    ear piercing 319
    eyebrows/eyelashes 191–2
    make-up 236
    manicure services 277
    pedicure services 277
    spa treatments 344
    waxing services 306
contra-indications 16–17
    ear piercing 311–12
    facial treatment 125
    make-up 199
    spa treatments 341
    treatment 16–17, 18
    waxing services 286–7
contracts of employment 56
*Control of Noise at Work Regulations
        (2005)* 14
*Control of Substances Hazardous to
        Health (COSHH) (2004)* 12
corns 248
corrective make-up techniques
    eye shape 225–7
    face shape 215–19
    lip shape 229
*Cosmetic Products (Safety)
        Regulations (2004)* 15
cramp, muscle 97
credit cards, customer payment 45
cross-infection 4, 22–4, 200
cutting (hair removal) 283

D
day make-up 234
debit cards, customer payment 45
depilatory cream 283
depilatory waxing 282
dermatitis 28
dermis, skin 75–7
desquamation 123
diabetes 18, 249, 286
diet, skin effects 130–1
disinfect 254
disinfection 22–3
distilled water 159
doctor's referral notes 18–19, 286
dry flotation, spa treatment 327, 330,
        338, 343
dry-heat sterilisers 24
dry nails 253

E
ear piercing 310–21
    aftercare advice 318–19
    assessment 320–1
    consultation 311
    contra-actions 319
    contra-indications 311–12
    equipment 312–14
    infection and irritation 319
    keloid scarring 319
    legislation 317–18
    materials 312–14
    preparation 314–15
    procedures 315–16
    products 312–14
eczema 28
effectiveness 50–9
    assessment 58–9
    procedures 56–7
    roles 54–6
    skills 51–3
    targets 57
    teamwork 53–4
effleurage, massage 147, 270–1
eggshell nails 249
elastin 72
Electricity at Work Act (1989) 13
electrocution 8
electrolysis (hair removal) 284
embolism 111
emollients 144, 156, 257
*Employers Liability (Compulsory
        Insurance) Act 1969* 15
environment, skin effects 134–5
Environmental Protection Act (1990)
        14
enzyme peels, facial treatment 145
epidermis, skin 73–5
epilepsy 120

EPoS systems, customer payment 45
epsom salts, spa treatment 330
erythema 26, 107, 191
evening make-up 234
exfoliation, facial treatment 144–6
eye make-up 220–7
eyebrow pencils 224
eyebrows 166–94
    see also eyelashes
    assessment 193–4
    consultation 167
    contra-actions 191–2
    equipment 173–7
    materials 173–7
    pre-16 restrictions 192
    products 173–7
    service times 168
    shaping 168–9, 174, 178–83, 191
    skin sensitivity tests 171–2, 173
    tinting 169, 175–6, 183–4, 191
    waxing treatments 301–2
eyelashes 166–94
    see also eyebrows
    artificial 168, 172–3, 176–7, 187–
        90, 192
    assessment 193–4
    consultation 167
    contra-actions 191–2
    equipment 173–7
    flare lashes 168, 189–90
    materials 173–7
    pre-16 restrictions 192
    products 173–7
    service times 168
    skin sensitivity tests 171–2, 173
    strip lashes 168, 187–9
    tinting 170–2, 175–6, 184–6, 191
eyeliner 221–3
eyeshadow 220–1

F
face and skull bones 88–9
face powder, make-up 211–12
face shape, corrective make-up
        techniques 215–19
facial primers, make-up 205
facial treatment 122–65
    see also make-up; skin
    aftercare advice 162–3
    analysis, skin 128–9
    assessment 164–5
    astringents 143
    benefits 123
    cleansing the skin 138–43
    comedones 162
    consultation 124–5
    contra-indications 125
    enzyme peels 145

equipment 125–7
exfoliation 144–6
factors affecting skin 130–7
fragrances (perfumes) 157
hydroxyacids 145
male skin 136, 158
masks 126, 152–5
massage 146–52
materials 125–7
microdermabrasion 145
milia 162
moisturising the skin 156–8
preparing clients 127–37
preservatives 157
procedures 138–62
products 125–7, 158
skin analysis 128–9
skin blockages removal 161
skin toning 143–4
skin types 128–9
steam treatment 159–61
toning 143–4
towel treatment, hot (warm) 161–2
warming the skin 158–62
waxing treatments 300–3
Fango therapy, spa treatment 328
feet
    see also pedicure services
    bones 92–4
    disorders 245–54
    massage, feet/legs 270–4
    muscles 103
    paraffin wax treatment 275–6
    thermal boots 276–7
fibrositis, muscles 97
Finnish saunas 323–4
Fire Precautions Act (1971) 10–11
first-aid, Health and Safety (First Aid) Regulations (1981) 8–9
first impressions, reception duties 34–6
flare lashes 168, 189–90
flotation, spa treatment 327–8, 330, 338–9, 343
foam baths 327, 330, 336–7, 342
folliculitis 25
foundation, make-up 208–10
fragrances (perfumes), facial treatment 157
freckles 27
French manicure 265–6
fungal infections 26–7

G
gift vouchers, customer payment 46
glass-bead sterilisers 24
glycerol 209, 256
gout 249
grievance procedures 56

H
haemoglobin 106
haemorrhage 199, 286
hair 79–82
    alopecia 82
    hirsutism 82, 306
    terminal hair 80–1
hair follicles 75
hair removal 281–309
    see also waxing services
    permanent methods 283–4
    temporary methods 282–3
hamams 325
hammer toes 249
hands
    see also manicure services
    bones 91–2
    disorders 245–54
    massage, hands/arms 270–4
    muscles 102
    paraffin wax treatment 275–6
    thermal mitts 276–7
hangnails 244, 250
hazards, health and safety 2–5
head, face and neck
    blood vessels 108
    bones 88–9
    muscles 98–9
health and safety 2–33
    code of ethics 16
    codes of practice 16–21
    cross-infection 22–4
    hazards 2–5
    insurance 15
    laws and regulations 5–15
    risk assessment 3
    skin conditions 24–30
Health and Safety at Work Act (HASAWA) (1974) 5–6
Health and Safety (Display Screen Equipment) Regulations (1992 and 2002) 8
Health and Safety (First Aid) Regulations (1981) 8–9
Health and Safety Information for Employees Regulations (1989) 6–7
heart, cardiovascular system 104
heat treatments, spa treatments 322–7
helix, ear 317
hepatitis 112
herbal wrap, spa treatment 328
highlighters, make-up 214–15
hirsutism 82, 306
HIV/Aids 112
hormones, skin effects 130
humectants 156–7, 257
humidity 128, 129

hydrogen peroxide, tinting, eyelashes/eyebrows 175–6
hydrotherapy 326–7, 337
hydroxyacids, facial treatment 145
hypoallergenic 199

I
impetigo 25
industry code of ethics 16
infection and irritation, ear piercing 319
infectious/non-infectious skin conditions 24–30
infestations 27
infrared saunas 324
initiative 51
insurance, Employers Liability (Compulsory Insurance) Act 1969 15
intense pulsed light (IPL) (hair removal) 284
iris, eye 180

J
job descriptions 54
joints 94–5
    arthritis 246

K
keloid scarring, ear piercing 319
keratin 79
Kneipp hoses, spa treatments 325
knuckling, massage 148

L
laconium saunas 324
Langelier Saturation Index, spa treatments 333
lanolin 156, 257
laser hair removal 284
lateral side 88
laws and regulations
    ear piercing 317–18
    health and safety 5–15
    selling 68
legally binding 56
legislation see laws and regulations
legs see limbs, lower
lessons, make-up 238
leuconychia (white spots) 250
ligaments 72, 87
limbs, bones 91–4
limbs, lower
    bones 92–4
    muscles 103
limbs, upper
    bones 91–2
    muscles 101–2
link selling 67

lip gloss 228–9
lip liner 228
lip products, make-up 228–9
liposuction 72–3
lipstick 228
lobule, ear 317
Local Government Act (1982) 15
Local Government (Miscellaneous Provisions) Act (1982) 15
lymph 75, 113
lymphatic circulation 116
lymphatic system 113–16
    oedema (fluid retention) 116
lymphocytes 95

M
make-up 195–241
    see also facial treatmaftercare advice 237
    application 206–33
    assessment 239–41
    blushers 212–14
    bridal make-up 235
    bronzers 214
    brushes 202–4
    concealer 206–8
    consultation 196–8
    contouring cosmetics 212–14
    contra-actions 236
    contra-indications 199
    corrective techniques, eye shape 225–7
    corrective techniques, face shape 215–19
    corrective techniques, lip shape 229
    day make-up 234
    different client groups 230–3
    different occasions 234–6
    equipment 200–4
    evening make-up 234
    eye make-up 220–7
    face powder 211–12
    facial primers 205
    foundation 208–10
    highlighters 214–15
    lessons 238
    lip products 228–9
    materials 200–4
    order of make-up application 206
    palettes 204
    photographic make-up 236
    preparation 200–5
    preparing clients 204–5
    products 200–4
    service times 198–9
    shaders 215
    skin sensitivity tests 199
    special occasion make-up 234–5

sponges 204
    treatment rooms 200
male manicure 266
male skin, facial treatment 136, 158
Management of Health and Safety at Work Regulations (1999) 8
manicure services 242–66
    aftercare advice 277–8
    assessment 279–80
    benefits 244
    consultation 245
    contra-actions 277
    disorders 245–54
    French manicure 265–6
    male manicure 266
    massage, hands/arms 270–4
    nail polish 264–5
    nail shapes 264
    paraffin wax treatment 275–6
    preparation 254–9
    procedures 259–66
    routine, quick glance 263
    thermal mitts 276–7
    warm oil treatment, nails 275
Manual Handling Operations Regulations (1992) 14
manual tweezers 174
mascara 223–4
masks
    facial treatment 126, 152–5
    non-setting masks 154–5
    setting masks 152–4
massage
    effleurage 147, 270–1
    facial treatment 146–52
    feet/legs 270–4
    hands/arms 270–4
    knuckling 148
    petrissage 147–8, 271
    tapotement 148, 271
    vibration 148
Material Safety Data Sheet (MSDS) 255
matt, make-up 209
medi-swabs 313
medial side 87
medical conditions, skin effects 134
medications, skin effects 134
melanin 75
melanocytes 30, 135–6
melanoma 30
merchandising strategy 67
microdermabrasion, facial treatment 145
microorganisms 22, 202
    spa treatments 329
milia 28
    facial treatment 162
mitosis 72

moisturising the skin, facial treatment 156–8
moles 30
monocytes 95
motor nerves 75, 76
muscles 95–103
    conditions 97
    cramp 97
    fascia 96
    feet 103
    fibrositis 97
    hands 102
    head, face and neck 98–9
    limbs, lower 103
    limbs, upper 101–2
    muscle tone 96–7
    shoulders 100
    strain 97
    tearing 97
    temperature effects 97
    trunk 99–100

N
nails
    see also manicure services; pedicure services
    Beau's lines (transverse furrows) 247
    black nails 253
    blue nails 247
    brown nails 253
    bruised nails 247
    disorders 245–54
    dry nails 253
    eggshell nails 249
    hangnails 250
    leuconychia (white spots) 250
    onychauxis (thickened nail) 250
    onychia (infection of the nail) 250
    onychocryptosis (ingrowing toenail) 250
    onycholysis (nail separation) 251
    onychomycosis (ringworm of the nail or tinea unguium) 252–3
    onychophagy (bitten nails) 251
    onychorrhexis (split or brittle nails) 251
    paronychia 251–2
    polish, manicure services 264–5
    pterygium (overgrown cuticle) 252
    ram's horn (club nail) 252
    ridges 252
    shapes, manicure services 264
    structure 82–4, 254
    warm oil treatment 275
nervous system 117–20
    central nervous system (CNS) 118–19

conditions 120
nerves 117–18
neurons 117–18
peripheral nervous system 119–20
neurons 117–18
non-comedogenic 208
non-pathogenic 24
non-setting masks 154–5
nucleus, cells 71

O

oedema (fluid retention) 116
oestrogen 130
onychauxis (thickened nail) 250
onychia (infection of the nail) 250
onychocryptosis (ingrowing toenail) 250
onycholysis (nail separation) 251
onychomycosis (ringworm of the nail or tinea unguium) 252–3
onychophagy (bitten nails) 251
onychorrhexis (split or brittle nails) 251
osteoporosis 86–7
oxidation 176

P

palettes, make-up 204
papules 153
paraffin wax treatment, hands and feet 275–6
Parkinson's disease 341
paronychia 251–2
pathogenic 24
payment, customer 43–6
pedicure services 242–3, 266–70
aftercare advice 277–8
assessment 279–80
benefits 244
consultation 245
contra-actions 277
disorders 245–54
massage, feet/legs 270–4
paraffin wax treatment 275
preparation 254–9
procedures 266–70
routine, quick glance 269–70
thermal boots 276–7
warm oil treatment, nails 275
peripheral nervous system 119–20
personal presentation 20
Personal Protective Equipment (PPE) at Work Regulations (2002) 12–13
petrissage, massage 147–8, 271
pH, skin 76
phlebitis 112

photographic make-up 236
pigmentation
disorders 27
skin 75
pinna, ear 317
plucking (hair removal) 282
posts, ear piercing 312
posture 21
powder, face, make-up 211–12
preservatives, facial treatment 157
pricing, reception duties 46–7
procedures, effectiveness 56–7
products
ear piercing 312–14
eyebrows 173–7
eyelashes 173–7
facial treatment 125–7, 158
knowledge 61–3
make-up 200–4
promoting 60–70
reception duties 46–7
selling 62–3
stock levels 40, 46–7
waxing services 287–8
professional behaviour 21
promoting products and services 60–70
assessment 69–70
knowledge 61–3
laws and regulations 68
sales techniques 64–5
treatments and products 65–7
promotional campaigns 67
Protection of Children Act (1999) 14
Provision and Use of Work Equipment Regulations (PUWER) (1998) 13
psoriasis 29
pterygium (overgrown cuticle) 252
pulse 109–11
pustules 153

R

ram's horn (club nail) 252
Raynaud's disease 120
reactions *see* contra-actions
reception duties 34–49
appointments 40–3
assessment 48–9
cashing-up 46
communicating with clients 37–40
first impressions 34–6
payment, customer 43–6
pricing 46–7
products 46–7
services 46
stationery and materials 36
record cards 17–18

red blood cells 105
regulations and laws 5–15
Reporting of Injuries, Diseases and Dangerous Occurrences Regulations (RIDDOR) (1995) 10
resin 257
ridges (nails) 252
ringworm (*Tinea corporis*) 27
risk assessment, health and safety 3
roles 54–6
rosacea 29

S

sales commission 63
sales figures 40
sales techniques 64–5
salt glow, spa treatment 328
sanitisation 202
saunas 323–4, 329
preparation 333–4, 342
scabies 27
sebaceous gland disorders 28–9
seborrhoea 306
selling, legislation 68
selling products 62–3
sensitivity tests, skin 43, 171–2, 173
sensory nerves 75
service time 17
services
knowledge 61–3
promoting 60–70
reception duties 46
setting masks 152–4
shaders, make-up 215
shapes, eye, corrective make-up techniques 225–7
shapes, face, corrective make-up techniques 215–19
shapes, lip, corrective make-up techniques 229
shapes, nail 264
sharps box 14
shaving (hair removal) 283
shoulders, muscles 100
skeletal system 84–95
skills
continuing professional development (CPD) 62
improving 51–3, 62
required 55
sales techniques 64–5
skin 73–9
see also facial treatment
ageing 135–6
alcohol 133
allergies 28
analysis, facial treatment 128–9
botox 133

caffeine 133
cancer 30
Caucasian 136, 137
colour 136–7
dermis 75–7
diet 130–1
environment 134–5
epidermis 73–5
factors affecting 130–7
functions 78–9
hormones 130
male 136, 158
medical conditions 134
medications 134
melanocytes 30, 135–6
pigmentation 75
smoking 133
stress 130
subcutaneous layer 77–8
sunlight 130
types 136–7
types, facial treatment 128–9
skin blockages removal, facial
    treatment 161
skin conditions 24–30
skin sensitivity tests
    eyebrows/eyelashes tints 171–2,
        173
    make-up 199
    reception duties 43
    waxing services 285–6
skin tags 30, 287
skin toning, facial treatment 143–4
skull and face bones 88–9
smoking, skin effects 133
spa pools 326, 330, 335–6, 342
spa treatments 322–46
    aftercare advice 344
    assessment 345–6
    body wrapping 328, 331, 339–40,
        343
    caring for clients 342–3
    cleaning and maintenance 329–33
    consultation 340
    contra-actions 344
    contra-indications 341
    flotation 327–8, 330, 338–9, 343
    heat treatments 322–7
    hydrotherapy 326–7, 337
    Langelier Saturation Index 333
    microorganisms 329
    saunas 323–4, 329, 333–4, 342
    spa pools 326, 330, 335–6, 342
    steam baths/rooms 325–6, 329,
        334–5, 342

water safety and testing 331–3
special occasion make-up 234–5
SPF (sun protection factor) 63, 277,
    278
spinal cord 118–19
spine 89–90
sponges, make-up 204
squamous cell carcinoma 30
stationery and materials, reception
    duties 36
steam baths/rooms 325–6, 329,
    334–5, 342
steam treatment, facial 159–61
sterilisation 22, 23–4
stock levels, products 40, 46–7
strengths/weaknesses, personal 51
stress, skin effects 130
strip lashes 168, 187–9
strip sugar treatment, waxing
    services 303–5
styes 25
subcutaneous layer, skin 77–8
sugaring (hair removal) 282, 303–5
sun protection factor (SPF) 63, 277,
    278
sunlight, skin effects 130

tapotement, massage 148, 271
targets, effectiveness 57
teamwork 53–4
telephone answering, reception
    duties 38–9
tendons 72, 87
terminal hair 80–1
testosterone 86–7, 130
thalassotherapy, spa treatment 328
thermal boots, pedicure services
    276–7
thermal mitts, manicure services
    276–7
thoracic cavity 91
threading (hair removal) 282
thrombosis 111
thyroid 134
tissue 72–3
toning, facial treatment 143–4
towel treatment, hot (warm) 161–2
training, continuing professional
    development (CPD) 62
treatment rooms 19–20, 200
treatment/service plans 18
trunk, muscles 99–100
Turkish baths 325, 330
tweezers, manual/automatic 174
Tyrolean saunas 324

U
ultraviolet (UV) cabinet 23
unhappy clients 39
urea 97
urticaria 28

V
varicose veins 111
veins 106–10
    phlebitis 112
    varicose veins 111
verrucas 253
vibration, massage 148
viral infections 26
vitamins, skin effects 131
vitiligo 26, 27

W
warm oil treatment, nails 275
warming the skin, facial treatment
    158–62
warts 26, 253
water safety and testing, spa
    treatments 331–3
waxing services 281–309
    see also hair removal
    aftercare advice 307
    arm wax treatment 300
    assessment 308–9
    bikini line wax treatment 296–8
    consultation 285
    contra-actions 306
    contra-indications 286–7
    effective waxing treatment 293
    equipment 287–8
    facial waxing treatments 300–3
    full leg wax treatment 296
    half leg wax treatment 294–5
    hot wax treatment 289–90
    materials 287–8
    products 287–8
    roller wax treatment 292–3
    service times 285
    skin sensitivity tests 285–6
    strip sugar treatment 303–5
    underarm wax treatment 299–300
    upper lip and chin waxing
        treatment 302–3
    warm wax treatment 290–2
weaknesses/strengths, personal 51
wet flotation, spa treatment 328, 330,
    338–9, 343
white blood cells 105
white soft paraffin 257
work appraisals 51–3
Workplace (Health, Safety and
    Welfare) Regulations (1992) 7

Photo acknowledgements

Alamy p.14 (Indigo Images), p.61 (Media Blitz Images), p.67 (Jeffrey Blacker), p.67 (logo), p.134 (Ilja Dubovski), p.282 bottom left (Inspirestock), p.283 (Helen Sessions), p.298 (Adam Jones); **Bobbi Brown** p.206, p.212, p.214; **Caflon** p.313, p.318; **Chanel** p.265; **Dermalogica** p.138; **Ellisons** p.162, p.174, p.256 a, c, e; **Finders Health** p.339; **Floatworks (UK) Ltd** p.339 a; **Fotolia** p.9 (Woodsy), p.16 (Maridav), p.56 (Stephen Coburn), p.60 (Sakala), p.65 (Sakala), p.163 (Naka), p.200 (Stanislav Komogorov), p.255 b, p.256 b (Coprid), p.258 a (Serghei Velusceac), p.316 c, p.318 (Jennifer Walz), p.325 a (Aysun Ozcan); **Getty Images** p.209, p.327; **Health and Safety Executive** p. 7; **Hive of Beauty Ltd** p.288, p.300; **HSBC** p.45; **IPC** p.159 (PSC IPC Plus Syndication); **iStockphoto** p.6 (Matej Michelizza), p.7 (Willie B. Thomas), p.9, p.10 (Pablo del Rio Sotelo), p.11 bottom right (Mark Richardson) p.15 (Daneger), p.24 (Sebastian Kaulitzki), p.27 e (Fanelie Rosier), p.47 (Willie B. Thomas), p.54 (Victor Zastol`skiy), p.66 bottom left (Miranda Salia), p.123 (Stígur Karlsson), p.126 (Valua Vitaly), p.132 (Jack Puccio), p.136 (Geber86), p.139 a (Famke Backx), b (Amy Dunn), c (Julia Savchenko), d (Famke Backx), p.143 (Ewa Brozek), p.144 (Jo Unruh), p.155 (Sheldunov Andrey), p.156 (Diane Diederich), p.167 (Dmitry Gerciks), p.168 (Hadel Productions), p.170 (Anton Zabelsky), p.172 (Valua Vitaly), p.186 (Hongqi Zhang), p.195 (Julia Savchenko), p.196 (Goldmund Lukic), p.197 (Darren Baker), p.198 (Valua Vitaly), p.201 (Slobodan Vasic), p.204 (Imagetwo), p.220 a (Mark Wragg), b (PLAINVIEW), p.221 (Inga Ivanova), p.222 a (Dave White), b (Jakub Pavlinec), p.222 (Kolupaev), p.223 bottom right (Gremlin), p.224 (Chris Bernard), p.228 (Alexey Avdeev), p.228 (Daneger), p.234 a (Ariwasabi), b (Julia Savchenko), p.235 (Natalia Maximova), p.236 (Alexandr Zadiraka), p.243 a (Valentin Casarsa), b (Valua Vitaly), p.250 a (Clayton Cole), p.255 a (Nikola Miljkovic), c, d (Travellinglight), p.256 d, p.257 (Cagri Özgür), p.260 a (Iconogenic), b (Cagri Özgür), p.263 a (Andriy Bezuglov), b (Serghei Starus), p.266 (Esolla), p.282 (Mark Fairey), p.289 (Jo Unruh), p.310 (Eva Serrabassa), p.316 a, b (Quavondo), p.317 (Quavondo), p.322 (Blend_Images), p.323 a (Marcela Barsse), p.332 b, p.334 (MatkaWariatka), p.341 (Olivier Lantzendörffer); **Jane Iredale** p.202; **Martin Sookias** p.12, p.13, p.20 bottom left, p.50, p.51, p.63, p.160, p.214, pp.230–233, p.238, pp.260–262, p.266 (bottom left), pp.267–269, pp.272–275, p.276, p.277, p.287, p.323 b; **Mediscan** p.251 a, c, p.252 c, p.306 a; **Nicholas Yarsley** p.8, p.20 top, p.22, p.34, p.35, p.36, p.37, p.38, p.39, p.52, p.53, p.57, p.62, p.66, p.127, p.140, p.142, p.143, p.145, pp.147–153, p.157, p.162, p.171, p.178, pp.183–189, pp.265–266, pp.289–292, pp.294–295, pp.296–297, p.299, pp.301–303, pp.304–305; **North East Pool Centre** p.332 top; **Photolibrary** p.325 b, c (Tom Pepeira); **Prestige Medical** p.23; **Rex Features** p.209, p.223 top right (Martin Lee), p.258 b (Sonny Meddle); **Robert Baran** p.251 b; **Ryan McVay** p.335; **Science Photo Library** p.14, p.24, p.25 a (ISM), b (Western Opthalmic Hospital), c (Dr P Marazzi), d (Biophoto Associates), e (Dr Chris Hale), p.26 a (Science Source), b (Dr P Marazzi), p.27 a (Dr P Marazzi), b (Dr P Marazzi), c (Dr P Marazzi), d (Custom Medical Stock), p.28 a (Dr P Marazzi), b (CNRI), c, d (Dr H C Robinson), p.28 a, b (Dr Harout Tanielian), c (Dr P Marazzi), d (Dr P Marazzi), p.30 a (Dr P Marazzi), b (Girand), c (James Tevenson), p.116 (Dr P Marazzia), p.125 (Dr P Marazzi), p.129 a (Helen Mcardle), b, c & d (Ian Hooton), e (Lea Paterson), f, p.130 (Daniel Sambraus), p.133 (Joti), p.135 (Joti), p. 11 (Mark Sykes & Cordelia Molloy), p.246 a (Dr P Marazzi), b, p.247 a (Pascal Goetgheluck), b, c (Pascal Goetgheluck), p.248 a,(Alex Bartel), b, (Mike Devlin), c (Jane Shemilt), p.249 a (Dr Harout Tanielian), b (Dr P Marazzi), c (Dr P Marazzi), p.250 b (Dr P Marazzi), c (Mike Devlin), d (Dr P Marazzi), p. 251 d (Dr P Marazzi), p. 252 b, d, p.253, p.284 aAJ Photo/Hop Americain), b (Michael Donne), p.286 (Dr P Marazzi), p.306 b, c (Dr P Marazzi), p.319 (Dr P Marazzi), p.329 (Eye of Science); **Sorisa** p.161; **Sukar** p.293, p.304; **Thalgo** p.337; **Wikipedia** p.131, p.252 a.